YOU MEAN I GET *PAID* TO DO THIS?

YOU MEAN I GET *PAID* TO DO THIS?

by

Jim Taylor

Horsdal & Schubart

Horsdal & Schubart Publishers Ltd.
Victoria, BC, Canada

Cover photographs: Jim Taylor, Donovan Bailey, Pavel Bure, Paul Kariya, Silken Laumann, Mark Messier and Dennis Rodman courtesy of Chris Relke.
Wayne Gretzky courtesy of Deborah Taylor.
Tonya Harding courtesy of Jeff Vinnick.
Evander Holyfield and Mike Tyson provided by the author.

We acknowledge the support of the Canada Council for the Arts for our publishing program.

This book is set in Galliard.

Printed and bound in Canada by Kromar Printing Ltd.

Canadian Cataloguing in Publication Data

Taylor, Jim, 1937-
You mean I get paid to do this?

ISBN 0-920663-54-0

1. Sports. I. Title.
GV707.T399 1997 796 C97-910621-4

Printed and bound in Canada

***

For Jim Coleman and Eric Nicol —
national treasures who can still
write your socks off.

***

CONTENTS

INTRODUCTION

"Backwards write to have I mean this does?" I asked.

"No," they told me.

"Sure you?"

"Absolutely. Just because the sports section now starts at the back of the front and works toward the middle doesn't mean you have to write that way."

"Doog! Lufrednow! Suodneputs!"

"Cut that out!"

"Yako."

Well, you couldn't blame a guy for worrying. Sure, the *Province* sports section was going to be bigger and I might be able to stay on the same page days at a time so it didn't take a Sherpa guide and two St. Bernards to find me, but back-to-front takes a little getting used to. Particularly after a traumatic experience in Tokyo.

It was the publisher's launching party for the Japanese translation of the Rick Hansen *Man in Motion* book — which, in the Japanese manner, opened from what North Americans would call the back. When the publisher presented me with a copy I handed it to a translator North American style. Rather than make me look like a jerk, that was where she started to read. Hansen crossed the finish line on Page 2. It can shake you.

But it worked, and the more I think about it, it was kind of symbolic. First the sports section went backwards, then the coverage.

As the English language sinks into a sea of rap, and video games foster a generation with trigger-quick reflexes and the attention span of hummingbirds, today's sports-page fan seems more concerned with numbers than with the people putting them up. Ask not whether your team won or lost, but how many points you got in the pool.

This isn't a complaint, really. Tastes change, and at a time when newspaper circulation is imploding, sports editors give the people what they think they want: Page after page of ERAs, RBIs, SOs, GFs, GAs, PENs, Ws, Ls, Ts and Pts. Mostly, these numbers are aimed at the barely-past-Clearasil generation, who communicate in grunts and think "He da man!" is one with Shakespeare. It is one of the enduring myths of modern journalism that kids buy newspapers. They don't. Mom and Dad do. Or did, when the words came first.

Me, I like words. I like the way they can paint pictures, the way they can make you laugh and cry and think and react. Numbers are smoke that blows away to be replaced by new smoke tomorrow. Words last. Properly assembled, they can march like armies and change the world.

The words in this book, scribbled and typed and telephoned and lap-topped in too many press boxes to remember, will not do that.

Mostly they are funny, or meant to be. When sport makes instant millionaires out of kids who can hit a ball or a puck with a stick or run up and down the floor in shorts bouncing a basketball, what's not to laugh? Sometimes they are sad. More than once the screen or paper blurred in the writing.

They are about good guys and jerks, strivers and fakers, journeymen and giants playing games for a living with the world peering into the fishbowl and bigger, stronger, faster challengers coming at them every year.

Following them has been mostly a joy and sometimes a pain. But staring at blank paper or empty screen with deadline looming, trying to make the words assemble and march and sing — ah, that's been magic.

Enjoy it. I did.

Jim Taylor, July 1997

Chapter One

LET THE GAMES BEGIN

It was Grade Two, I think. Miss Guysler, a dark-eyed young teacher for whom I had the hots, wrote, "The sun is setting in the west" on the blackboard, asked us to add a second line that would make it a poem, and a kid named Johnny Lukoni shot his hand up and said, "The birds are singing in their nest."

"Suck-hole," I whispered.

It never worried me saying things like that, not even to the tough kids. Sure, there was recess and noon hour to get through afterward, but who was going to beat up on a chicken-boned little kid with sticky tape on his glasses — two weeks covering one lens, two weeks covering the other and, later on, the top half of both lenses all the time? ("Lazy eye," the doctor called it. "This will strengthen it." It never did.)

They could tease, and they did. In the few times I tried to learn to skate they could wait until my blind side was toward the ice and smash me into the boards. They did that, too. But they couldn't hit me. Not a four-eyed, half-blind wimp. Besides, they were my friends. And a sharp-tongued little brat could always get his own back in class.

So I needled Johnny Lukoni — until I noticed that Miss Guysler, my fantasy love, was applauding and all the other kids were looking at him as though he'd just invented jawbreakers.

Jeez, all that for one lousy two-line poem when she gives him the first line?

When she asked us all to try to write our OWN two-line poem, I pulled out a sheet of that lined foolscap paper they used to give us that was so rough it still had pieces of pulp sticking out, and wrote one that ran EIGHT lines. Eat this, Lukoni!

I can still remember every word:

I have the cutest little pup,
On his hind legs he stands up.
He never, ever runs away,
For he is very happy and gay.

My pup can do a lot of tricks.
He brings me the paper, he picks up sticks.
And you may be sure that he walks with me,
And brings me home in time for tea.

Of course, I didn't drink tea. I was seven years old, for God's sake. And I didn't have a pup. In Nipawin, Saskatchewan (pop. 2,300), the paper only came once a week, and I was the kid who delivered it. But Miss Guysler patted my head and said, "Look, class, Jimmy has written an EIGHT-line poem! Let's all give him a big clap!"

She pinned it on the blackboard — my first published work. People read it, and nobody thumped me at recess. Maybe I was on to something here ...

RIGHT MAN FOR THE JOB

September 20, 1995

In a time when it would be so easy to believe that the entire world of sport is going to hell in a handbasket, it gives me great pleasure to report that one professional team has finally gotten it right.

Flamingo, Brazil's most popular and successful soccer club, has fired its coach and replaced him with — wait for it — a sports columnist.

The new man is Washington Rodrigues, a 59-year-old columnist for Rio's highly respected sports newspaper, *Journal Dos Sport*. He has never coached a team.

A surprising number of people would consider this a disadvantage. Not so. Rodrigues may be a rookie at coaching, but he is a veteran at that most important aspect of soccer as it is played and observed in South America: second-guessing the man who is coaching.

In South America, the second-guess is the profession of every soccer fan — man, woman or child. They may have other jobs necessary to put bread on the table, but their profession is second-guesser.

North Americans think they are among the world's greatest fans. They aren't even close. Suicides are not unknown when Brazil loses.

Reporters following the World Cup matches in California took a $40 cab ride to a scheduled Brazil practice. There'd been a mix-up. There was no real practice. All they found was the backup goalkeeper, a few rookies — and about 400 Brazilian fans pressing so determinedly against the chain-link fence trying to get closer to their heroes that a harassed policeman finally used his handcuffs as a padlock to snap shut the gate.

No one has second-guessed better than Washington Rodrigues, a firm exponent of the Brazilian media credo that victory is expected, draws tolerated, and losses grounds for South America's version of the triple play: Blindfold, cigarette and bullet.

In North America, the home-town media at least put up a pretense of impartiality. In South America, forget it. Brazilian media arrived for the World Cup final against Italy wearing official national team jerseys. They sang fight songs in the press room. When Brazil won it in a shoot-out they hugged and kissed. There were tears of joy. You think Don Cherry looked silly kissing Doug Gilmour? These guys were serious.

Given all this, it is only logical that Flamingo should replace Edinho, who actually played the game, with Rodrigues, who has not.

With one deft stroke, they eliminate the middle man. Rodrigues can begin second-guessing as he lathers up in the morning to shave. He can put his own soccer theories to the test. If they work, he can nominate himself as coach of the year. If they don't, he can blame inferior talent. If, God forbid, the team should lose badly, he can cover up that 3-0 drubbing with a column pointing out that if it hadn't been for those three lucky goals and incompetent officiating, the match might have ended in a draw.

Edinho could do none of those things.

Okay, he could bounce the ball off every part of his body and keep it in the air for 20 minutes, or use his head to pound it into the top corner. But could he un-split an infinitive or reel in a dangling participle? Had he polished those skills, the guy on the phone after that last 2-1 defeat might have been a judge awarding him the Pulitzer instead of the team owner telling him not to bother coming home.

Naturally, we in the writing dodge wish him every success. No profession this side of high fashion is more slavishly trendy than professional sport. The guy makes good, I could be coaching the Canucks. But I warn you now: I will not play kissy-face with the media. Or, for that matter, with Gino Odjick.

OVERS HERE, OVERS THERE

September 21, 1994

Australian cricket officials plan to experiment with revolutionary new rules that could transform the limited-overs game. Under the new format, limited-overs will be split into four innings instead of two. — News item

"Guess what?" I shouted across the newsroom. "Australian officials are going to experiment with revolutionary new rules that could transform cricket!"

"Cricket? Didn't she used to be on *77 Sunset Strip* with that Kookie Byrnes. She must be — what, about 112? Kind of old and breakable for experimenting."

"What are they going to do, put in a rule that says the game has to end in the same decade it starts?"

Clearly, they didn't understand the magnitude of the moment.

"It's the limited-overs," I explained. "They're splitting them into four innings instead of two."

"Well, you know what Yogi said: 'It ain't overs 'til it's overs.' "

Frankly, I do not understand their indifference. How can any sporting heart not beat faster upon reading the details of the proposed revolution in a game so historic that one of its most hallowed competitions is for an urn full of ashes, reportedly those of early spectators who withered away waiting for the first match to finish?

Just listen to the proposed changes and tell me this will not raise the adrenaline to the pulse-pounding levels of a Stanley Cup final or a heavyweight title fight: "In a 50-overs match under the experimental rules, the team batting first will face half its allotted overs before effectively being forced to declare. The opposition will then take its turn at bat for 25 overs before both sides bat again for the remainder of their allotted overs ..."

Got that?

The move to loosen up the game has come, explains Australian Cricket Board chairman Alan Crompton, because "there's a suggestion that some matches lose their interest early in the piece, particularly if the team batting first are about 70 for six after 25 overs."

I couldn't have put it better myself.

Oh, we could argue about the precise point where the matches lose their interest. Mr. Crompton opts for the point where the team batting first are 70 for six after 25 overs. My own interest wanes when the team batting first actually shows up. But then, as Mr. Gershwin put it so well, "You say toMAHto, I say toMAYto." In cricket, as in any sport, the dozing-off point is in the eyelids of the beholder.

My own exposure to the game has been limited by a frightening experience in the early '80s.

I was sitting in a bar in Australia waiting for Rick Hansen to get his wheelchair fixed for the next 70 miles of the Man in Motion tour when the bartender turned on the telly.

"Cricket," he explained. "Give it a go. Good way to get your feet wet. It's one of the short matches."

"How long?" I asked.

"One day," he replied.

Suddenly, I felt dizzy. A game that took a whole day to play? That could be slower than baseball!

"You like this stuff?" I asked.

"Not really," he said. "But I sell a hell of a lot of beer."

HERE A RAT, THERE A RAT ...

October 21, 1996

Most sports wilt in the glare of logical thought.

Curling is a game in which a fat man can be narrow and a skinny man wide. Baseball outlaws the spitter as a pitch but forgives it as a player. Canadian football awards a point for missing a field goal. Tennis says love means nothing, then goes ga-ga over Andre Agassi and Brooke Shields.

But for sheer dumb, I'll take golf against the field. Which brings us, inevitably, to Taylor Smith.

Taylor Smith is the rookie golf pro disqualified in the final round of the Disney Classic because his playing partner, one Lennie Clements, noticed that the two grips on his putter weren't quite round and — in the finest tradition of the game — ratted on him to officials.

At that, he's probably lucky. Had that putt he sank on 18 for an apparent tie for the lead and a playoff with Tiger Woods counted, some PGA official would have been duty-bound to shoot him on the way to the scorer's tent. In the Year of the Tiger, the first rule is that anything or anyone standing between Woods and victory shall be considered an unnatural obstacle and removed forthwith.

Golfers are always tattling on each other and sometimes on themselves, mostly over violation of rules so piddling they would reduce athletes in physical contact sports to gales of helpless laughter.

Greg Norman once refused to sign playing partner Mark McCumber's scorecard, accusing McCumber of cheating because he pulled a blade of grass away from his ball before attempting a seven-foot putt.

"I was just swatting at an insect," McCumber protested.

"Right, then," said the PGA man. "Play on."

Twice, Norman disqualified himself, once in Australia in 1990 when he had a four-shot lead with 36 holes to play, for signing an incorrect scorecard, and again this year at the Greater Hartford Open when he was testing balls for Maxfli that bore different stamps for identification purposes and the stamp on the ball he used wasn't on the PGA-approved list.

On at least one occasion, golfers watching a tournament on television phoned to fink on a player seen in close-ups to be violating a rule so obscure the guy who wrote it probably couldn't remember why.

And then there was Roberto De Vicenzo, the ever-charming Argentine, who was ratted on after the final round of the 1968 Masters by Tommy Aaron, the guy who actually screwed up.

De Vicenzo apparently had a tie and a playoff with Bob Goalby at 277 after shooting a final-round 65. But Aaron, De Vicenzo's playing partner and thus his scorekeeper, put down a 4 instead of a 3 for the birdie Roberto made at 17. He also totalled the second nine at 35 instead of 34, and the round at 66. Aaron noted the goof and went running to the officials.

Aaron's mistakes, all three of them. But De Vicenzo, caught up in the excitement of the moment — the guy had a playoff going for the Masters jacket, for Pete's sake! — signed the card without checking it closely. The rules say what you sign is what you shot. So De Vicenzo shot a 66 instead of a 65, and Goalby won the Masters by a single stroke.

Contact sports are governed by a simpler code: Games are won on the field of play and anything undetected by officials is legal.

Referees do not accept the word of opponents. Leroy Blugh doesn't rat on himself. ("Excuse me, Mr. Referee, but I do believe I hit the quarterback late and with malicious aforethought. I demand that you march off 15 yards and throw me out.") Patrick Roy doesn't confess that his pads are too wide. If the people in charge don't see it, that's their problem.

Fortunately for Lennie Clements he's a golfer, where ratting out is socially acceptable. In any other sport, he might be in hospital today, having a bat, ball or hockey stick surgically removed.

SEWERPERSON

May 20, 1992

My wife is crewing in the Swiftsure yacht race. Training-wheels division.

"I'm navigator," she explained. "And sewerman. I get to haul in the sail and fold it."

This from a woman who hates to fold my shirts. A woman whose unerring sense of where she is and how to get where she wants to go is sometimes nullified by instructions along the lines of:

"Go left right here."

"Left?"

"Right."

But she has a cousin and he has a boat and Swiftsure has a lot of classes. Besides, their three-race record is 1-1-1: one win, one motor-in and one "We didn't race, actually, we spent all day getting the boat ready for next weekend." That's how I know she's ready. Sailors jump in their little sailboats and sail. Yachtspeople stay on the dock fixing their boats for next weekend.

"You want to crew for us?" she asked hopefully.

She knows I can't swim, hate water, and failed miserably in my only attempt to navigate a canoe. I was headed for Shawnigan Lake. It was on top of my car and fell off. At 5 p.m. In the middle of the Oak Street bridge. On to the hood of another car. I think she's after the life insurance.

But I'm behind her in this Swiftsure thing. Yessir, boy, there's nothing like the feel of a pitching deck as you run from the front end of the boat to the back end, upstairs and downstairs, looking for a place you can toss your cookies without getting it all over the hardy crewperson below (See: Sewerman). Those of us staying behind to lie down on the couch and watch the Stanley Cup are as green with envy as they'll be with *mal de mer*.

There were, however, a couple of questions.

"Does your Sophia work?" I asked.

"My what?"

"Your Sophia. That navigational thing that picks up from a chain of stations all over the place that tell you whether you're approaching Race Rocks or the lobby of the Pan-Pacific."

"It's not a Sophia," she said. "It's a Loran. With an 'a'."

"Whatever. Does it work, or do I have to ruin my weekend in some bumpy Air-Sea Rescue helicopter staring down at the water hoping to find you before the sharks do?"

"It works perfectly," she said in that skipper-to-landlubber tone that says you should kill yourself because neither your jeans nor your genes have salt in them. "Except when we were installing it and pushed an extra button and it thought it was somewhere off Tokyo."

"Kind of the long way around to get back to Victoria."

"Stow it," she said nautically.

But I'm supportive, especially since I found out amateurs can actually win. Bill Koch, who'd never entered before, won the Americas Cup on the weekend off San Diego. Cost him only $64,000,000 compared to $100,000,000 for second-place Italy, which only goes to show what kind of bargains there are out there in Yachtland if you really shop around.

A wonderful thing, technology. In Long John Silver's day you loaded a wooden boat full of swabs and went looking for treasure. Today you spend a treasure on the boat and go looking for a trophy that would make a hell of a hubcap if you could figure a way to flatten it.

Which reminded me.

"How much is this gonna cost us?" I asked.

"Ferry fare over and back with the car," she said. "And I've got to pack a lunch."

"Hey, no problem. I read *Treasure Island*. Barrel of water, barrel of flour, easy on the weevils. A tot of rum for the swabs. What can it cost?"

"Man overboard!" she screamed.

"Huh? Where?"

"Come out back," she said sweetly. "I think we should check out the pool."

INDY! MY HERO!

September 3, 1994

In all modesty, I know almost everything there is to know about Indy. Loved him in *Raiders of the Lost Ark.* Cool hat, great bullwhip. Sequels weren't bad, either, especially the one with Sean Connery playing his dad.

'Course, that's just the current Indy. Before that I saw *Gandhi* twice, and even before that I pulled for Sitting Bull in every Custer movie. Any day now you can expect to hear my fight song for the new Indy land-claims settlements, "The Big Bands Are Coming Back."

Yessir, you'll have to get up pretty early in the morning if you're gonna sneak an Indy question past me.

Except for the business with the cars.

What is all that, anyway? Once a year a bunch of guys hit town in cars obviously held together with decals, with such shoddy paint jobs they have to be redone after every race. Lousy mileage, no leg room, and you could look all day and never find one set of angora dice on the rear-view mirror or a doll-on-a-spring on the dash.

Did the guy on the used-car lot see them coming, or what?

"Got a great little deal for you, folks. Half a mil puts you behind the wheel of this little beauty right here, I swear only driven on Sundays. One owner, completely rebuilt. Well, actually, the *car* is completely rebuilt. The owner they're still working on.

"Unique styling, no clutter, just bare-bones efficiency. In fact, that's one of the bare bones right there. Looks like a femur, don't it? Musta wedged there after the last cra ... uh, maintenance check.

"What? No, madam, there is no driver-side air bag. There is an optional driver-sized body bag, but we don't encourage our customers to buy it. After all, ha ha, if you're ever in a position to need it, you're beyond worrying about who pays for it, right?

"Radio? Tape deck? Rear-seat speakers? Actually, madam, the engineering on this baby has eliminated the need for expensive options like that by eliminating the entire rear seat. Also the passenger side seat. And once you get behind the wheel and take 'er on the open road you'll see how a sound system would be a waste of time anyway. Get 'er up past 60 and it's so noisy you can barely hear your own screams.

"Spare tires? Of course it has spare tires. Two or three sets, which is about how many you'll need on a really fun weekend. Yes, madam, there is a reason you can't find them. They're not on the car. They're right there in the one optional extra you'll need to ensure top performance hour after hour: a full pit crew of expert, highly paid mechanics. Shouldn't run you more than, oh, about another half mil a year. Plus equipment.

"But there's a definite plus to it, madam. When you pull into that pit for a tire pump and an oil change, I guarantee there'll be no waiting. You'll be out of there in 90 seconds, tops.

"You'll take it? Great. Now, since I know you'll want to drive 'er right off the lot, I'll just go ahead and get a few other little extras you might want to consider in case a teensy little problem or two happens to crop up. Let's see ... fireproof suit, crash helmet, St. Christopher medal, and your complete list of Indy Driving Tips. That should about do it.

"What's that? Well, yes, there is only one tip on the list, but it is important: Have You Considered Taking a Bus?"

INDY EXPLAINED

September 1, 1995

Due to my acknowledged automobile expertise (as a teenager I once got eight people into my Austin A40. Strangers when they entered, they were intimate friends upon exit. In fact, two got married), I have been asked by Troubled Reader to explain one important aspect of the Vancouver Indy.

To wit: How do you watch a race where the cars keep passing each other when they're around a corner where you can't see them, and come back in an order so confused that you are reminded of the Biblical admonition that many who are last shall be first?

Dear Troubled: You have come to the right person.

For many years I, too, was troubled by the stubborn refusal of Indy drivers to proceed in orderly fashion in their assigned lanes and pre-determined order, thereby allowing once-a-year fans to holler things like "We're No. 8!" without drawing hoots from nearby know-it-alls reporting that you are now actually No. 14 or spread in sections in a pile of rubber tires on a corner.

Given some respect for order by the men behind the wheel, a certain spectator at the last Indy — dentists with pliers could not extract his name — might have been spared the embarrassment of cheering wildly as his favourite car roared over the finish line long before anyone else, only to learn that it had been lapped by everyone but the pace car.

Fortunately, Troubled, today's auto fan has access to the Internet, libraries, and newspaper special sections bigger than the Manhattan phone book which offer in excruciating detail the answer to every possible auto-racing question.

Except yours.

Nowhere can you find a simple explanation of how to keep track of cars that keep running around in circles, are out of your sight more times than they're in, and invariably choose the other side of the B.C. Place oval to lap each other.

You can search the world over. Michael Jordan's second question to that monk in the Gatorade commercial, right after the one about the secret of life, was the secret of watching an Indy. The response? "Shuddup, my son, and drink your Gatorade."

The only clue is a rumour, whispered in muffler shops and car washes when the clanging and the splashing mask the words from strangers, of an ancient rite held in certain grease pits on nights when the moon is eclipsed by the passing of the Goodyear blimp. There, to the incantation of retired pit crews ("Oldfield-Vukovitch-Granatelli! Oldfield-Vukovitch-Granatelli!"), the secret is passed down, car-fan father to car-fan son.

Unfortunately, this leaves those of us who don't know brake shoe from break dance sitting there in the sun wondering why we're wearing this crazy T-shirt ("I Drive Indy! Your Garage or Mine?") and watching our ice cream melt.

There are, however, solutions.

*Listen to the public-address man telling you who's ahead. If you feel stupid, having paid to sit in the sun essentially trying to listen to a radio drowned out by passing race cars, hum the old Allan Sherman song, sung to the tune of "Alouette":

Al and Yetta
Watched an operetta.
Leonard Bernstein
Told them what they saw ...

*Sit next to someone with a deep Scottish accent. Tell yourself it's Jackie Stewart.

*Stay home. Pour your own beer. Sit in front of the TV set. Tape the first 10 minutes and replay it on a loop. Figure out how long the race will take. Set the alarm. Wake up and find out who won.

Y're welcome. Always happy to help.

SMALL BOY, BIG TIGER

December 18, 1992

"If a kid has the right kind of friends, maybe when they start teasing him about figure skating and calling him a fag and a queer and all those things, he can sit down with them and explain what he's doing and why he's in the sport and what it takes to be good at it. If they don't listen and keep it up, well, maybe he should take another look at the kind of friends he has."

— Kurt Browning, three-time world champion

It has always taken a special, extra brand of courage for small boys with big dreams to put aside the hockey sticks and pull on the figure skates. That's what made the story so hurtful.

It was a bad story — outdated, sensationalized, backed by nebulous statistics purporting to show an apparent relationship between AIDS and figure skating.

It was written in Calgary and picked up in abbreviated form by the wire service. In the judgment of our sports department, where the sport is followed, it was not worth running. In the judgment of our news department it was worth a front-page headline:

TRAGEDY ON ICE.

Skating world savaged by deadly disease. Page A5

It ran under a white-on-red banner: THE SPECTRE OF AIDS.

"A sport of grace and beauty has been invaded by a monster," the story began. Then it claimed that "at least 40" male skaters and coaches in North American figure skating have died in recent years from AIDS-related diseases. The key names: former world junior champion Dennis Coi of Vancouver, three-time Canadian men's champion Brian Pockar, and 1988 Olympic dance bronze medallist Rob McCall.

The phones at the B.C. Figure Skating Association went ballistic. "Mostly it was fathers or mothers of skaters," says BCFSA sport developer Ted Barton, "telling us their sons had come home from school saying they had just spent the worst day of their lives."

It was all the old stuff recycled: "If you figure skate you've got to be gay." "Careful where you bend over, boy." Limp-wrist waves and falsetto cooing. Kid stuff — unless you're a kid and peer pressure is the greatest hurt of all.

The sport will survive. Rational thought will prevail. The words and excellence of a Kurt Browning ultimately will be measured against the unsubstantiated bleatings of someone called Arthur Luiz, co-president of "the newly formed International Gay Figure Skating Union". ("I don't even know who he is and I've never heard of this association," says American pro Brian Boitano.)

But there will be damage, because figure skaters *have* died of AIDS. So have doctors, lawyers and journalists — but their professions don't carry the baggage of the '70s and '80s, when CFSA officials admit the percentage of gays in the sport was far, far higher than today.

The CFSA has educational programs in place, including seminars with some of Canada's top male skaters there to assure the kids there's no stigma in wanting to skate, that it's just a sport like any other, with the same demands and work ethic and rewards. About 70 boys listened to Elvis Stojko, Michael Slipchuck, Patrick Brault and Doug Ladret at a recent session in Abbotsford. "They went away proud," says Barton.

But now it's all mixed up: the old stories, the new AIDS fears and the ignorance and misinformation that come with them. And the peer pressure.

I asked Kurt Browning about that. He'd just come off the ice in Toronto, where he's launching his comeback from back problems for another assault on the Worlds.

"Sure, it can be a problem," he said. "Especially when you hit 14 and the testosterone starts acting up and you'll be expected to hang out with The Guys chasing girls and being the king hockey player.

"It's just perception. They'll see you going off to figure skate and they'll make cracks. What they WON'T see is the 14-year-old boy going off to take part in a sport where the ratio is 8 to 1 girls!"

Kurt Browning played hockey, captained his team, and still frets that he can't find the time to play more. He chose one sport over another without apology.

"You have to ask yourself if it's worth the ribbing," he said. "Because those people always will be there. Me, I'm glad I didn't listen to them — because where are they?"

For the little kids with the big dreams, that's the rock to which they must cling: In sport as in life, there will always be tigers. And the goal is always worth the battle.

THE ROARING GAME

February 15, 1997

It's playdown time in curling, the only sport in creation where a game can be decided because somebody picked up a hair.

Over the years the occasional quip has crept into this space about what used to be called the Roaring Game back when they used brooms instead of carpet sweepers. I can't help it. It's a family curse.

My mother, my sister and my brother all played the game for years. Their idea of a really good time is a few hours spent discussing the relative merits of the in-turn freeze-dried draw as opposed to the double out-turn hold-the-fries takeout with hack weight. Or something.

At family dinners everything on the table would wind up at their end so they could stupefy the rest of us with descriptions of key shots in the C event mixed spiel where they kicked ass against the family down the street. ("The salt shaker is the button, see, and they're lying three with the knife, the fork and the cream jug. But I take the pepper shaker and pull a hit-and-roll on the napkin ring and sneak in behind the knife for shot!")

I, on the other hand, am a throwback to the Far Side of the family in which a great-uncle several times removed — but never far enough — had his tongue frozen to a boulder during one of the milder Saskatchewan winters, causing him to roll down the only hill in Nipawin with said boulder bouncing off his skull.

One look at a sheet of perfectly good hockey ice with bull's-eyes painted at each end and not a net or a faceoff dot in sight and this loathsome thing creeps over me. Strange words pour out of my mouth — words like "Eskimo bowling," "Overshoe shuffleboard" and "Yes-yes-off-off-no-no-hard-hard-hard-was-it-good-for-you-wanna cigarette?"

During Brier week thousands of people who know nothing about the game suddenly will be glued to their TV sets. For them, this curling primer:

CURLING: A game invented by Scotsmen too cheap to buy bowling balls who took to the sport by the thousands once they discovered that the rocks on the hillside were free. Wives soon insisted that they be allowed to play, too, despite male protests that when God gave woman a broom he meant her to stay in the kitchen.

(Note: Scots are also famous for inventing GOLF, a game in which people in overpriced sweaters hit a ball with an assortment of expensive clubs so they can go find it and hit it again.)

SWEEPING: The act of cleaning the ice just before the dirty rock goes over it and gets it dirty again. (Curlers are not here on scholarship.)

RINK: The place where they curl. Also the name for teams that do the curling. (See "scholarship" above.)

HOUSE: Not to be confused with RINK. The house is the place inside the rink (the building, not the curlers) where you're supposed to put your ROCKS and figure out the best way to remove the other rink's (the curlers, not the building) rocks so the people watching between drinks from the lounge above can second-guess and call you an idiot.

THE GAME: Four players on each rink play 10 ENDS (innings), throwing two rocks apiece from one end (the ice, not the inning) to the other end, where they either hit each other's rocks or they don't. Then they all go to the other end and throw them all back to the end they just left. When they've done this 10 times it's the end, unless the score is tied, in which case they throw all their rocks to the other end and keep doing it until somebody wins, at which point it's the end.

SUMMATION: Scots believe curling is a wonderful game. Mind you, they also serve their traditional meal using a sheep's stomach for a casserole dish.

SMALL TOWN THINKING

March 9, 1997

The Brier is in full broom, so let me tell you the story of how my home town put the game on the map.

I was nine years old and thus not invited to town-council meetings, but I'd hear the people talking about it in the Kozy Korner coffee shop as I tried to sleep on the old wooden breadbox while my mother kept them happy with the best donuts in town: In January, 1947, Nipawin, Saskatchewan (pop. 2,300), was going to hold the world's first carspiel.

Entry fee would be $100 per team. Because the matched granite curling stones were available only on a quota basis in those post-war years, entrants had to bring their own. Prize money would total an incredible $10,000, and to the winning rink: four brand-new, sleek and shiny 1946 Hudson automobiles!

There was considerable outrage. The old guard wanted nothing to do with it. "Do you know what this will do?" they fumed. "It will turn the game professional!"

Was this why they built the town's first one-sheet rink back in '24 — built it with slabs and stuffed the cracks with straw? They pumped the water in for the ice with an old stock pump — by hand, of course, the electrical kind was just too damned expensive — and hung gasoline lanterns at each end and one coal-oil lamp from the ceiling over the middle of the ice — so it could lead to this?

Why, this was 1925 all over again! Remember that, Bert? Some damned fool decided to charge us to curl — two dollars a season!

But the nay-sayers quieted down when they heard the reason for what was to be billed as "The World's First Automobile Bonspiel": Money was needed to complete the new six-sheet rink then under construction. Besides, wouldn't you like to see how we measure up to the rest of the prairies?

So they held it, and drew 103 rinks. Five additional sheets of ice were made in the arena adjacent to the usable but still unfinished six-sheet rink. Because the local hotels (there were, I seem to recall, two of them) could never handle the visiting curlers, let alone spectators, billets were arranged in private homes. And away they went with an event that would be held every winter through 1954.

Winnipeg's Howard "Pappy" Wood (with Al Derrett, Howie Wood Jr. and Bob McFarlane) won the cars, and Nipawin was the talk of curling and, indeed, the sport world-wide. Only it didn't know it yet.

It wasn't until later that the impact of the Autospiel on the game was truly measured. Walt Riddell, *Saskatoon Star Phoenix*: "Up until the Nipawin car bonspiel, there was hardly any coverage of curling in newspapers and radio beyond a local level. But by gathering the world's finest curlers and putting up cars for competition, Nipawin caught the fancy of the entire country. People as far away as Vancouver were staying up until 2 a.m. just to hear Bill Good's reports from Nipawin. This was the start of creating tremendous public relations in curling."

Twenty years later, Bill Good — "Breathless" as Jack Wells called him — would become my friend and mentor. His son, Bill Jr., and I would cover the Sapporo Olympics and go to Moscow for the first

Canada-Russia hockey series. But back then, scrunched up on the breadbox waiting for Mom to close the Kozy Korner so we could go home, I could only wonder what the fuss was about.

Go out today and see. And if you get a minute, drink a toast to the dreamers in the little two-sheet rink in Nipawin where you might say the whole thing started. Better yet, have a donut.

O! MIGOODNESS

May 1, 1997

Dennis Rodman, the Peck's bad boy of pro basketball, says he plans to have his name legally changed to Orgasm.

He offers this dazzling decision in his best-selling bathroom book, *Bad As I Wanna Be*, a tome so odious that Oprah Winfrey, who has been known to offer guests along the lines of split-personality cross-dressers who argue with themselves over what to wear, cancelled his scheduled appearance on her show because it wasn't worth discussing.

That may well be — but inquiring minds DO want to know, and Dennis has left out one key detail in his plan to alter his birth certificate: Is Orgasm to be his first name, or his surname? Either way, the disaster potential is reasonably high.

If it's to be his first name, are the Chicago Bulls — not to mention the NBA — ready to deal with a PA announcer blaring out "At forward — from Oklahoma State — ORRR-Gasm ROD-Mannn!"

And if it's his last name, does he become Dennis Orgasm, or change his first name to something really colourful, like Premature, or Multiple, or something exotic like Neverhadan?

The simplest, easiest and most sensible way to handle Dennis Rodman is to ignore him, to reach the logical conclusion that a man who changes his hair colour more often than his socks, a guy who goes out in public wearing a nurse's uniform and a platinum wig, is several bricks shy of an outhouse and let it go at that.

But Rodman is not stupid.

Wacked out, maybe. Bizarre, okay. Rubber-room candidate, with any luck at all. But there is a mind, however twisted, under that food-coloured do. Rodman knows that all those people pawing through the tabloids in the checkout lines are not just killing time while the clerk prices out the radishes. *National Enquirer* sells millions based on the public's fascination with celebrity, the more lurid the better. If you're shameless enough to market your depravities, you can sell a lot of books.

Take away his weirdness and Dennis Rodman is just a tattooed tall guy who grabs rebounds. That's not a book. Hell, it's not a chapter.

How many books would the long-retired Wilt Chamberlain have sold in 1991, discussing what it was like to go through life bumping your Adam's apple on doorjambs? But throw in the claim to have slept with 20,000 women, as The Stilt did — Pow! The talk shows clawed to have him even if the figure didn't stand the test of reality.

When Wilt's book came out I did the math. Setting an arbitrary starting age of 15, it would work out to 1.2 women per day, and that's not even allowing for nights he had a headache. Maintaining the average would require sleeping with TWO women one day out of every five. No wonder he preferred to be called The Big Dipper.

That's not even taking into consideration the obvious disadvantage of being 7' 1". Car conquests would be out. Picture the teenage Wilt trying to make out at a drive-in movie. The date would end with a chiropractor and the Jaws of Life.

Was he exaggerating? Probably. But people saw him make the claim on talk shows, read it in the tabloid reviews, and lined up to buy the book in hope of even more detail.

Dennis Rodman is operating on borrowed time. Soon he'll be 36. The Bulls are growing weary of the act. Given his lifestyle he's not likely to have put much of his millions aside for a house in the suburbs, a wife and 2.1 children. Dennis Rodman, cross-dressing superstar, is a curiosity. Dennis Rodman, cross-dressing private citizen hitting the job market, is something else.

Ignore him. If you really want to, and if you can. Dennis and his publisher are betting that you can't.

GET THEE TO A CLOSET ...

March 21, 1996

Mahmoud Abdul-Rauf is upset with America, the country that pays him better than $2,000,000 per year for stuffing leather balloons through fishnets.

"The Star Spangled Banner", he says, is a symbol of tyranny and oppression in America and though he will stand when they play it before NBA games he will no longer listen. Instead, he will pray to Allah.

This is a definite softening of his original stance, which was that, as a protest against the injustice rife in America, he would no longer rise with the rest of his Denver Nuggets teammates when the anthem was played. The NBA could suspend him, he said, but his religion was more important than money.

Two days later, after deep meditation and consultation with religious leaders — and quite possibly his accountant — Abdul-Rauf (who was Chris Jackson before he found Allah) graciously consented to stand from the "Oh, say can you ..." clear to "the home of the brave", thereby allowing his career to continue and the cheques to keep rolling in. I trust you are as relieved as I.

Three nights later, Iron Mike Tyson, another Muslim convert who has yet to change his name — although for three years he had to change his area code — fell to his knees in the middle of the ring and gave thanks for the strength and ability to beat the living snot out of another human being. Given the current state of the heavyweight division, it may be the only way anyone ever sees him hit the canvas.

I've always had trouble with the concept of fighters who thank whatever Lord is theirs for the ability to smite more quickly and effectively than they are smitten. Tyson was a thug and a rapist when he went into the Indiana pen. He came out as a Muslim, which may have done wonders for his peace of mind but took no noticeable steam out of the mugging he gave the hapless Frank Bruno.

Is this really what Allah had in mind when he helped a mugger see the light? Is a Maker with an entire cosmos to run really so concerned about who holds the heavyweight title that He allies Himself with one corner rather than the other? What happens when two fighters of equal religious fervour do battle? Is it an automatic draw?

Abdul-Rauf is a different kettle of convictions.

I myself have nothing against "The Star Spangled Banner" once you get past the fact that you need the vocal range of a coyote to sing it. When it is played I stand at attention — not necessarily as an expression of belief in everything for which America stands, but because it is the anthem of another country and thus due the respect. But there is a jarring hypocrisy to scooping millions from a league and a country with both hands and simultaneously spitting on the system that allows it to happen.

Here's a thought: If the man is so concerned about the poor and oppressed of America, why doesn't he give them all his money? That way he, too, could be poor and oppressed, giving him an opportunity to do first-hand research in the field. Who knows, he might even be able to write a paper on it, get a grant, and write the whole thing off under advertising and marketing when he pays taxes on his next $2,000,000.

Religious conviction is laudable. You could argue that it takes courage to make a public stand, to reject an anthem or begin every press conference or post-fight interview with a 30-second commercial for your Maker. But I seem to remember a line in the Bible in which the Lord instructed us how to pray: "Enter into thy closet, and when thou hast shut thy door, pray to thy Father which is in secret ..."

Nowhere did He mention centre ring or centre court.

Chapter Two

LOOK, MA, I'M A JOCKWATCHER!

Consider my qualifications to run all over the world criticizing professional and amateur athletes.

I cannot skate, let alone play hockey. I have never played a game of basketball. In my house, jam was a word that came after "bread and". When I dribbled, Mom changed me. The one time I got into the paint it was scrubbed off with turpentine. To this day I cannot clean a paint brush without flashback.

I have no size, no speed, no reflexes, no conditioning, no desire to play hurt or healthy. I am all but totally devoid of depth perception. Playing tennis involves seeing the ball at the top of the other guy's serve and not seeing it again until you hear it bounce. You'd be surprised how many get through.

I do play golf. Started a few years ago. Took every cent of the money I won in the office Super Bowl pool and bought a Sega 16-bit video game with golf cassette. (In my house it is a given that when God drops easy money on you He does not mean you to make an extra mortgage payment, get the roof fixed or buy your wife a new vacuum cleaner. He means you to buy toys.) Got the 10-year-old next door to hook it into my TV, positioned my easy chair equidistant between coffee and junk food, and settled into a serious exercise regimen: 36 holes a day, winter and summer, no matter what.

I would play more, but recently my silken thumb-stroke on the button has developed a bad case of the yips. I'm stabbing at it instead of following through, and can't putt worth squat.

"You mean that game where you have to book 24 hours in advance for a start time so early you've got to wear a hat with a lantern on it?" I ask. "That game where you hit a ball, go look for it, hit it again, then go to the bar when you've finished and bitch because you had to hit it so often? Go get caught in the ball-washer."

Actually, I played real golf when I was a kid in Winnipeg. There were two reasons I quit: My left eye and my right eye, which refused to synchronize.

My record for swings at a ball without actually touching it stood at 16 when I quit. For the first three tries the people in the foursome behind us found it quite amusing. "Look at that cute little kid trying to hit the ball," they said. By swing No. 8 they'd turned ugly. At 16, I ran like hell.

This chronic inability to do anything athletic was a Godsend in that it helped forge my career.

"Mom," I said, "I can't run, jump, hit, tackle, throw or catch. I was born to be a sportswriter."

"Put a cool cloth on your forehead," she advised. I tried, and missed. "Maybe you're right," she conceded. "A lack of talent like that shouldn't be wasted."

So I did, and one of the first things I covered as a rookie sports writer for the *Daily Colonist* in Victoria was the city amateur golf championship. "Amazing," I thought. "These guys hit the ball every time they swing."

Things did not go all that well. The night before, I'd taken a girl out in my brand-new 1959 MG convertible. We'd stopped for too much pizza and wine. "I'm gonna be sick," she said as we drove home, and promptly threw open the door, leaned out, and upchucked.

The next day I parked my car at the Oak Bay Golf Club, arriving early to get a spot in the lot, and spent the day covering the tournament.

The temperature hit 85. I'd left the top down. When I got back to the parking lot it was still crowded, but my car was in the middle of a huge empty circle. It seems the girl hadn't quite gotten the door all the way open after all. The side pocket was full. It had been exposed to the heat all day. Driving home was not a lot of fun. Anyway, I stick to Sega golf these days. Shorter hours, no green fees, and if you get off to a bad start you just push the button and start over. Oh, and that girl who barfed in my MG? I fixed her wagon. I married her.

The point is, I am not and have never been an athlete, yet I make my living reporting and often criticizing the performance of the finest athletes in the world. My colleagues, most in the same boat, see nothing wrong with this. But how would they react if athletes were given newspaper space to criticize us?

"Taylor is good on the long words but can't get in there and handle the short ones. His sentence structure looks like something out of an ESL class, and he spells like he shakes the Alpha-Bits box and lines 'em up as they come out. He can't parse and thinks a clause should have a Santa in front of it. Besides that, he's bald and looks like he hasn't paid his syntax."

Maybe that's why the technical end of sport has never been as much fun as the oddball: because it takes (or should) considerable expertise to discuss zone traps and weak-side locks and nickel defences, but any fool can wonder aloud what would happen if there was a shoemaker draft and why Donald Duck doesn't wear pants. "Who, what, where, when, why and how!" editors tell the kids coming in. Me, I prefer the "What if ..."

HELLO, DOLLY

March 10, 1997

One of the side-effects of the birth of Dolly the Duplicate Ewe is that sports fans the world over are dreaming of all-Jordan, all-Gretzky, all-Maradona, all-Griffey Jr. teams laying waste to sets of athletes unfortunate enough to have been conceived in passion rather than in a petri dish.

Even allowing for the obvious flaw (cloned M.J.s would grow and develop at the same rate as the original, and what franchise, let alone coach, can afford to wait 20 years?), they are missing the point: If cloning athletes ever becomes possible, the people doing the cloning will become more important than the athletes themselves. Figure it out: Who would you rather have, one Gretzky or the guy who can build you as many as you like, Gretzky willing? No, the key figures in sport's Brave New World will be the scientists, not the athletes.

Some of us have seen it coming.

In 1992 two Alberta university professors told the Canadian Space Agency meeting in Edmonton that Canada's brightest young scientists should be drafted and paid like NHL stars. They were a decade late. In 1982, I myself devised a marketing plan for the Faculty of

Science at Simon Fraser University, whose funding slash was taking a back seat to the save-the-football-team campaign.

Hold an academic pep rally, I said. Cheerleaders, marching bands, the whole thing — and tailor the cheers to fit the need:

Look up-court and whadya see?
The boys from Biochemistry!
They've cloned a guy who's 9' 3"
And now he's jumping centre.

They've made a tackle five feet wide,
Designed for speed and action.
Except, they put the feet inside,
And he can't get no traction.

They'll cure that cancer, wait and see,
It's there on their agenda.
Right now it's no priority,
They're building a tight enda.

I was ahead of my time. But Dolly has changed everything. Maybe it is time scientists were paid jock money, despite the inevitable salary disputes.

Who should get more — a scrub nurse who wins the Golden Rubber Glove Award for keeping the operating theatre germ-free for an entire season, or the superstar surgeon who goes one-for-four on tummy tucks?

How would you judge the relative worth of the scientist who perfects the gene-splicing technique that crosses Lee Iacocca with Julio Gallo to produce a car salesman who'll never sell you a lemon? And the developer of the spray for telephone mouthpieces that burns out the tongue of any caller who begins with the words "Is this James E. Taylor? And how are you today? That's great! James, I'm calling on behalf of the Association for ..."

There is, however, the problem of acceptance by the general public of intellectual superstars who haven't broken a sweat since the day they found out they had tenure.

I would suggest a program in which they learn to do the things that set athletes apart in public perception. They could start by learning to pout and spit.

TOY DEPARTMENT

February 22, 1997

A recent suggestion that curling is not exactly a sport for Mensa candidates has raised considerable ire, much of it burning out my E-mail circuits.

It's understandable. A fine lot, curlers, and some of the great party people of this or any other day. But between the shots on the ice and the shots in the lounge their humour glands tend to wind up pickled in specimen jars.

Maybe it's all that time their curling parents spent inhaling the smell of overheated overshoes and steaming breeches as they huddled around the pot-bellied stoves that were the social hubs of every rink before someone invented second storeys, lounge chairs and Scotch. Whatever. Mock curling at your peril. This is serious stuff. Honey, can I borrow your broom?

What they don't understand is that every sport is wide open to mockery. And in an era when hyper-pituitarial giraffes forgo their senior year of collegiate Basket-Weaving, Square-Dancing and Rap Lyrics 101 to accept millions of dollars to slam-dunk and endorse sneakers; when 18-year-olds who think high school is a classroom with more than two floors and matriculate on the bus between Melfort and Yorkton are suddenly pulling on NHL caps and deciding whether to buy the Mercedes or the Hummer, I find it increasingly difficult to keep a straight face.

Take a step back and look at some of the games people play:

BASEBALL: Grown men are paid millions to swing a stick at a ball thrown by a man who has three pitches and shakes off four signs. Its two biggest events:

(a) No-Hitter or Perfect Game: Two guys basically play catch while a bunch of other guys swing at pitches they can't hit and tame announcers don't talk about it lest they jinx the guy doing the throwing.

(b) Home Run: A millionaire puts a ball in orbit while nine guys look disgusted, then TROTS around the bases because he's too rich and too lazy to run.

GOLF: The quintessential dumb game. Exorbitant green fees to hit a ball and walk yourself into cardiac arrest chasing it so you can hit it again.

Here's a tip that will take a minimum 60 strokes off your game: Place the ball on the ground in your back yard. Hit it on TOP, driving it into the ground. Go to the kitchen. Have a beer. When you come back, it'll still be there. Hit it again if you feel like it. No green fees. No caddy to pay for an afternoon of frustration. No lost balls.

NHL HOCKEY: Twenty-six teams play a total of 1,066 games so 16 of them can start all over. Ticket prices are so high kids have to knock off a 7-11 on the way to the game. A basically one-legged Finn named Esa Tikkanen with 10 — count 'em, 10 — goals wants a new contract for $3,000,000 a year. Mario Lemieux, the best player in the game, wants to quit and play golf.

TENNIS: A sport played by people who can't count to three and think love is nothing.

NFL FOOTBALL: Canadian football with one less player and one more down, played on a postage stamp by superstars who've been busted so often they can't go to the post office without looking on the walls for their picture.

CRICKET: Played in "overs", but never is.

SOCCER: Now wait just a darn minute. Don't you be knocking soccer. That's MY game.

A MATTER OF PRIDE

July 17, 1996

Oh, but they'll be arguing up a storm in Miami, and you can understand why.

The Miami Heat signed free agent Juwan Howard to a seven-year contract which Miami papers say was for $98,000,000. But the *New York Post* says the deal is worth better than $100,000,000. Meanwhile, the Heat also came to terms with Alonzo Mourning on another seven-year deal which everyone agrees is for $105,000,000.

And there's the problem: Which guy is basketball's first $100,000,000 man? Howard definitely signed first, so if the *Post* is correct then he gets the title. But if the *Post* is wrong and he settled for a paltry $98,000,000, then Mourning is the champ.

You can see where this is important. I mean, how will the loser be able to hold his head up back home in the 'hood — a kid in his early 20s, hanging out at the playground trying to impress the locals when every kid on the block knows he's only No. 2?

Basketball is a trash-talking, chest-butting, in-your-face, don't-you-be-bringin'-that-stuff-to-my-house metaphor for life in which one guy is No. 1 and everybody else is No. Nuthin'. The first guy to sign for $100,000,000 is a big deal. The second is that dude who had to make do with a couple of million less.

What's he supposed to do with the rest of his life — hide in the custom-built Lamborghini? Join the *National Geographic* team exploring the uncharted floors of his mansion?

When the shame grows too burdensome will he have the courage to ask the chauffeur to drive him to the nearest MMA (Multimillionaires Anonymous)?

"Hi. My name is Juwan, and I'm stinking rich!"

"HI, JUWAN!"

"I guess it all started when Alonzo signed that contract bigger'n mine. Right away I started pretendin' like I was really rich like him, y'know, 'sted of havin' that eight-figure deal to his nine? Pretty soon I was carryin' American Express cheques in brown paper bags where I could peek in at 'em when no one was lookin'. "

"WE'VE BEEN THERE, JUWAN!"

Or, on a night when the shame grows too heavy to bear, will he simply say to hell with it, tie his money belt around his neck and throw himself off his wallet? Difficult times, indeed, for players like Mourning and Howard, living with the knowledge that only one can have this moment in the sun — and a fleeting moment at that, because whichever the winner, he knows the title will be his for only as long as it takes Shaquille O'Neal to decide whether he wants to stay in Orlando or move to Los Angeles.

The Lakers have offered seven years for $95,000,000, the Heat reportedly countering with $110,000,000 to keep him. The Lakers are now reviewing their offer with a view to upgrading.

Well, of course. No matter where he signs, O'Neal will have to get more than Howard or Mourning. He's the Shaq! Bad enough that Michael Jordan has that $25,000,000 one-year deal, which makes him the highest-paid guy per season. Could Shaquille live with the knowledge that he was also No. 2 or 3 long-term?

Of course not. It's a pride thing. After all, man cannot live on $100,000,000 alone.

A CALL TO ARMS

September 30, 1994

Since all my favourite ath-a-leets are spendin' more time on the front page than the sports page, I bin readin' the rest of the paper myself. And boy, there's an issue out there bigger'n hockey and baseball combined: The right to bare arms.

First time I seen it was on the editorial page, which is like the comics only with just one cartoon. The letters to the editor are full of it: guys sayin' the average citizen shouldn't be allowed to have 'em, others sayin' if we don't have 'em we won't be able to defend ourselves if somebody tries to take over the country — which, considerin' the way things are goin' lately, might not be a bad idea.

So, seein' as how I probably got no hockey pools to worry about because some American midget they flew in from basketball wants to play tough guy and shut down the NHL, I figure it's time I took a stand on this bare arms thing.

I'm for 'em.

We were born with bare arms, and dependin' upon whether you want cremation or your relatives want you to look dressy in the open casket and won't go with the I Like Beer T-shirt, we're gonna die with bare arms. Why should we stand by and let the government decide how we dress?

Take me, for instance. All my life I've had bare arms. I got baby pictures to prove it. For a while I even had bare legs. I didn't know how to use 'em at first, which is why me and my brothers were forced into long-sleeved stuff with crocheted animals on it. But that wasn't the Commies, that was Grandma, and we spat up on 'em as soon as she left.

Okay, we wore long sleeves in the winter. I grew up in northern Saskatchewan, man. You left your arms bare for more than 30 seconds and the huskies would use 'em for popsicles. But once spring came, we bare our arms. Now I'm, like, adult, and sometimes I'm forced to wear shirts. Funerals, weddings, poshy restaurants on two-for-one night ... but in the daytime or when I'm in the pub with the guys, I bare arms with the best of 'em.

It hasn't been easy, 'cause mine are kinda weenie. They got hair all over 'em, and I got no tattoos 'cause needles make me barf. Truck drivers ask me to arm wrestle against their baby fingers. Or their baby sisters. But I bare arms, man. It's a pride thing.

Now we got people tellin' us we can't, 'cause it causes accidents and triggers violence. You wanna see violence? Send some swishy fashion designer into a truck stop yellin' "Ruffles, anyone? Long sleeves with ruffles?"

Besides, we let people start tellin' us we can't bare arms and pretty soon they'll be tellin' us a bunch of other stuff we can't do. They're already tryin'. It's right there in the letters to the editor. Makes a guy realize how much he's missed, readin' nuthin' but the sports pages.

Take tree huggers. You got people sayin' they're environmentalists and people sayin' they're terrorists. Me, I figure everybody's sexual preference is their own business. Different strokes for different folks. They can't get a real date, let 'em go pat an ash.

But one fight at a time. Right now, we all got to get out there and stand up for our right to bare arms. With all those millionaire jocks on strike or locked out or threatenin' to suck their thumbs until they die, we got lots of time to prepare. Remember: When the cops come at you wavin' a long-sleeved shirt and demandin' you put it on, don't fight. Just stretch your arms up in the air and keep 'em there. That way, they'll never get the cuffs on you.

WHAT PRICE A BUTTOCK?

June 23, 1992

I suppose you could call it a form of sexual harassment, and maybe Vance Johnson's lawyer should have done just that. The headlines would have been bigger, and Confucius did say, "The bigger the headline, the bigger the payoff."

He didn't? Well, he should have, and I'm sure he would have had he thought of it or anticipated a time when retroactive humiliation would become the lawsuit of choice.

Whatever the reason, Johnson did not go that route.

Instead, the Denver Broncos' wide receiver had his lawyer file a plain, ordinary lawsuit against the Home Box Office pay-TV network for showing locker-room footage in which viewers were given a front view of his person including that geographical area normally covered by his jockstrap or, at the very least, his Fruit-of-the-Looms.

"It was embarrassing and humiliating to Vance," lawyer Mike Burg is quoted in sports pages across the land, "because it showed total frontal nudity. It was certainly discernible to the public. His mother-in-law has seen it. His sister has seen it."

Omigod! Not his mother-in-law! His sister, okay. She probably shared a tub and rubber duck with him when they were little. But his mother-in-law? What if she laughed? What if reporters come to her about the lawsuit and she calls it much ado about nothing?

I'd say the humiliation potential is immeasurable, except that old Vance has already measured it. He wants the network to pay him $50,000. Presumably that would give him enough to assuage his humiliation with a new toy or two, with maybe even enough left to buy a bath towel.

I do have a couple of questions.

First, football season ended four months ago and training camp hasn't started. When did this indignity occur and why did it take so long for old Vance to whip up a batch of humiliation? Did he need prompting? Hey, maybe his mother-in-law did laugh.

Second, Vance Johnson has been a pro football player, and a star at that, since 1985. Before that he went through a high-profile college program at Arizona, where he drew enough attention to become a second-round draft pick. At some point in that time, even if he was taking Basket-Weaving 10 and Parking Lot 100, he must have noticed the occasional TV camera in the dressing room.

Is it not reasonable to assume that he might have figured out that the cameras are there to take pictures, and that if it bothers him it might be a good idea to drape himself in a towel? Or wasn't Towel 10 on the curriculum?

The way things work these days he'll probably win the lawsuit and come away with the $50,000 and endorsement deals with Fleecy and a bath-towel manufacturer. Which leads to my final question: How do I get in on this? *Playboy* hasn't phoned. Or *Penthouse*, or *Hustler*, or even one of those drugstore tabloids where they put the little black bar across your eyes so no one will recognize you except everyone you've ever met.

I'm not saying I'd go full frontal nudity for 50 grand. My mother-in-law would come back from the grave to laugh. But I'm willing to negotiate. Say, $10,000 for a tantalizing glimpse of hairy buttock?

No?

How about $10,000 for an ankle shot?

No?

Okay, final offer: For $5,000 I bend over and let you shoot the bald spot made famous by former Premier Bill Bennett, who once stood at a banquet and said he got the idea for B.C. Place Stadium on a camping trip as he saw me crawl out of a tent. "Fortunately, Jim didn't back out," he said, "or we'd have had two domed stadiums."

CONTRACT TALKS

January 24, 1994

Mr. Brian Butters,
Editor-in-Chief,
The Province.

Dear Brian:

Further to our conversation — okay, my conversation — last year on a contract renegotiation that would make me a millionaire: I now see where I went wrong.

My mistake was comparing my salary to what Petr Nedved wanted from the Vancouver Canucks. Your brilliant riposte ("He's young and athletic and has female subscribers swooning over him. You're none of the above"), left me defenceless. But now — NOW I've got you.

We've just learned that John Madden has agreed to terms with the FOX network to do colour commentary on its NFL games for the next four years — for $32,000,000! His broadcast partner, Pat Summerall, has also signed for big dough, and the word is out that Terry Bradshaw, the CBS analyst from back at Mission Control, will join them for double the $600,000 salary he earned last year.

Madden's getting $8,000,000 per year, Brian. Troy Aikman, the Dallas quarterback, is the highest-paid player in the NFL, and he's scraping by on $6,250,000 per season. Being a fair-minded man and a trained journalist, you will realize instantly what this means: *The people who cover sports are more important and thus worth more than the people who play them.*

No doubt this will make you reconsider my bid for contractual rich-guy status (See: "FAIR-MINDED" above). Allow me to help with the following comparisons between myself and the Madden-Bradshaw analytical team:

Madden is a former fat guy who has lost weight. I have found it.

Bradshaw is bald and looks terrible on TV. My hair is thinning and, except for that tiny picture next to the stadium ("Dome and Con Dome," as a former friend put it), my face is not necessary to my work.

Madden does Ace Hardware commercials. I once wore a crest on my back saying I bowled for Washing Machine Parts and Services Ltd.

Bradshaw once did a pilot for a TV situation comedy in which he and stuttering country singer Mel Tillis played good-old-boy dirt-track racers. It lasted one episode. I did a TV show with a bearded chap named Greg Douglas which was often uproariously funny, sometimes even when we planned it that way. It ran 64 weeks.

Madden talks a lot. In all modesty, I have been talking almost since birth.

Bradshaw was a great quarterback, Madden a great coach. Thus, their work is always getting cluttered up with information. As an athletic nonentity with no sporting experience whatever unless you count that time in the bath house in the Sapporo Olympics in '72, I am under no such handicap.

Being a man of great perception (did I mention fair-minded?) you cannot help but agree that my credentials for sports-related wealth are impeccable. I am prepared to open negotiations at any time.

Sincerely,
JT.

BAD HAIR DAY

January 10, 1996

Phineas T. Barnum, who gave the world a midget named Tom Thumb and an elephant named Jumbo, built his circus and his fortune on the belief that "No one ever went broke underestimating the intelligence of the general public."

Barnum always denied the other quote attributed to him, "There's a sucker born every minute, but none of them ever die." But he never disputed the sentiment. Make it big enough, make it gaudy enough, make it wacky enough, and the people would line up to buy it whether they needed it or not.

Barnum would have loved a recent night at General Motors Place. It was there that 350 Vancouver Grizzlies fans, including 18 women, waited in a lineup for the privilege of having their hair given the flattop cut favoured by Bryant "Big Country" Reeves. They did this in exchange for a free seat for the game between the Grizzlies and the (nudge, nudge) Los Angeles CLIPPERS ("Get it, Martha? It's, like, the Clippers in town and we're getting, like, clipped, haw, haw!").

As it turned out, they didn't really have to, because the lineup was so long the team wound up letting the rest in anyway. But they did it, and willingly. They had their hair cropped to where they could sing tenor for the Crewcuts, just so they could watch one NBA game. Ah, Phineas, you were born too soon.

The kids, you could understand. High-school hoopsters wear their hair cropped anyway. For them, it was a free haircut to go with the free seat. Adult males might do it, if only for bragging rights down at the pub. ("Yeah, Big Country gave me this. Him and me, we're like that.")

But women?

Picture this: A guy walks into the dining room Sunday night after a hard day on the couch watching NFL playoffs. And there stands his wife, looking like third runner-up in a k.d. lang lookalike contest. The girl he married, she of the long blonde hair, *butched.* Paint windows on her face and she could pass for the Flatiron Building.

Right away, the guy's in a no-win. He can't compliment her. The man's not blind. Frantically, he considers possible reactions.

"What in hell have you done to your hair?"

"My, you're looking wonderfully flat-headed tonight, darling."

"Jeez, I'm glad it wasn't a football game. You'd probably shave the whole thing off, paste Lions decals over your ears and go as a helmet."

"Do me a favour: pretend it's a Canucks game and you're a goalie. Put on a mask until it grows back in."

"Stay inside, honey. Four Spitfires are in holding patterns waiting for clearance to land."

No, the man is helpless. Worse yet, he knows this is only the beginning. If she's enough of a fan to turn her head into an aircraft carrier because the Clippers are in town, what's she going to do when the Washington Bullets hit town — spend $300 on a flak jacket? Line up to be sawed in half for the Orlando Magic?

You can't blame the Grizzlies, who are already putting on a show so good that the game is often an afterthought — which, on many a night, has been a good thing. When you're short on steak you sell the sizzle, and no one does it better than the NBA.

The Grizzlies aren't going to win much. As the season goes on, it may get tougher to keep the customers coming. Hence, the smoke, mirrors and haircuts. It's crazy — but when 18 women line up for haircuts that will make them look more like a 290-pound man ... well, maybe it's just as well Barnum didn't make that crack about a sucker born every minute. Whoever did obviously underestimated.

LIGHT IN THE WINDOW

July 29, 1994

Once in a while a guy has to exit the toy department and become involved in something more meaningful. This is the day, and I have chosen the objects of my involvement.

Hookers.

Not in the physical sense, you understand. No, indeed. Not in the move-'em-here, move-'em-there game of musical beds that has passed for Doing Something about them for generations. As a member of the second-oldest profession, I simply feel a duty to assist practitioners and proponents of the first.

In that context — average citizen just trying to help — I offer today a simple, cost-effective way to handle a complex situation to the betterment of all concerned. To wit: A perfect site for the controversial "safe-stroll zone", where favours can be offered and purchased in an atmosphere of cleanliness, comfort and safety, free from the harassment of police, pimps or outraged residents.

I nominate GM Place.

Okay, it takes a little getting used to. But think about it. Here we have this beautiful, big, 20,000-seat luxury sports palace now under construction as a playpen for the NHL Canucks and the NBA Yomommas. Even allowing for playoffs, you're talking a maximum 120 game nights. That leaves 245 nights that Arthur Griffiths and friends must fill to make the operation fully viable — 246 of them in Leap Year when, under my plan, February 29 would be designated Leap Night with specially reduced rates and truly amazing gifts.

Consider the advantages to turning those nights over to the ladies of the evening:

* Two red lights are already in place, one at each end.

* Arthur and partners could rent the building to the city (which would write off the costs against money saved by cutting patrols on Richards and Seymour), take a flat fee from the occupants or, in the same entrepreneurial spirit with which they launched the NBA franchise, gamble on a percentage of the take.

* The celebrity boxes would give the place that touch of old Amsterdam, with the ladies sitting back-lit in the windows in fetching outfits that would say "Come hither" and dare a john to yawn.

* With 20,000 comfortable seats — not a bad view in the house, it promises in the brochure — even the nights when demand over-

whelmed supply could turn into a plus as hot-dog and beer vendors worked their way through the crowd peddling wares of their own at prices only slightly less staggering.

* GM Place designers, rightfully proud of their creation, have said from the beginning that the communication system will be state of the art. How tough would it be for a john to dial the number listed on the front of the celebrity box in which lounges the lady of his pro-tem dreams, whisper sweet figures in her ear and arrange a tryst? For an extra $10, management could even offer her enlarged photo on the big-screen scoreboard.

* With the celebrity boxes equipped with TV, washroom and food and beverage service, the ladies could even rent one for the evening, thus eliminating those awful and unsightly late-night traffic jams as johns try to drive away from the current curb-side negotiations with one hand on the wheel and the other holding their hats over their faces.

* The rink is not in a residential area. There's plenty of parking. Keeping the ladies safe from harassment would be as simple as stationing an usher at the stairs leading to the celebrity-box floor. One policeman could handle the whole night.

Give it a go, Arthur. If it works, you might even consider expanding to include game nights. You might not win the Stanley Cup, but you'd lead the league in post-game shows.

DADDY'S BOY

May 1, 1996

It's May, that wonderful time of year when college freshmen and sophomore and junior basketball stars must decide whether to stay in school or skip their remaining collegiate years and take the NBA money right now.

It is also the time of year when educators — many of whom have spent the year fighting to maintain the athletic eligibility of gargantuans who believe staying above C level means keeping your head above water — suddenly feel the PR department knives poking into their spines and trumpet to these young men the virtues of staying in school as poverty-stricken Oral Communication, Kitchen Management and Psychology of Square-Dancing majors.

"Get your degree," they plead, "and someday, should you come upon a square-dancing bus boy longing to communicate, when he says, 'Allemande left to your corners, y'all,' you'll be able to answer right back, 'Dosi do, bro!' With an education, you can make a difference!"

It is a stand supported and appreciated by coaches who were fortunate enough to have out-bribed other coaches to get these phenoms into their program and who can see a shot at the Final Four flying out the window if they leave.

"You've been like a son to me, Alonzo, and ..."

"Al-FRAY-doh, coach. Mah name's Al-FRAY-doh, with a r-a-y in the middle and one of them aitches on the end."

"Whatever. The important thing is, you stay around one more year and you'll go even higher in the draft. Go now, and long-term you lose BIG money! Think of your future, son! More important, think of MINE!"

So far, 10 collegiate stars and one kid fresh out of high school have resisted the temptations of more years avoiding the study hall and declared themselves eligible for the NBA's June draft. The high-schooler, one Kobe Bryant, has seen Kevin Garnett make the leap and believes he can, too. The scouts say he's wrong, that he needs collegiate competition, so he's probably making a mistake.

But the rest of them?

If I had a son who'd completed one, two or three years of college and was already good enough to attract the attention of NBA scouts, I would sit him down and give him one of those pieces of survival lore that have been passed from father to son since cavemen first began exchanging pretty pebbles for pieces of T-Rex meat.

"Son, this is your father speaking, so listen carefully: TAKE THE MONEY!

"I know you're really enjoying that sociology course, *Baywatch*: Cultural Landmark or Skinflick, and I'm not saying that Gym Decoration won't be of great value down the road. And there's no denying you owe Embraceable U a debt of gratitude for getting those nerds to take your other exams so you could concentrate on your jump shot.

"In fact, you'd make your mother and me really proud if you went back to college in the off-season and took some courses in a foreign language like, say, English.

"But the NBA will pay you NOW. How much is it going to pay you in a year if you blow a knee playing in college for nothing?"

And if he agreed, with tears in my eyes I would reach up, pat him on the head and say, "There's a good boy. Now you go right down to that agent, sign that letter saying you're turning pro, and stay there until draft day.

"And on the way home, stop in and buy your old dad a Mercedes."

Chapter Three

WILLIE AND THE SAXONS

In 1066, William the Conqueror took on the Saxons in a best-of-one series and won England. Nine centuries later, in exactly 1,066 games, 26 National Hockey League teams reduce their number by 10 and win the right to start all over again.

Obviously, Willie and the Normans had a better system than Gary and the Governors.

Suppose, after that first battle, King Harold the Saxon had told the local scribes, "Okay, that's one. But this is a best-of-seven war, and when the going gets tough, the tough get going. There's a lot of pride in our tent, and once we get our guys playing to a defensive system where they duck those arrows instead of throwing their chests in front of them ..."

Would England have been any better for a best-of-seven? Before the first battle horn blew the smart money was on the Normans. Everybody knew they had better equipment, more size and a deeper bench. If there'd been a Vegas, the Saxons would have been 200 to 1.

And there were no prelims. William and Harold didn't have to stop off at every Pimple-on-Thigh and Water-on-Knee hamlet to squash the local tough guys on the way to Hastings for the final. This was pre-expansion. They weren't just the best, they were the only. So they had the fight, got it over, and the peasants went back to the villages muttering, as villagers always have and always will, "Normans, Saxons, big deal. We all know who's gonna get pillaged in the end. Us — the bloomin' spectators!"

"Too right! You see that Saxon doin' the barterin', floggin' those flippin' white towels? Wanted my cow, 'e did, and I was savin' 'er for an ale."

"You call that a battle? I tell you, they've gotta do something about the violence. There ain't nearly enough of it."

Nine centuries later, we haven't learned a thing.

Twenty-six teams start the hockey season. They play 1,066 league games for admission prices Joe Average can't afford. Coaches are handed lousy teams, and get fired because they don't win. Players go through two-thirds of the season on cruise control because they know nothing matters until March.

And then, as the flowers bloom on the west coast and the ice floes begin to crackle and shift in the east, all but 10 of them start all over again.

If all 15 series were to go the maximum seven, that would mean 105 playoff games — one entire season's worth of games plus 23 for one team — culminating in the Stanley Cup Finally (just when you think it's never going to end, it's finally over) which runs through mid-June, thus winning the annual battle to get hockey season over before the summer solstice.

And no matter how the seasonal turtle derby ends, several teams in each conference will march triumphantly into the playoffs having lost more league games than they've won.

Is this not a job for the Better Business Bureau? Shouldn't there be some competency level to be attained before you are allowed to inflict yourselves on the playoffs? Would not winning more games than you lost during the regular season be a reasonable place to start?

When the league had six teams, four made the playoffs. When it expanded to 12, the top four in each division qualified — eight of 12. It stayed that way through expansion to 18, then ballooned to 16 in 1979 when four WHA teams were graciously allowed into the lodge in exchange for everything they owned and options on their first-born. And now every playoff series would be best-of-seven.

Why has all this happened? Why has the NHL drifted away from logic and ever closer to consumer fraud? Because it has discovered to its delight that come playoff time the pigeons have short memories and deep pockets. When in doubt, follow the money.

HELLO, DR. PAVLOV?

April 23, 1996

It's a Saturday. The Canucks and the Avalanche are locked in a 4-4 tie with five minutes left in the third period. The Orca has orked, The Fiddler has fiddled, the Blues Brothers have blued, the banjos have duelled, the lounge lizard has slithered, and 32 people have gone into full pretzel trying to keep up with the Macarena.

Suddenly, on the four message boards on the Orcavision scoreboard — where only seconds ago the giant white-gloved Mickey Mouse hands were showing people how to clap — a new cartoon appears: people throwing themselves from the upper tiers. Below them, one word: "JUMP!"

How many people do it?

My bet is that the body count would break the record set by dead fish (two), and maybe even approach the dead-rat total in Florida. In the brave new world of the Pavlovian Hockey League, to read and to hear is to obey. And if you pumped the 18,033 customers full of truth serum and asked them what happened, they'd say, "Hey, we got to have another party!"

And another hockey game?

"Oh, yeah — that, too."

There are those — and I'm one of them — who contend that the NHL has overdosed on sizzle, that with its credo of no-second-unfilled it has broken the link between team and fan and made the game secondary to the entertainment.

Once there was time to turn to your buddy in the stands and marvel at a Corey Hirsch save or the obvious ancestry of the guy with the whistle. Now, you say, "Wasn't that ... oops! Sign says it's time to make noise! YEAAAAH!"

Once you didn't need a sign telling you when to clap and when to make noise. If you felt like clapping, you clapped. If you wanted to yell, you yelled. The decision was yours and yours alone. Now you see people actually looking up at the sign like kids at a crosswalk waiting for the light to go green. God forbid they should jump the count with unauthorized decibels.

You think it isn't conditioned response? Ask yourselves how many times you've seen the talk-show scene from *Slap Shot* flashed on the screen. You know every word, every French-Canadian nuance of the guy's speech. But when he says, "You feel shame ... and then you are free," you laugh. Every time.

Why? Because you're not there to watch hockey, you're there to have fun while you're watching hockey. What Orca Bay has done, along with the marketing mavens in all the other arena-cum-Palace-of-Versailles showplaces springing up around North America in all their corporate-sponsored splendour, is reverse the priorities of the over-paying customers.

But repetition is shifting those priorities, bleeding away the spontaneity.

When the Macarena first began to catch on, the people jumping up and trying to do the hand gestures were hockey fans caught up in the moment. Now they're people who arrive in make-up, wait until they see themselves on the screen, and go into a routine so rehearsed they could join the Radio City Rockettes.

And isn't it funny how the same faces always seem to show up? More than 18,000 people in the joint, and the camera just happens to find those same two girls, over and over again. Truly, technology is a wonderful thing.

You can see Orca Bay's point. In the world of Sega and Genesis, Internet and interactive — a world that only the young truly understand — the attention span darts and dives like a demented bluebottle. When you're charging big bucks you titillate the senses full time or the minds switch channels and you may never get them back.

This is not so much a complaint as an observation, a cry for lost spontaneity, perhaps, or lost youth. But someday I will tell my grandchildren stories of chilly rinks with real ice and nights when hockey was the only thing on the menu. No rockets, no electronic scoreboards, no video monitors, no gigantic inflatable whales. Just hockey.

They will look at me strangely, not knowing what they've lost.

THE PUCK STOPS HERE

February 18, 1997

To: All Staff
From: Head Office, *Hockey Night in Canada*
CC: CBC
Re: Foster Hewitt dead rumours.

It has come to our attention that a radical group of western viewers upset with our mandate to follow our beloved Toronto Maple Leafs on their inexorable drive to the Stanley Cup are spreading a scurrilous rumour that Foster Hewitt is dead.

Further, these nagging nabobs of negativism, in league with the national media, are producing on a daily basis standings showing the Leafs in last place in their division, an inept band of under-achievers with no chance of reaching the Cup final without buying tickets, and charging that we at *HNIC* are living in the past.

Their stated objective: To force *HNIC* to telecast Saturday-night games that do not involve the Leafs.

Instead, they would have us foist upon this nation games in which participating Canadian teams are actually battling for playoff positions, including those based in cities west of the Great Lakes.

Allow me to respond.

1. Foster Hewitt is not dead.

Although we do not attend games personally, we know that he is still in the gondola providing those thousands of children sprawled on the floor in prairie farmhouses with his matchless descriptions of Teeder and Turk and the Big M and awarding the third star to Dave Keon, who always plays a good game. If he wasn't, Harold Ballard or King Clancy would have called to tell us.

2. The Leafs are definite contenders for the Stanley Cup.

Anyone with any understanding of mathematics realizes this. With six teams in the NHL and four of them advancing to the playoffs all we (excuse me, they) have to do is finish ahead of two clubs, which should be even easier with the rumoured injuries to Jean Beliveau and Bobby Hull.

3. Proposed telecasts of games involving NHL teams west of the Great Lakes.

There are no NHL teams west of the Great Lakes — or anything else, for that matter. Every schoolchild realizes that anyone crossing the Saskatchewan-Alberta border falls off the edge of the earth into a flaming pit, to be devoured by dragons. This is all anyone in the east knows about the west, or cares to.

Westerners, on the other hand, hunger for any crumb of information regarding life in Toronto in general and the Leafs in particular. Here at *HNIC* that is our mandate, and we are committed to its relentless pursuit.

4. Lost touch with the NHL?

Deep in the Molstar bunker in Toronto, crack teams of trained senior citizens who can recite the rosters of every Leafs team from Conn Smythe to Punch Imlach are crouched over their crystal sets on 24-hour alert for reported sightings of non-Toronto Canadian NHL franchises — all part of *HNIC*'s commitment to remaining on the cutting edge of hockey coverage.

Further to this commitment to stay abreast of the hockey scene, we plan to launch a series of *HNIC* profiles of up-and-coming players who might someday be Leafs. Segment One: a 14-year-old in Brantford named Wayne Gretzky.

CALAMARI TO GO

May 12, 1996

True love, Stanley Cup style:

In Detroit, a Red Wings fan prepares for the trip to the Joe to see his team dump all over those Blues guys from St. Louis who had the gall to turn this thing into a series and cost him all kinds of extra ticket bucks.

He stands in front of the mirror, sucking in his gut like Lee Marvin did dressing for the showdown in *Cat Ballou.*

He pulls on his Red Wings jersey, the one with Stevie Y's name and number on the back.

He paints his face Red Wings red and pulls on his Red Wings cap.

He goes to the bathroom. Got to keep the old bladder empty. Leaves more room for the beer.

Then he runs a check list:

Gretzky Sucks sign. Check.

Go Wings Go towel. Check.

Keenan Sucks sign. Check.

White towel. Check.

Hull Sucks sign. Check.

Dead octopus ...

"Honee! Where'd you put the octopus?"

"They didn't have any."

"They what??? Game Seven, and they're out of octopus? What kinda wimp supermarket you dealin' with?"

"Well, actually, they did have some, but they jacked the price, so I settled for squid."

"Squid! You want me to go to Game Seven with my buddies, and when the Wings score they're all throwin' octopus and I'm throwin' squid? What kinda hockey fan you think I am? They'll laugh me out of the Joe!"

"Uh, maybe they won't notice. See, I saw how squishy and drippy and oozy the damn thing was, and I thought 'What the hell, there's got to be a drier squid than this.' "

"And ...?"

"And I talked to the butcher, and he said no, there wasn't, and please apologize to you for him, but the rest of the idiots got there first. So ..."

"Wait a minute! You said you got me a squid!"

"Well, sort of. See, I went over to the specialty counter and they had a sale, so I bought you a whole *bunch* of squid. Here!"

"What's this?"

"It's a bag of calamari."

"Calamari? I send you out for octopus and you come back with deep-fried squid?"

"But honey, they've got holes in the middle! Think of them as squid donuts. They're aerodynamic. You can spin 'em like Frisbees. You'll get lots better distance than your buddies. You might hit the referee right in the head and do some real damage!"

"There is that," he conceded.

"Sure! And what you don't throw, you can eat. Let's see those lowlifes try that with their stupid octopus."

"I love you," he says, throwing his arms around her.

"Careful," she says. "You'll squash your ammunition."

She stands in the doorway, waving goodbye and wondering where and when the man she loved became a fruitcake. Then she shrugs. After all, it could be worse.

Her sister is married to one just like him, and they live in Florida. It must be tough finding deep-fried rats.

EVERYBODY OUT OF THE POOL

September 5, 1995

I have in mind the perfect hockey pool.

You prepare hundreds of copies of the previous season's NHL statistics and this season's entry form. You encase them in waterproof packets, sink them to the bottom of the Vancouver Aquarium pool, and tell all would-be poolsters that they have to jump in to get them.

Then you fill the pool with piranha.

Within hours the pool would be placid, the silence broken only by the burping of contented cannibal fish, and the Canadian gene pool would be considerably strengthened by the elimination of an ever-growing number of people who obviously have the intelligence level of potted plants.

"But wait!" I hear you shouting. "Your very own newspaper is running perhaps the finest hockey pool of them all! Surely you jest?"

I do not jest. And stop calling me Shirley.

My newspaper is, indeed, running an excellent hockey pool. The fact that I am free to criticize such intellectual aberrations stands as a shining example of the democratic manner in which this organization is run (he said, tap dancing furiously).

Why, just yesterday I was saying to Brian Butters, our beloved editor-in-chief: "To paraphrase Mr. Voltaire, I disapprove of what you do in this matter of hockey pools, but I will defend to the death your right to do it."

"It may work out that way, at that," he agreed.

Cloaked in this vote of confidence, I feel free to offer a piece of advice to the thousands upon thousands of people who will no doubt enter our hockey pool and the thousands upon thousands of similar pools that now infest the continent like prairie grasshoppers and rap: It is not too late. There IS a cure.

From the list below, select the profession, job or lifestyle into which you currently fit. Proceed to the bathroom, gaze into the mirror, and repeat the words that follow your designation.

Average citizen:

"For seven months I am going to court eyestrain reading newspaper six-point type to follow the hockey fortunes of a bunch of people I have never met nor will ever meet.

"I am going to spend inordinate amounts of time fretting over their slumps, crying over their injuries, and adding up everybody's points every day in case the designated statistician in our pool screws up or cheats."

Secretary or low-echelon office employee:

"For seven months my boss is going to have me clipping hockey summaries or phoning the newspapers the night before so I can have an up-to-date pool report on his desk when he gets in every morning.

"Naturally, the boss will expect me to do this in addition to my regular work load, because it's really great for office morale to have a hockey pool, as long as he wins it. If he doesn't win it, it will be my fault."

Non-playing husband/wife:

"I got married for *this*? A Significant Other who seven months of the year thinks foreplay is the National Anthem?

"The dining-room table covered with hockey summaries? Listening to Don Cherry's Grapevine like it's the Sermon on the Mount? Trying to cheat his best friend by trading Gretzky to him before he hears about the bad back?

"I've had it. Either we cancel the *Province* or I cancel him. And I *like* Calvin and Hobbes. Now, where did I put the rat poison ...?"

At first it will be hard to face that mirror. But don't give up. Repeat the process morning and night. At the end of the week you should be able to walk right up to it and shout, "My name is John. I'm a Poolaholic!"

Trust me, you'll feel better. And think of all the time you'll save for drinking and gambling.

FOREVER HOUSE

February 4, 1993

Calgary traded right wing C. J. Young to Boston for left wing Brent Ashton. — Transactions, *The Province*, February 2, 1993

Susan Ashton calls it her Forever House. It sits empty in Saskatoon, waiting for the summers when hockey's over and the family can come home for a few months before the phone rings again and they move heaven knows where.

"We bought it, but we don't rent it," she says. "It's just there. We open the door, and we're home. And one day when this is over we're going to move in and stay forever."

"This" is the life of a hockey Gypsy, where time is measured in packing cases and team jerseys and you're almost afraid to make friends because you know that goodbye comes too soon after hello.

"This is not real life," Susan Ashton says without a trace of self-pity and a barely detectable hint of regret. "It's like you're waiting for your life to start."

She is on the phone from Boston, where Taylor, four, and Carter, two, and a 125-pound German Shepherd named Fletcher make background sounds as she packs for the umpteenth time, heading this time for the Forever House, which will be close enough to Calgary for visits back and forth.

Her husband has just been traded to his ninth National Hockey League club, Boston to Calgary. For Susan Ashton, who remembers the jumps less in terms of cities than moving companies, it is a point of pride that, though he'd begun this season with the Providence farm club, the Bruins weren't trying to get rid of him; the Flames came looking.

But then, it's always been that way. For 14 seasons, from Vancouver to Colorado to New Jersey to Minnesota to Quebec to Detroit to Winnipeg to Boston and now to Calgary, Brent Ashton has epitomized that bedrock of the working class, the skilled journeyman.

Want a winger who'll skate all night, kill penalties, work the power play, check relentlessly, do his share of the rough work and end every game with his uniform soaked in honest sweat? Phone whoever's got Brent Ashton.

Need a guy who can fly in today, play tonight, get along in whatever dressing room he happens to be in, fights for his worth but never whines or goes public, and just might be that extra part you need for the stretch? Where's Brent Ashton these days?

He has the skills that make him handy enough to be valuable, but not too valuable to lose. So the phone rings, the GM gives him the word, and Susan Ashton looks around Whatever House in Wherever City, and calls another van line.

"The kids are still too young to realize," she says. "The dog knows every time. He sees a duffel bag or a packing case, he sits by the door and doesn't move. Me — I've done it so often the moving companies don't tell me how it works, I tell them."

Moves are measured by the places she's unpacked. New Jersey was easy because the whole team was moving from Colorado. Minnesota was six weeks in a hotel and two houses in 18 months. Quebec was moving 11 days before Christmas, farther east than she'd ever been, more snow than she'd ever seen.

In Detroit, they bought a house. Seventeen months later they were in Winnipeg. "You believe them the first time they say you're not going to be traded," she says. "After that, you just wait."

There have been good times. Susan Ashton has learned that every city is beautiful in its way if you take the time to look and savour new experiences. "Here in Boston we rented Wade Boggs' condo," she says. "I'm looking out the window right now and can see the beach where we can walk in the winter."

She had talked to Brent, who'd played his first game as a Flame the previous night. "He said he got to play a lot and was aggressive," she says, the pride coming through. "It looks like it's going to work out pretty well."

She said goodbye and thanks. There were suitcases to fill, and Forever House was waiting around one more twist in the road.

NEW DIGS, OLD MEMORIES

August 23, 1995

The first thing you notice about the entrance to the press box at GM Place is a distinct absence of ladder. And ants.

Well, maybe not if you're semi-old or younger. In that case, you might notice that the joint is a lot bigger and more comfortable than the one in Pacific Coliseum. But if you're old enough to have worked in the box at the Vancouver Forum, you never enter a new press box without thinking of the ladder and getting sympathy pains in your scalp.

The Forum was the second press box of my professional career — third, if you count clinging to one side of an Esso oil truck with my notepad on a baby Austin in the middle of a snowstorm at the western Canada intermediate football championship game in Fort William, Ontario.

It was my first road trip. "So this is the bigs," I thought, blowing snow out of my nose and banging my ballpoint against the Austin's paint job to keep the ink flowing. "I wonder if Red Smith ever did this."

The Forum was the pre-Coliseum home of the pre-NHL Vancouver Canucks.

To get into it you climbed a ladder — not set at an angle as God intended, to allow a guy some balance, but nailed flat into the wall.

The ladder led to a trap-door entrance cunningly designed to look about four inches wider than it actually was. The four inches were occupied by a two-by-four — black, so it would blend in and look like empty space.

The way it worked, you climbed a few rungs, pushed off to poke your head into the box, and smashed your skull into the two-by-four. You could always tell the beat men. They were the guys with the cuts on their scalps that never quite healed, more noticeable on some of us than on others.

We used to dream of the day that Vancouver would get an NHL franchise, because that couldn't happen without a new arena.

"Some day," the really old guys would tell us, "there'll be press boxes with chairs that don't fold and catch your privates, which you don't notice for a while because they're already frozen to the metal. There'll be room to work, maybe even heat ..."

We wrote them off. Too many times into the two-by-four.

There was a little room behind the press box where we could get coffee and sandwiches before the game or between periods. One Sunday in 1964, waiting for the Western Hockey League Canucks to play, we noticed snow coming down from the ceiling onto the sandwiches. Only it wasn't snow. It was sawdust, provided through the efforts of a termite chewing its way through the plywood.

We complained to Canucks' PR man Hugh Watson.

"Not ours," he said, examining the ant. "Must be with the visiting team."

We shook off the sawdust, ate the sandwiches, and trooped in to watch the game.

The next day, we got a report from a member of the Forum staff.

"It wasn't a termite," he said indignantly. "It was a carpenter ant."

We agreed that was good to know.

Funny thing, progress. When Pacific Coliseum opened the year before the Canucks made it to the NHL, it was considered palatial. Thirty years later, it's written off as a tawdry old bawd with too much rouge and her mascara running, too used up to draw a glance in a sports world gone Hollywood. The same thing happened with the opening of B.C. Place, when sagging old Empire Stadium, site of so many glories, became the butt of jokes and was allowed to die alone and untended.

We are the better for it, both fans and the spoiled brigades of the press box. But there is a cost. The old stories of carpenter ants and drafty buildings and bloodied scalps will fade away, to be replaced by — what? Tales of the night the air conditioning failed, or one side of the scoreboard went dead?

Legends are built of memories and perishables. They'll be harder to grow in wonderland.

THE DREAM GAME

March 29, 1992

Twenty-one things to do on game night if the strike means they have to call off the Stanley Cup playoffs:

1. Turn on TV set in den. Lower sound, colour and picture levels until all you have is a blank screen.

2. Close door. Warn wife and children that if that door opens other than to admit bearer of beer and junk food, house had better be on fire.

3(a). Three minutes after what would have been telecast opening, place hand over heart, rise, and sing "O Canada."

3(b). If this would have been a road game in an American city, invite a couple of insufferably cute little kids over to sing "The Star Spangled Banner." Badly.

4. Yell at wife to get move on with the beer before they drop the puck.

5. Make up imaginary forward lines. Second-guess them.

6. Announce that the opening faceoff is brought to you by a brewery.

7. If you have false teeth, remove them.

8. Spit.

9. Five minutes into what would have been first period, run full-tilt into wall. Jump up, pull off sweater, and beat the stuffings out of chesterfield pillow.

10. Sit in chair in corner for five minutes.

11. Spit.

12. Commercial break. When wife brings in beer, pretend she is voluptuous 22-year-old blonde with brow never furrowed by a single cogent thought. Hold bottle in air. Tilt head back. Smack lips. Do not, under any circumstances, drink the beer. (No one in beer commercials ever tastes the beer. They've all got bottle and mug fetishes.)

13. Spit.

14. Yell "He shootshescores!"

14(a). For Canucks goal, say, "The Russian Rocket! Isn't he something, Jim? He went around that defenceman so fast the guy didn't have a prayer. Is he something, or is he something?"

14(b). For opposition goal, blame defence.

15. Spit.

16. Intermission. Call youngest boy into room, tell him his name is now Ron McLean and his job is to sit down and look bored. You be Don Cherry.

Say, "Yeah, Pavel Bure. Not bad for a Red. Reds are better'n Swedes, y'know. Like I was sayin' to Cam Neeley — great kid, Cam, know him well — the trouble with this league is that it's bringin' in too many foreigners to steal jobs from good Canadian kids like Gretzky, who is pretty good even if his grandfather did come from Russia and ...

"Tonight's game? Shuddup, I'm talkin' ... You think *Hockey Night in Canada* pays me all this money to talk about tonight's game? They pay me to act like a redneck, beer-swilling know-it-all ... Now, you take that Ulf Samuelsson, when is somebody gonna GET that guy?"

17. Pretend to turn off sound.

18. Repeat items (9) through (15), making sure that the great goals by Is-he-something-or-what? outnumber the soft goals caused by defensive lapses.

19. Two minutes before you figure game should end, start singing "Na-na-na-na! Na-na-na-na! Say he-ey! Goodbye!" Then jump up and down screaming, "Yessssss!"

20. Turn off set. Return to living room. Do not spit.

21. Warning: As you sit there alone staring at the blank screen recreating the game, DO NOT under any circumstances attempt the Wave. People will think you're crazy.

HOCKEY NIGHT IN AMERICA

March 31, 1996

FOX television unveiled the new, improved version of its electronically enhanced hockey puck during a St. Louis-Detroit telecast. Instead of putting the puck in a blue halo, they put it in a white halo. Science marches on.

The difference was staggering. Where once the puck looked as though it was embedded in a blue beach ball, it now looks as though it's died and gone to heaven. ("Look, daddy, the puck's an angel! Let's go outside and kill my football!")

Yes, the wonderful folks who brought you *Baywatch* and proved beyond a scientific doubt that helium-inflated chests do not lead to premature evacuation have done it again.

Undaunted by public reaction to the puck's debut at the All-Star game, where many rated it a tool as least as useful as the John Ziegler Action Doll (Wind it up, it does nothing), the FOX lab rats have toiled day and night, weeks on end, to achieve a scientific breakthrough: They have modified their million-dollar monument to American myopia to the point where, without so much as lifting a finger, you can miss most of the game's finer points while simultaneously developing eyestrain and a migraine headache.

Isn't that exciting? Doesn't it make you want to rush to the FOX penthouse executive suite, grab the hand of the beaming CEO, and play crack-the-whip to send his body crashing through the window to the street below while you lean out screaming, "Halo that, you bastard!"?

Not that I expected any improvement on the original model. We are talking here about people who gloated at the original press conference that, with the click of a mouse in the Puck Truck — that's what they said: the Puck Truck — the halo can take on any shape or colour.

"With computer graphics," chortled FOX VP Jerry Gepner, "it can look like anything from Roger Rabbit to Gumby." Still need a little work on the medication, do we, Jer?

So, there they were on national TV, putting a glowing white halo around the puck, watching it slip off, catching it again, running it across the crowd four rows up so we'd know when the puck was actually up against the near boards where the camera couldn't see it, swooshing that red streak whenever somebody hit the puck really hard ... boy, things must have been really jumping in the old Puck Truck ...

"Uh, you sideline commentators — Jer here in the Puck Truck — All right! The smartass who said Truck Off! I want his name!

"Listen, could you maybe wave to the crowd to keep the noise down a little? We're trying to keep this bleeping halo on this bleeping puck for all 67 American viewers and the three Canadians who aren't heaving into their toilet bowls in disgust, and how are we supposed to concentrate when ...

"What's that? They scored a what? A goal? Is that like g-o-a-l? Who cares — we're working down here!

"Hold it a sec. Got a call from the studio. Early results of our FOX fan participation poll. Let's see: 92% of viewers want James Brown to do 'I Feel Good' between the second and third periods ... lady in a trailer park in St. Petersburg says somebody keeps squishing mosquitoes and leaving blood smears across the screen ... that's the puck speed SWOOSH, you senile old ... John Ziegler says 'Keep it up and they'll want me back in no time' ... five-year-old in Vancouver says he's sorry the puck died, but what did you expect when people keep hitting it ..."

But we must not despair. The FOX scientists are still working on modifications.

"We shape the thing like Pamela Anderson, see. Two halos, and they jiggle. Our ratings will go off the board. And we get rid of the puck. Who needs it when we've got Pamela? Hockey! I love this game ..."

"I WANNA MAKE A MOVEMENT!"

March 29, 1995

Vancouver Canucks hold private players' meeting to discuss team's recent record and current problems. — News item, *The Province*

Minutes of emergency team meeting, Vancouver Canucks, March 28, 1995 ...

Chairman Trevor Linden calls meeting to order, notes that only four players are in attendance, and orders a change of venue. "I should have known better than to hold the meeting in front of the net," he apologizes. "At least, not without issuing maps."

Full team gathers in dressing room. Chairman Trevor asks for reading of the minutes.

Gino Odjick: "Uh, 11.15. No, wait: 11.16. That big hand moved when I wasn't looking."

Chairman Trevor asks each player to assess his own play to date. Final count is 10 bleeping greats, four not bleeping bads, two I've been bleeping hurts and four how-the-bleep-am-I-supposed-to-bleeping-do-anything-when-I-never-get-on-the bleeping ice?

Chairman asks for suggestions to get the team back on the winning track, reminding membership that when the going gets tough the tough get going; it's not the size of the dog in the fight, but the size of the fight in the dog, and it ain't over till it's over.

Motion for him to shut the bleep up. Carried. Unanimous.

Chairman pleads with team to remember the good old days in the playoffs when they were one bleeping team on and off the ice and the coach used to say how maybe some of the guys weren't all that talented, but they were great in the room.

Chairman is reminded that the room is not the problem. "It's the ice. They keep making us play on it."

Chairman polls the room for suggestions.

Cliff Ronning: "I think it's time we all looked at ourselves in the mirror. Except Gino, of course. With all those stitches and his tongue swollen, he should stay away from mirrors as long as possible."

Sergio Momesso: "One million and one, one million and two, one million and three ... uh, pardon?"

Tim Hunter: "We've just got to stop saying we're gonna play well and start DOING it. We've got 19 games left. We can still nose our way into the playoffs."

Dave Babych: "Easy for you to say. You could stick your nose in the Eastern Conference without even leaving the room."

Geoff Courtnall: "Tim's right. We all do our own jobs and stop worrying about the other guy's, and ..."

Greg Adams: "What IS my job anyway?"

Chairman: "See this rubber thing? You're supposed to dent the twine, blink the red light, put the old biscuit into the basket, hit the old five hole, go tweeners ..."

Adams: "Oh, yeah. It's been so long, I forgot."

Pavel Bure: "Is big waste of time, this meeting. We've been here 15 minutes, nobody says anything about my haircut."

Chairman Trevor: "The chair apologizes to the honourable millionaire from Moscow. We didn't know it was a haircut. We thought it was cradle cap."

Kirk McLean: "I've got an idea! Why don't we try stopping somebody? Half you guys think defence is de guy you sell de stolen jewellery."

Courtnall: "Some goals would be nice, too. I know I certainly plan to score some, once I find out where I'm playing."

Chairman: "How about scoring some THIS season, Geoff?"

Courtnall: "Interesting concept."

Chairman Trevor: "I'd like to thank you all for coming, and for clearing the air with this meaningful dialogue. Is the chair safe in assuming the membership wishes to reach the usual conclusion? All in favour? Opposed?

"Okay, it's unanimous. We blame the coach."

NATURAL DISASTERS

April 11, 1995

When my son was six years old he would rise with the dawn, check out the Roadrunner cartoons, then watch the reruns with me several hours later and make bets on what would happen next to Wile E. Coyote.

"My son's trying to past-post me!" I'd boast to my horse-racing friends. "The kid's gonna be all right!"

It all came rushing back this week with word that the National Hockey League, apparently hell-bent on a policy of naming new franchises after natural disasters, has agreed to the new moniker proposed for the departing Winnipeg Jets. By the time they get to Phoenix, they'll be Coyotes — or possibly Coyot-EES.

There is some confusion about this. Ian Tyson, in his wonderful audience-participation song, "The Coyote" — the one that allows small children to shout "Sonofabitch!" with impunity — pronounces it Coyot-EE, but I distinctly remember Gene Autry referring to "that no-good coy-OTE." Whenever I shouted the question to Wile E., on the Roadrunner show, he was too busy falling off a cliff or getting hit by an anvil to answer.

Whatever. What matters is that the soon-to-be-former Jets are to be re-christened as Coyotes and lumbered with a logo that looks like a junkyard dog painted by Picasso after a hard night with the grape.

The logo, we're assured by the marketing mavens, is "electric" and will trigger a lemming-like rush to buy Coyote T-shirts, caps, cups, waste baskets, pencil sharpeners, lunch boxes and all the other paraphernalia no true fan could be without. And don't forget the cute connection, they say. See, the old Western League team used to be called the Roadrunners and now hockey is back in Phoenix as the Coyotes!

Lord, I hate cute.

The bigger question, however, is what triggered the acute depression that apparently has gripped the NHL Board of Governors. Have they been watching the Ottawa Senators again? Is Don Cherry starting to make sense? What's with this sudden affinity for disaster?

Quebec Nordiques move to Colorado and are named after the Avalanche, an event in which rocks start at the top of the heap and roll clear to the bottom, where they remain forever as more and more other rocks bury them ever deeper.

And now the Coyotes, named after an animal that looks like a dog after a trip through the car wash and has a history of being beaten, pummelled and made to look stupid by a bird whose entire vocabulary consists of "Beep-Beep"; an animal so dumb that it hasn't yet figured out that when it comes to things that explode, the Acme store is not the best place to shop.

I predict nothing but trouble. Every adult in Phoenix grew up learning that the Coyote never wins. If they've followed hockey at all they also know that the Jets are semi-terrible, and that when they get to Phoenix a more appropriate logo might be a Coyote baying at the top half of the standings. And these are the people being asked to buy tickets. They'd have to be dumber than coyotes.

There is, however, one bright spot. We can now start dreaming up disaster names for new franchises (the Dallas Book Depositories, the Waco Standoffs, the LA Tremours) as once we used to pick names for expansion teams in Europe.

Who will ever forget those wonderful sessions coming up with teams like the Rome Antics, the Paris Ites, the Bali Highs, the London Derrieres, the Bern Baby Berns, and the famous Manila Envelopes?

We were doing fine until we got to Bangkok.

THE HOLLYWOOD WAY

August 26, 1994

The last time I spoke to Bruce McNall he was presiding over lunch at the Forum Club in the Great Western Forum in the hours before his LA Kings were to face the San Jose Sharks.

Even then, the storm clouds were gathering on the horizon. The Kings were in the process of missing the NHL playoffs. McNall was now team owner in name only, his holdings reduced to 23% after his ever-growing money problems had crunched him into a corner where he had to sell the rest to Jeffrey Sudikoff and Joseph Cohen. There was talk that federal officers were about to seize his books over unpaid debts in the millions and suggestions of mail fraud and conspiracy charges in the works.

But he sat there like a man in a time warp, living in a bubble where nothing had changed.

Hollywood heavies kept interrupting his lunch to discuss Wayne Gretzky's charge toward Gordie Howe's goal-scoring record. Business associates who knew he was in trouble kept coming over to talk potential deals as though they were still there to be made. And Bruce McNall smiled and laughed and joked, the same affable, obliging owner who'd been a public and media hit since the day he swung the Gretzky deal that hoisted southern California into the hockey biz for good.

"Yeah, I was going to fire [coach] Barry Melrose," he laughed. "But then I thought, 'Why should he get away? Let him stay here and suffer like the rest of us.' "

The sale of controlling interest in the Kings was actually a good thing for him, he confided. Sudikoff and Cohen were more concerned with the construction of a new rink, which they would own as landlords for the Kings and the basketball Lakers. This was all about getting the rink built, he said. He'd be much better off with a small piece of the team and a good rink deal than the whole team and the current lease that was crippling him despite sellouts in the Great Western Forum.

"It will all work out," he said confidently, then turned to more important matters. "Walter," he said to Wayne Gretzky's father, "have you tried the desserts here? They're fabulous."

In March I'd visited him in his offices in Century City, which covered one entire floor. The place was a-buzz. "It's coming together," he said then.

In July, on an off day for the World Cup, I returned to the offices. The big oak main doors were locked. Pinned to them was a note with directions. You went down a narrow hall past what looked like the office cafeteria, and through a small door into what was once an outer office. There were packing cases everywhere and one man, apparently the sole occupant.

"Bruce isn't available right now," he said. "He has a lot of things on his mind."

"What do you think?" I asked.

He shrugged his shoulders and held up one hand, fingers crossed.

The next time I saw Bruce McNall he was on television at centre ice, presiding at the reception honouring Gretzky for breaking Howe's goal record. When all the other gifts had been presented, he gestured to the end of the rink, the gates swung open, and out came a black Rolls Royce convertible, approximate value $325,000 Cdn.

The feds and the bankers were closing in. He had to know that jail was a distinct possibility. It didn't seem important. It was a Hollywood Moment, and it required a Hollywood response. Bruce McNall revelled in Gretzky's stunned reaction to the gift and basked in the applause. Tomorrow the sky might fall, but tonight, in that moment, he was the happiest man in the world.

HOCKEY NIGHT IN HOLLYWOOD

June 13, 1995

The wire stories were just a bit too Hollywoodish: Bruce McNall's soon-to-be ex-wife selling off his designer neckties in a garage sale in Los Angeles because she and her two kids were short of cash.

It was like something dreamed up by some hack pitching a B movie concept: "See, the guy was a multimillionaire. Everybody thought so, anyway. Jet planes, hockey team, race horses, mansion, the works. Family sharing the good life with him. Ozzie and Harriet in Beverly Hills.

"Then it turns out the whole thing was a bubble. Guy has to sell off everything, the feds close in and hit him with bank fraud, the family breaks up, he plea bargains and pleads guilty, she files for divorce while he's waiting to see how much time he does — and the closing shot, she and the kids are selling off Daddy's ties in a garage sale 'cause they got no money. I tell ya, Manny, there won't be a dry eye in the house."

Maybe it isn't that bad. Maybe the ties were just one item in an ordinary garage sale, and some writer in search of an angle mixed them in with the pending divorce and McNall's upcoming appearance for sentencing, and came up with a heart-tugger.

I'd like to think so. Because there is another, better memory of Jane Cody McNall, peeling the wrapper off a pack of bubble gum and sharing the prize with her husband, back when the world seemed theirs to keep.

November, 1988 ...

The girls in the gownless evening straps arrive early on Hockey Night in LA, filing into the owners' box wearing mega makeup, brittle smiles and eyes bright with the thought of Actually Being There.

They look barely old enough to vote. If they did, it was probably for Ricky Schroeder. When Jerry Buss enters with one on his arm, the rest swarm over him like starlets over the casting couch.

Buss, the 60-ish-looking zillionaire who owns the Forum and the basketball Lakers and used to own the hockey Kings, has a reputation for dating and enjoying fresh young faces and their assorted accessories. On this night, there is no shortage of applicants. When one of them leads him out in triumph midway in the game, the crowd surrounding the box — actually a section of stands separated by an iron railing — gives him a rousing cheer.

"Way to go, Jerry boy!"

"Hell of a choice, man!"

"Aw-*right*!"

Down in the first row of the box, seated in front of a floor-model TV set so they can catch the replays, Bruce and Jane Cody McNall are poking through the new hockey cards in the bubble gum a fan handed her as she climbed the stairs.

A visitor taps his shoulder and gestures to the girl who'd come in with Buss — briefly alone now, and somehow older.

"What happens to the ones who don't make it?" he asks.

"Farm club," McNall replies, straight-faced but obviously uncomfortable with the fuss and its cause. "Down to the minors."

He is having trouble watching the game. People keep coming into the box to say hello. Peter Weller, the man who played the lead in *Robocop*, sits down to discuss a possible deal. Pat Valenzuela, the hottest jockey in the country, is there to congratulate McNall on the Kings' success. A young black actor says hello to Weller and suggests they should do a movie together. Fans lean over the railing seeking McNall's autograph, high-fiving him for signing Wayne Gretzky.

He is on top of the world, and enjoying every second.

"Look!" yells Jane Cody McNall, professor of classics at USC, waving a card under her husband's nose. "I've got Wayne! And you paid $15,000,000 for him!"

They break into the giggles. Life is good, and will surely stay that way.

Six and one-half years later, it's all gone — the Kings, the planes, the houses, the fortune, the marriage. Bruce McNall is awaiting sentence, and Jane Cody McNall is selling his ties in the driveway. It ain't all jam in the bigs.

THE MIGHTIEST DUCK

June 6, 1996

Paul Kariya wears his fame the way he wears his second set of new teeth: It looks good, it feels good, but it comes with no guarantees.

He scoffs at the mantle that has been draped over his shoulders almost from the day, three years ago, when he became a Mighty Duck: Paul Kariya, the next Gretzky, the next Lemieux, the next Canadian dazzler who's going to take the game back from the Europeans who seem about to steal it and make it theirs.

"It doesn't bother me," he says quietly. "I just don't think it's correct. I've played one and one-half seasons in the NHL. I've never been in a playoff game. I've got a lot to prove before any mantle is put on — but then, that's what the media like to do, isn't it? They're doing it with 15- and 16-year-old kids, kids coming into the draft: this is the next whoever.

"It's unfair," he concludes. "You're never going to be the next anyone. You're only going to be who you are."

Who he is at the moment is a 21-year-old living with a bad rap: Kariya is unco-operative. Kariya won't live up to the responsibilities that go with being a pro. Kariya won't ...

Kariya will. But not if it gets in the way of his hockey.

"The whole thing is a misunderstanding," he says quietly. Everything about him is quiet: the answers, the laughter, the expression — until that store-bought new smile breaks the stillness like sunshine.

The unco-operative tag, he believes, began with a scheduled *Hockey Night in Canada* interview with Don Cherry.

"I don't do interviews during games," he explained. "Once I get into the dressing room, I focus on the game. That's just me. I come in early to do pre-tapes, but I won't do live, between-periods interviews, which aren't effective anyway because you're huffing and puffing and out of breath.

"*Hockey Night in Canada* wanted me to do a pre-tape. I arrived on time, but Cherry was late. They said he was doing Coach's Corner. I waited 15 or 20 minutes, then the team meetings were starting so I apologized and left. Apparently they came looking for me a half-hour later, and I was in the meetings.

"Ironic, isn't it? Don Cherry's late, and he was the one who ripped me in the paper for not doing the interview."

He is not upset, merely bemused.

"There are guys so relaxed they could do interviews sitting on the bench," he says. "That's not me. From the time I leave the hotel I don't want any distractions. I realize that can be misinterpreted, but that's the focus I need to perform at the level where I want to be.

"I hope people will come to understand that — that I'm going to do the interviews, but it's a matter of timing."

So far, the timing has been perfect, so perfect you'd think the Disney people designed him, scripted him, and then made him a Mighty Duck.

At 21, he's been a winner at every level he's played: American college player of the year, star of Canada's national and Olympic teams, 50-goal scorer in his second pro season in Anaheim, soon-to-be member of Canada's entry in the World (*née* Canada) Cup competition — he has it all.

More importantly, he realizes what he's got, how he got it, and what it will take to keep it.

Talk to Paul Kariya and you hear the word "focus" a lot. It's in his approach to life, his approach to the game that is now his profession, and to the trappings, necessary and unnecessary, that surround it. Maybe that's why, out of nowhere, comes this media perception of a kid who might have gone big-headed, who dekes his way out of interviews the way he dekes around defencemen.

He stays away from off-season promotional or marketing activities. They could interfere with a rigorous training and conditioning program. "I have to work hard in the summer to be ready to compete," he says. "If I had to fly to Anaheim every couple of weeks to do a promo thing, it would really get in the way."

Later, perhaps, when he's truly established not as the Next One or the New One, but as Paul Kariya, NHL standout. But not now. Now is for getting better, for learning how to play and how to live in a lifestyle with too much idle time for someone used to the rigours of combining school and play.

"It's not a negative, it's just what you do," he says. "If I work out at the rink from 8 to 2 and then have lunch, there's still the rest of the day to do something. I'm reading a lot now, trying to stay occupied. The travel ... on the long trips I don't even know the names of the hotels we stay in. If I got lost in the city, I'd be done."

There is also the matter of toughness, mental and physical. Which brings us to the brand-new smile with the brand-new teeth.

He takes a fair amount of ribbing about that smile.

Early in the season the bottom teeth were broken. ("Brad May in Buffalo, I think.") The big one came in the second-last game of the season when Joe Niewendyk high-sticked him in the mouth.

"A total accident," he grins. "I'm sort of at elbow height of most players, stick-in-the-mouth range. The problem was that because of the work on the bottoms the tops weren't aligned and they had to take six teeth out.

"I'd just gone through two months of dental work to get the new tops. Finally they've got the permanents in place, and I'm joking around with the guys saying how good they look. The next day Joe takes four of them out."

The temps went back in, and off he went to the world championships. Now the second set of replacements is in place — but for how long?

"I can't wear a mouth guard. I can't talk on the ice and it almost makes me gag. Even the form-fitted one doesn't feel good. The way I figure, the teeth are all fakes now anyway, so what difference does it make?"

Down in Disney Hockey World, expectations are huge. Kariya's personal timetable hasn't changed.

"The way I judge a year," he explains, "is if I can say at the end of it 'I wish I was this kind of player at the start of the season or any point in between,' I'll know I've done my job in terms of improving my game, of becoming a better player."

The tape recorder clicks off.

"Thank you," says Paul Kariya. The store-bought smile flashes again and he is gone.

"Nice kid," the photographer says.

You betcha.

WALKING WITH STANLEY

July 25, 1996

They were two of the youngest recruits in hockey's version of the Seven Years War, two 17-year-old kids who passed each other in transit, never dreaming that they were about to carve a chunk of history.

It was November, 1978, and Wayne Gretzky's professional hockey career in Indianapolis had lasted eight games and 53 days.

Nelson Skalbania's plan to generate excitement by signing the kid phenom from Brantford to an attention-grabbing four-year contract (a $25,000 signing bonus, $100,000 for the first season, $150,000 for each of the next two and $175,000 in the fourth? Outrageous!) hadn't worked. Indianapolis still refused to get excited about the Racers or the World Hockey Association. So: he would sell Gretzky to Peter Pocklington, use the money to bring in some new faces, and start over.

One of the new kids was a bull moose named Mark Messier.

Messier's stay in Indianapolis was even shorter than Gretzky's. After five games he moved on to Cincinnati, where he finished out both the season and the league. By fall he was an Oiler, the Oilers were in the NHL, and The Kid and The Moose were ready to fly.

They're ready again as New York Rangers, but age and perception have altered the ground rules.

Gretzky moves to New York with terms like "The Grey One" and "The Not-So-Great One" burning his ears after what is perceived as a year that drew him back to the mortal pack. Messier now has a Greatest of his own, as in The Greatest Leader in Sport. He, not

Gretzky, will wear the C for the Rangers. It won't bother either man, but it could further warp a couple of perceptions already bent out of shape:

*Gretzky had a bad year, Messier had a good one. Ask anyone. But Gretzky, playing on two mediocre clubs, finished with three more points (102-99) than Messier, who was with a club viewed as a Stanley Cup contender.

*Gretzky is 35, and age has eroded his once-awesome talents. Messier is the heart of the Rangers, their long-term ace in the drive for another cup. But Messier is the same age as Gretzky. In fact, he's eight days older.

Their friendship is case-hardened by triumph and disappointment. Neither man has ever hidden the thought that it would be nice to end their careers together as they'd begun. Perhaps Gretzky was ready to become a Vancouver Canuck, but you can bet the idea of Gretzky as a Ranger was never far out of mind.

Not that friendship alone would ever have been enough. No amount of money could have persuaded him to go to a rebuilding team, or to one without a shot. Gretzky burns to win one more Cup. By definition, any team for which Messier plays will share that commitment because Messier will tolerate nothing less.

The philosophy was carved in stone one May morning in 1984, the night after the Oilers won their first Cup. The party had been long, loud and liquid, but Gretzky's orders to Messier, Kevin Lowe, Paul Coffey and a visiting writer had been firm, if hoarse.

"My place, 8:30 this morning," he croaked, thereby allowing for a generous three hours' sleep. "Bacon and eggs. Then we take Stanley for a walk."

Everyone showed up, in itself a triumph of spirit over spirits, and off we went.

They carried the Cup from cafe to coffee shop to watering hole, setting it on table or bar, posing for pictures, even pouring in an illicit beer or two for those who might like to sip out of hockey's most storied trophy. "It's yours, too," they'd shout. "Drink up!"

It went on for what seemed like hours. Coffey was the first casualty, cajoled by two lovely young ladies to head off and tell them all the secrets of his success.

Finally, it was time to crawl home.

"Mess," said Gretzky, "let's do this again next year."

"No," growled The Moose. "Let's do it a LOT."

OF PALACES AND LEGENDS

March 11, 1996

"Nostalgia ain't what it used to be. What's more, it never was."
— Lee Hays, The Weavers, Carnegie Hall reunion, 1980

It's probably not the best time to repeat such heresy, the nation being awash with warm and fuzzy memories, real and imagined, of a Montreal Forum that not one-10,000th of the country could ever have visited. After all, the remark was made by a man who opted for cremation and stipulated in his will that his ashes be scattered over his compost heap.

But most nostalgia does not stand up to close scrutiny.

Parents who tell their kids they thought nothing of trudging miles through the snow to get to school forget that they froze their butts doing it, or that crying over chilblains was the price of finally getting warm. "I never had a car when I was your age" should, in the interest of veracity, be followed by "but I would have killed to have one."

The Montreal Forum hasn't been marvellous for decades (sit high enough in the stands and the girders blocked your view). The marvel lay in the history written in it by a team inextricably woven into a country's cultural fabric, the pre-helmet Canadiens, their dashing francophones blazing down the wings, hair swept back in their own jetstream.

Even that memory suffers from comparison. Visit the Hockey Hall of Fame. Look at the tapes of the old games. The first thing you notice is that compared to today's model, the players are (a) small and (b) slow.

It's a natural progression. Paul Henderson, hero of the first Team Canada-Russia series, says the first thing he notices today when he looks at tapes of those games nearly a quarter-century ago is how slow they look. "I remember them being really fast, and they were for the time," he says. "I remember believing we had a great transition game. But compared to the way the game is played now — forget it."

Buildings are — buildings. Maple Leaf Gardens was a magical place as described by Foster Hewitt. As a sports writer I couldn't wait to visit. Gazing out of the press box at the wooden-backed seats — several rows of former reds newly painted gold so that Harold Ballard could charge more for them while keeping his word that prices in the various sections would not go up — my first thought was "What a dump."

Memories paint us into corners. They insist that I loved the old Vancouver Forum with the ladder to the press box nailed flat to the wall, the trap-door entrance with the hidden beam that routinely cracked your skull, the metal folding chairs that pinched the unwary in places no one wanted to be pinched, and the carpenter ants that drifted sawdust onto the sandwiches on the old card table.

Would I give up the elevator to the cushioned swivel seats and the perfect sightlines, the endless coffee supply and the buffet dinner that's there for the asking if there's no time to go home? Yeah, right.

The sadness in the loss of so many of the NHL's landmark buildings is that they are losing their individuality. The Boston bandbox with the parquet oak floor for the Celtics games, so storied that you hardly noticed cracks big enough to lose a rat. Chicago Stadium, with the pipe organ built into the very walls, its matchless, ear-splitting sound replaced by something just as loud coming out of a boom box. Maple Leaf Gardens, where Foster painted word pictures better than the games themselves from a gondola Ballard later ripped out and burned.

The new palaces are better, but all alike. We spoil easily. Even luxury can grow tiresome, and living with the brand-name sponsorship will take some getting used to. If the Romans had thought of it, would the Coliseum have been Cato's Chariot House?

But in the end it's the games and the players that matter. Eventually, all buildings fall. Legends live forever.

ONE OF A KIND

August 22, 1996

Listen! Close your eyes and listen to the sound of the skates as Team Canada finishes its morning drill. Listen to the slap of blades hitting ice — the chop-chop strides of the workhorses, the glide-chop-glide of the ones to whom it comes so much more naturally. Listen for the special, gliding sound. Listen for the swoooooosh ...

He was 11 years old, and he couldn't go to hockey camps.

It wasn't the money, it was the time. Hockey camp meant leaving home for a week in the summer, maybe more, and summer was for playing lacrosse and baseball and all the other joyous things that brought you home scuffed and dirty and bone-weary, to fall into bed and count the hours until you could go out and do them again.

So Paul Coffey stayed home and took power-skating lessons. It was like handing Picasso a paint brush, or Jesse James a gun.

Thirteen all-star game appearances, including eight in a row. Three Norris Trophies as the NHL's top defenceman — a bit of a hoot, that, when you remember in the early years the knockers said he couldn't play defence, he was just a forward playing back there. Four Stanley Cup rings, four first- and four second-team all-star selections, three Canada Cups, 11 assists short of passing Gordie Howe and moving into second place on the all-time list (trailing only a chap called Gretzky), eighth and climbing among point-getters, more goals, assists and points than any defenceman who ever played ...

But do a word-association test with anyone. Say "Paul Coffey". Almost always, the answer will be "skating".

For 16 years he has all but redefined the art. And now, when a premium is put on the skill as never before in the NHL, when most of the young guns coming in have taken power skating as a matter of course, here he is at 35, still the master, counted upon to be as big a factor in the first World Cup as he's been in the last three Canada Cups.

"The logic is that I have to have lost a step somewhere," he says, stripping off sweat-drenched practice togs. "It doesn't feel like it, but maybe. Or maybe it's that when you hit 35, what you've lost in speed you've gained in experience. All I know is that I feel good, and I feel ready."

He has noticed the difference. He sees it every year as fresh young faces appear under the helmets, asking advice or nodding respectfully, the shy ones just standing there looking at the man who was a star before some of them had donned their first skates.

"In the '60s and '70s," he says, "teams had two or three guys who were good skaters. Now almost everybody can roll. The game has changed: Basically, if you can't skate, you can't stay."

His father must have seen it coming, back home in Weston, Ontario.

"I did power skating for about four years, from 10 or 11," he says. "My dad wanted me to go, but he didn't tell me, he asked me. It would be hard work, he said, but it would improve my game. So I said sure. All my friends were at those exclusive hockey camps where you water-skied and other stuff like that. Me — I was at power-skating lessons."

He wasn't alone. The classes were full of kids in full hockey gear, putting aside the old figure-skaters-are-sissies prejudices and trying to emulate these people whose strides were so seemingly effortless, people they couldn't have caught in a taxi.

"I really enjoyed them," Coffey recalls. "Except for the part where they kept patting you on the ass. That was what they did — patted you on the ass and yelled 'Get moving! Get moving!' "

He did, and he's been moving ever since, while people shake their heads and wonder how he does it, how much is left, and how, with so many great skaters coming into the league, the all-but-silent, distance-eating Coffey stride is still the one by which the art is measured.

Maybe the answer lies in something he said a few days earlier about his fellow icons, Gretzky and Messier.

"People keep saying he isn't the old Wayne. What they forget is that neither is anyone else. The system simply hasn't produced another one like him, or Mark."

Or Paul.

Not yet, and maybe never.

Listen! Listen for the special sound. He's coming! Paul Coffey is heading up-ice! Listen for the gliding sound. Listen for the swoooosh ...!

A MODEST PROPOSAL

March 28, 1996

Early in the alleged showdown between the Calgary Flames and Vancouver Canucks, the $6,000,000 scoreboard flashed the message we've all been dying to see: Yet another guy in the crowd is about to propose to his girlfriend, right there on the big screen before our very eyes.

Gosh.

The camera zooms in, the guy pops the question. "SHE SAYS YES!" the sign screams out in letters big enough to signal the end to global warfare.

She kisses him. He kisses her. They both sit down to begin their new lives by watching the Canucks go down 4-0 in a game they couldn't have won if they'd been awake. Another Kodak Moment.

It was cute the first time. But like all acts in this era of Pavlovian-response entertainment ('fess up: when the clapping hands come on the screen, you clap, right? Even in games when the home team should be arrested for loitering), it soon wears thin.

Think about it: Do you really believe there's any risk involved here, that the guy would be proposing on camera if he wasn't 100% dead certain of the answer?

Statistics say that five years down the road he's likely going to be handing her the house, the car and custody of every living creature in the place up to and including the dog, the cat and the potted plants. Now he'll risk going to work the next morning and getting ragged on by co-workers shouting, "Give us an N! Give us an O! NO!"? I don't think so.

It's a set-up. He wants to pop the question in a memorable way. The bungy-jump joint was overbooked and the Canucks wouldn't let them crawl into the hyperbaric chamber. So he phones Orca Bay, tells them what he wants to do, gives them the names and his seat numbers, and sits there through the first few minutes, probably wondering if maybe this was the night he should have left her at home and brought the shop foreman.

Where's the suspense in that? Where's the comedic value?

The secret to entertaining hockey is that both teams must have a chance to win — a fact obviously not lost on spectators recently, when some left so early The Fiddler should have been playing the theme from *Exodus*. If the on-camera proposal gig is to last, it too must have an element of uncertainty.

So c'mon, Arthur, let's give it one.

Hold an Unmarried Couples Night with reduced ticket prices for all registering pairs. Put them in a special section. Pan the camera over them, pick a pair at random, and have a genial MC stick a mike in front of them.

"Now, then, Bob, for valuable Canucks merchandise and a chance to stay home next week, do you want to propose to Wanda here, or take Option B and be forced to watch the entire third period?"

He'll propose. Wouldn't you?

The poor girl, whether she's been seeing the guy for years or just dates him on nights the good teams are in town, will have to answer spontaneously and see her first blurted words flashed on the screen:

"SHE SAYS 'NOT IN A MILLION YEARS!' "

"SHE SAYS 'GREAT! I'M PREGNANT!' "

"SHE SAYS 'WITHOUT A PRE-NUP? NO WAY!' "

"SHE SAYS 'I'VE BEEN SEEING YOUR BEST FRIEND BILL!' "

The genial MC smiles his genial MC smile and shouts: "Sorry, Bob! She says no! But remember, you're still eligible, so find yourself another girl and give it a try next week. Meanwhile, for being such a good sport, we're refunding the full price of your tickets and letting you stay home for the Hartford game!"

You're welcome, Arthur. Next week: BIRD-DANCERS, AND HOW TO BREAK THEIR LITTLE ELBOWS!

Entertainment. It's my life.

MIRACLE '72

September 27, 1992

We made too much of it, of course.

Twenty years after the first NHL-Soviet Union hockey showdown, with Swedes and Finns and Czechs and Russians scattered through the NHL like seeds of a better, stronger, faster game to come, we should be able to look back at the wonder that was September of '72 and view it fondly and calmly as a hockey series that grabbed the national heart and squeezed.

We should be able to treasure the memories and perhaps laugh at ourselves a little for allowing it to transcend hockey and become a Them vs Us. We should be able to admit that as great as it was, as great as we remember it being, for sheer talent and pure speed it couldn't measure up to, say, the three-game Canada-Russia Canada Cup final of 1987. "When I look at that tape," says Paul Henderson, "I find myself thinking: 'We were so slow!' The speed today, the transition game ... we had great players, but the game today is so much faster it's unbelievable!"

But we can't do that.

The tapes of memory are always played fast-forward. The colours are brighter, the players bigger, the shots harder, the checking stiffer. Memory adds a sound track and a call to arms. We didn't fly to the Soviet Union, we rode great white steeds, our knights in shoulder pads on a crusade to right a great wrong, the nation's colours dangling from their lances.

The series we were supposed to win 8-0 stood at two wins, a tie and one loss for Them. A trip that was supposed to be a lark to add the last four kicks to the big Red corpse had become a desperate quest to win back NHL pride. Hockey series, hell. We were a nation at war.

You know what made the series? The 4-4 tie in Game Three in Winnipeg. Suddenly an eight-game series became a best-of-seven, a super Stanley Cup final. Barring another tie, there would be a winner. All we had to do was win three of the last four playing on the road.

We lost the first, won the next two, and now it was a sudden-death final and we were down 5-3 with one period to play.

In the concourse before the final 20 minutes, Alan Eagleson asked the interpreter to say to Mr. Gresco, the head of the Soviet delegation, "Wouldn't it be nice if Canada scored two goals and the game and this wonderful series ended in a tie?"

"Mr. Gresco says yes," the interpreter said a moment later, "because in that case we would win the series on the basis of goals scored."

"In that case," snapped the Eagle, "Tell him 'Bleep you!' "

Phil Esposito scored. Yvan Cournoyer scored. Henderson scored with 34 seconds left, the best-known goal in the history of hockey, the completion of an incredible hat trick: the winner in each of the last three games. The defence, all but forgotten in the years to come, held the Russians to five shots in that final, gut-wrenching 20 minutes.

And we won. I guess.

We won a series we were supposed to sweep on a goal with 34 seconds left in the final minute of the final period of the final game. And every year the memories of it grow more vivid, more dramatic, more wonderful, as those who were there swap Russian stories with those who were here and can tell you exactly where they were when Henderson scored that last goal.

I have my own memories.

I remember the laughter when the man from the embassy warned us before we left that the Soviets would have jackhammers going outside the hotel at 3 a.m. to distract the players, and Serge Savard said, "That's okay. We won't be in."

I remember the frantic search for spy bugs in the hotel room, when two players threw back the rug, discovered a flat metal disc, unscrewed it, and heard a tremendous crash as they released the chandelier in the room below.

I remember defenceman Gary Bergman snarling after Game Six: "People say these guys don't play dirty? Look!" And showing me a shinpad that looked like a dart board, jabbed by Soviet skates.

I remember coach Harry Sinden, getting up to go out and reason with disgruntled players who wanted to go home because they weren't playing. And John Ferguson snarling: "Let me reason with them. I'll send them home in a bleeping box!"

I remember Frank Mahovlich, in a game for which he wasn't dressed, standing behind the Team Canada bench singing "O Canada", over and over again.

I remember outraged Canadian fans screaming, "Let's go home! Let's go home!" and the soldiers ringing the ice, and Pete Mahovlich jumping over the boards to rescue Eagleson when it seemed we were seconds away from a riot.

And I remember the long plane ride home, the games replaying over and over again on the backs of my eyelids, thinking that hockey could never get better than that.

It did, of course, and will again. But never in memory. Memories like those are dipped in amber, to take on a golden lustre with the years, to be held and treasured forever. As they should be.

ONE LAST MEMORY

March 22, 1997

Close your eyes. Picture something or someone you loved and lost. Remember how tough it was to say that last goodbye.

Now tell me how terrible it is that Gordie Howe would want one more shift as a pro hockey player.

Okay, he's 68 and the idea is surface silly. One turn around the ice with the Syracuse Crunch, one shift, maybe two, against kids who could be his grandchildren — that's not playing pro hockey. Who's going to hit him? Show me the young pro, however jaundiced, however keen to attract the attention of the NHL parent club, who's going to board Gordie Howe, or rough him up in the corner as they go for the puck.

But to Gordie, this token appearance in a minor-league game will mean he's played professionally in each of six decades. "It's a record no one will ever touch," he says, and if that's important to him, so be it. No harm, no foul.

But it has been so terribly mismanaged.

First the Crunch announced that Gordie Howe had signed a contract to return to professional hockey. Just like that, one of the greatest players and finest ambassadors the sport has ever had was an instant laughing stock.

A lot of guff was written and broadcast. Some of it, I'm ashamed to say, by me.

Six decades? Why not seven? The Good Lord willing, why not eight? Put him out there with a walker in 2017. One shift. His centre carries the oxygen, his winger brings the IV pole. Pow! Gordie Howe, playing pro at 89.

But the contract is a technicality. To play with the team he has to be of the team. There was never any intent that Gordie be a player, although when you consider that the Crunch is a bunch of guys not good enough to be called up by the Vancouver Canucks, he might still be able to elbow his way onto the roster.

Howe says it will be just one game, perhaps just one shift. In effect, he will be a one-man old-timers team — Frank Sinatra standing to bow and wave from the audience, Pele taking a ceremonial kick-off. Standing O, a few dewy eyes in the audience, and exit, stage left, to his own private pinnacle in the history of the game that's been his life.

That's the way it should have been presented. Because it wasn't, the legend is left open to mockery. In part, it is the fault of the people closest to him, so fierce in their justifiable pride in his accomplishments, so reluctant to see his records supplanted as all records must be.

When Wayne Gretzky passed his NHL points record in 1989, Colleen Howe was quick to point out that it was only his NHL record, that with his WHA points included, Gordie was still Mr. Hockey. When Gretzky approached Howe's NHL goal-scoring record of 801, Howe's combined NHL-WHA total of 975 was quickly brought into play.

It was as though a war had been declared, a battle over who really was Mr. Hockey. "To me, that will always be Gordie," Gretzky said. But it was mutually hurtful, and unnecessary. Howe's place in the game has long since passed mere points.

So why is he making this essentially meaningless gesture, this one last trek from a pro dressing room, past the players' boxes and out onto the ice?

Not, I suspect, for the cheers. He gets those at card shows, at banquets, in hotel lobbies, from kids and parents and grandparents. The six-decade thing is a long-standing dream — but in the end it might draw a line in Guinness.

It's the game, the life. The dressing-room kidding, the warm-up, the travel, the endless card games: all those years, he loved it all. When you're in love, you never stop dreaming of one last goodbye.

YOURS TRULY, HIM

March 27, 1997

Boy, talk about your sore winners: Fifty-two years ago the Americans dropped two bombs on Japan. Now they're going to drop another one.

NHL commissioner Gary Bettman's announcement that the Vancouver Canucks and the Anaheim Mighty Ducks will play their first two league games in Japan next season was met here with stunned silence, broken almost instantly by a wail they must have heard in Osaka: "Whaddya mean, they're coming back?"

Due in equal parts to wishful thinking and the current Western Conference standings, there'd been a persistent rumour that cell-phone whiz John McCaw, the Howard Hughes clone who owns the Canucks, was shipping them to Japan in the manner that wealthy Brits used to boot their ne'er-do-well offspring to the Colonies. Remittance Men, they were called, in recognition of the cheques that kept coming to support them on the condition that they never return.

But no: Once those two games are out of the way and they've rejected the many hara-kiri kits proffered by Japanese fans who've watched their performance and expect them to do the honourable thing, the Canucks will return to GM Place to pursue their destiny. Which, given the direction their skate logo is pointing, seemingly involves a kamikaze dive into the root cellar.

And the question remains: If the NHL wants to dip a skate into the sports-crazed Japanese marketplace, why send the Canucks?

The Ducks are an obvious choice, what with Paul Kariya's part-Japanese ancestry and the enormous popularity he already enjoys in that country. Mickey and Donald and Goofy have already blazed the trail. You think Disney won't sell a few Mighty Ducks jerseys?

But the Canucks? Did Bettman get some bad sushi? Did his Toyota break down? It makes no sense.

What if the Japanese swarm out to see Kariya, watch the Canucks flailing around like Elvis Stojko on snowshoes, and somehow get the idea that this is the real National Hockey League? What will that do to attendance for Olympic hockey a few months further down the road in Nagano?

Mind you, they are great sports fans. On an off day at the '72 Winter Olympics in Sapporo we walked a downtown street and saw a lineup that stretched all the way around the block. It was a ten-pin bowling alley. "Waiting to get lane," our guide explained. "Very difficult."

The Japanese had a hockey team in those Olympics, which was more than could be said for Canada. We sat that one out, remember? The problem was, the Japanese kids didn't know.

They took one look at my hairline as I walked out of a rink after watching 16-year-old Mark Howe practising with Team U.S.A., nudged each other, and swarmed over me with autograph books outthrust.

"Bobby Hull," they screamed. "You Bobby Hull!"

I assured them that I was not Bobby Hull. They were having none of it.

"Bobby Hull!" they yelled. And now they were getting angry. Who did this Bobby Hull think he was, refusing to give them an autograph?

"You better sign," advised the CBC's Bill Good Jr. "You're making Canada look bad."

So I started signing: "Best wishes, Bobby Hull." "Best wishes, Bobby Hull."

The kids were delighted. Good — tall, dark and TV-handsome — was laughing himself sick.

I fixed his ass.

"Look, kids!" I yelled, pointing to him, "Jean Beliveau."

Now we were both signing. Okay, it was fraudulent. But the kids went away happy. Their kids should only be as happy watching the Canucks.

MARTY AND BUTTERBEAN

April 2, 1997

There was this biker named Schnoz. He had another name, but we were afraid to ask. We met in a Nanaimo pool hall where he won a lot because he tended to get upset when he lost.

Schnoz heard about one of those So You Wanna Fight cards in Vancouver, where tough guys checked their brass knucks at the door and did in the ring for money what they did in the pubs for free. "How tough can it be?" he thought. "They wear gloves for chrissake!"

So he climbed on the ferry, put his name on the list, and stepped into the ring with a guy who'd been there a couple of times before. It ended early. His blow-by-blow account later went as follows: "I bin hit with clubs, bats, chains, guns, you name it," he said. "But I never bin hit that hard. This guy hits me once in the chest, I think I'm gonna have a cardiac. So I think 'To hell with this!' and I leave."

Schnoz is no longer with us, which is a pity. A few minutes with him might have been instructive for Marty McSorley.

McSorley, who has smote many a ruffian upon the mandible as enforcer for assorted NHL teams, has somehow become convinced that it would be fun to step into the ring with a professional boxer named Eric Esch, who is known as Butterbean because Pillsbury Doughboy was taken. The collision is scheduled for the summer, possibly in Edmonton, where Marty did much of his best smiting on behalf of the Oilers.

This is not a good idea for several reasons.

Butterbean may look more like a hassock than a hitter. His 28-1 record may have been compiled at the expense of opponents who could barely fog up a mirror. His IBF super-heavyweight title may be so phony that the belt should be Styrofoam. The day he fights a legitimate contender may be the day the priest mutters, "Esch's to ashes."

But he can throw a punch professionally. Right there, he's ahead on points.

McSorley is a hockey fighter, which mostly means you drop your stick, step back, throw off your gloves and circle, all the while yelling things like: "You want summa me? Come and get it, you bleeping excuse for a hyphenated bleeper-bleeper!"

"Oh, yeah? You think you're tough? My mother is tougher than you!"

"Really? She didn't look all that tough in the bar last night. Mind you, the fleet was in!"

Then they lunge, each trying to pull the other guy's sweater over his head, and throw punches so roundhouse they're marked for next-day delivery. Both guys know that within 90 seconds tops, two linesmen will step between them and send them to the penalty box where they can rest for five minutes.

Not all hockey fights are like that. Some get downright bloody. But unless you're braced against the boards it's difficult to plant and throw haymakers on skates. Boxers have no such problem. They do not wrestle each other to the canvas when they feel like quitting. They do scientific things like hooking off the jab and beating on kidneys so hard and so often that even the winners pee in technicolour.

Hockey fights are mostly ritual — the home team's enforcer vs the visiting team's goon. "Sometimes you don't even have to fight,"

McSorley said once. "You just skate around the ice looking at guys, letting them know you're there."

For all his apparent deficiencies, Butterbean Esch is a professional fighter whose fists put bread on the table. McSorley is a hockey fighter who doesn't need the purse. For him, the fight would be a lark. Going in, Schnoz felt that way, too.

GOING COLD TURKEY

May 14, 1997

May 14, and no hockey telecast. That's three nights in a row. Already you're twitching like some puffy-sleeved guy with an accordion is playing "Lady of Spain" on your nerve-ends.

You try the world tournament, the puck junkie's version of methadone. Nothing. When you've seen the Rangers and Devils and the Avs and Oilers, where's the jolt in watching a bunch of leftovers who lead the world in hyphens and umlauts?

You've done things you've sworn never to do.

You've watched ringette, which is basically hockey with a hole in it. You've driven through street hockey games, and stopped when the kids yell "Car!" just so you could stare at the nets.

You've tossed and turned at 3 a.m., finally giving in to the loathsome urge to creep downstairs and watch Don Cherry videos. Sometimes it gets so bad you don't even turn off the sound.

You've stolen your kid's Gretzky jersey and tucked it in on one side. You've eaten a case of Messier's potato chips. You've found yourself longing for a glimpse of the FOXpuck bubble. You've grease-pencilled a rink on your picture tube.

In the throes of cold-turkey delirium, you've defended the new Canucks logo. ("Hey, it's an orca whale. They're slow and non-aggressive and prefer to stay on the bottom. If you're a Canuck, what's not to like?")

There is no relief. But there is hope. I know — for I have been there.

The secret is to find ways to kill the empty hours by doing things you haven't done since you bought the dish and subscribed to the six-game-a-week package in October. A few possibilities:

*Go into the kitchen and say hello to whatshername, the one you married before you found out she thought a faceoff was something you flew to Sweden for when your cheeks started to sag.

*Hold a conversation. Show her you're more than just hockey hype. Discuss current events. Ask her how that Ellen thing worked out. Was she gay or just really happy? That gold stock — Bre-something. Think maybe we should get in on it?

*Ask how the kids are doing in junior high. If she says they're in college, bluff. Say, "I knew that. It's just that I hate to see them grow up."

*Watch other sports. Try baseball. If nothing else, it will put you out for three or four hours.

*Go outside. You know — the place where they make all that light that reflects on your screen? Step on the green stuff. Take off your shirt. Feel the warmth. Listen to the birds sing.

*Say the S-word. Go ahead. You can do it. Start with a hiss like you're booing Koharski. Do an "Uhh!" That's your normal "Duhh!" but the D is silent. Give it an "Mmmm" like you've just sipped your next brewski. Then go "Er", as in "Er, whatdya say, honey? I'm watchin' hockey here!"

Put it all together. "Summer!"

Doesn't that feel good? Doesn't it make you want to run out and mow the lawn? Go play slo-pitch? Sit on a bench in the mall at lunch time and watch the secretaries go by?

No?

I see. You still want to go into a small, stuffy room in late afternoon, pull the curtains shut, send out for pizza and sit in semi-darkness watching itinerant workers hit a piece of rubber with a stick, and if Thursday doesn't get here soon you're gonna die.

You're sick, you know that? But there's a lot of it going around.

Chapter Four

LIGHTS THAT FLICKER AND DIE

On May 19, 1995, a Colombian boxer named Jimmy Garcia died in a Las Vegas hospital. Doctors who'd kept him on a life-support system for 13 days following the massive brain injuries suffered in his last fight finally gave up and disconnected him from what was left of the life he'd all but lost in the ring.

Boxing mourned briefly, then got on with the business of making money. Jimmy Garcia, boxer, became the late Jimmy Garcia, statistic: the fourth fighter in recent times to die of head injuries suffered in the ring. The fourth, but not the last.

Boxing's answer is, essentially, a shrug. It's a tough game. These things happen. When is Tyson gonna fight Foreman?

It should have learned from his death — as it should have learned from the others — that the human brain was not designed to take a series of blows to the head, that protective headgear should be mandatory. The Jimmy Garcias can't be brought back, but the sport has a responsibility to those who follow him.

It will never happen. No matter how many Jimmy Garcias die, it will never happen. Because in the minds of the people who run boxing — and in the minds of so many who pay to watch — headgear is for sparring sessions. The thrill of the sport, although they'd never admit it, lies in the possibility that one fighter will pound another into jelly-legged insensibility.

No one will pay to watch two men pile up points for the crispness of the jab, the beauty and effectiveness of combinations.

Pay-TV millions are made on knockdowns and knockouts, the bloodier the better. You wanna see some guy win on points, watch the Olympics.

Mike Tyson was never a boxer; he was an assassin whose self-proclaimed ambition was to hit an opponent so hard that the small bones in his nose would be driven up and back into his brain. People didn't pay millions to watch him box. They were there to see how quickly he could dispose of a Michael Spinks, and how much damage he could inflict in doing it.

Fight fans drooled over his return to the ring. Had prison dulled the killer instinct, or honed it? Promoters knifed each other for the privilege of staging the fight that would provide the answers. There was talk that it would be George Foreman. It was a no-brainer. Iron Mike the convicted rapist vs Old George, the support-hose Superman. Ex-con vs con artist. Pent-up rage vs golden age. It would be like printing money.

Boxing is fuelled by pay-TV, and pay-TV boxing is fuelled by living-room blood lust. The people who pay aren't looking for a win on points. Even now, Tyson-Foreman would sell, an assassin pounding a waddling old man. Put them in headgear and it might get 90 seconds on *Circus of the Stars.*

The death of Jimmy Garcia briefly renewed the cries for the abolition of boxing. It was and remains unrealistic. Man will always fight. He will fight in casino theatres or out in the parking lot, at Madison Square Garden or on a barge out beyond the clutches of the law. And there will always be those who'll pay to watch. For these people who have never taken a blow, gloves are a concession. Headgear is beyond consideration.

When my daughter suffered the injury that left her brain-damaged and quadriplegic, the bruise on the side of her head was no bigger than a dime. I asked the doctor how that could be.

The brain, he said, is like a ball covered with millions of glowing light bulbs, floating in liquid. Each time the skull is jarred, the ball rides the resulting wave and bounces off the bone on the other side. Bulbs are broken. And they can never be turned back on.

Headgear would not save all the light bulbs, but it would save some. Enough, perhaps, to save the lives of the Jimmy Garcias to come. The sad truth of boxing is that the Jimmy Garcias don't matter. Maybe they never have.

THE SWEET SCIENCE

August 16, 1995

LAS VEGAS — As our story begins, a convicted rapist promoted by a former numbers racketeer who served four years for manslaughter and is due in court October 1 to face nine counts of wire fraud, is about to launch his post-prison career against a patsy whose only claim to fame is that his father once was floored 13 times by Floyd Patterson.

The rapist is managed by two old-time buddies, a failed nightclub comedian best known for introducing the rapist to his first and short-term wife, Robin Givens, and a guy who apparently knows as much about boxing as the other guy did about comedy. These two have both worked in the past for the manslaughterer, to such a degree that cynics contend they are front men who actually work for him, not for the rapist, who did his training at the manslaughterer's camp.

Did we mention that the patsy is also part of the manslaughterer's boxing kingdom? Or that the rapist's conversion to Islam while in prison is viewed with some suspicion by those who recall that at another low point in his career he became a born-again Christian, which raises the question: Is he a new man of Islam, or the same old thug under a prayer cap? Or that his conditioning coach and diet supervisor is a stranger who says he's conditioned many other famous professional athletes, but refuses to name even one?

Welcome once again to the wonderful world of boxing. Starring Don King as the promoter, manslaughterer and controller of both fighters, with Mike Tyson as the returning rapist, Carlos "Who?" Blackwell as his conditioner, Peter McNeeley as the patsy, and Rory Holloway and John "The Comedian" Horne as the managers. All coming to you live on *Showtime* from the 15,222-seat Grand Garden of the $1,000,000,000 MGM Grand Hotel. Check your guns and disbelief at the door.

It's not that there haven't been crazy fights and gross mismatches before. Who can forget the televised two-country wrestlebox double-header, Muhammad Ali vs a forgettable Japanese guy, and Chuck Wepner, the walking blood bank, vs Andre the Giant. Big numbers, Manny. Big! When it comes to gullibility, boxing fans win easy.

But this one could top them all.

Tyson, the new man who just wants to be by himself, is succeeding so well that hardly anyone has seen him. Those claims that he was at his fight weight of 218 pounds two weeks ago and has been flattening sparring partners with awesome regularity come only from members of Team Tyson. The sparring partners are strangely silent.

Hardly anyone has seen him spar. Interviews have been scant and limited to favourites. On Monday he skipped two scheduled media appearances. Today he is supposed to appear at the final pre-fight press conference. The early betting is that he won't.

And Peter McNeeley? The patsy goes along with the hype, giving it the pro-wrestling schtick and the predictions of a monumental upset in which he wins by a KO.

This, mind you, from a man whose 36-1 record was manufactured at the expense of opponents whose school might as well be Cadaver U. In all, he's fought 29 men. Only four had winning records. Twelve of them didn't win even once. In his 14th bout he finally met an opponent with a winning record — sort of. Ron Drinkwater was 10-1 when he met McNeeley in 1993, but had been inactive for 15 years.

Another winner was Lorenzo Boyd, who'd been knocked out 10 straight times and hadn't won in seven years when he was fed to the man now being billed as a threat to Mike Tyson's return to pugilism.

You know the weirdest part of this? Unless he loses, it isn't going to prove anything about Mike Tyson. Boxing won't get a real look until November, or even early next year, when Team Tyson closes a deal to fight someone who matters, one of the current versions of heavyweight champ, probably the one who looks least capable of doing him harm.

But this one will sell, because people want to see the post-prison Tyson. Eat your hearts out, Sigfried and Roy, still working those white tigers at the Mirage. Sell 'em for fireplace rugs. The real circus is over here.

RETURN OF THE GYPSIES

August 17, 1995

"After the last fight, we partied till 7 a.m."
"Man, we partied a whole month!"
"You just the cutest thing!"
"Yes I am, momma."
" 'Cept, I got a tape recording says different."

— Crowd noise, Tyson-McNeeley weigh-in

LAS VEGAS — The fight Gypsies have arrived, wandering the halls of the world's largest hotel in search of celebrities, souvenirs, and that one slot machine that secretly hates the owners of the MGM Grand.

You see them at all the big fights, usually wearing one of the T-shirts from the last one, or the one before that, to show that they've been around. Outside the Coyote Cafe, they discovered that the price of being in has gone up.

"Yep, $15 for the souvenir program," a salesgirl at the fight counter says tiredly, pointing to the price list propped up on the counter, a revelation in itself.

A Tyson solo T-shirt cost $22, a Team Tyson $20, a Team Event $20. A tank top sets you back $20, shorts $25, cut-off sweat shorts $25. For the upscale-minded, there's a polo shirt for $40 and a rayon jacket for $100. There's a Tyson fanny pack for $10, a water bottle for $22, a duffel bag for $25. Tyson caps and event caps go for $20 apiece.

"Don't worry," a 60-ish lady in a "No Mas" Roberto Duran shirt assures her friend. "After the fight, they'll all go down."

They do not know about the big item yet to come. Perhaps it's just as well.

During the press conference, before Mike Tyson and Peter McNeeley and the rest filled up the 34 seats at the podium, a man from *Showtime* leaned into the microphone and instructed the managers of all fighters to meet and produce their "ringwalk CDs", the music that will be played as each fighter makes his way to the ring. It was "imperative" there be no delay. Fight ringwalks, coming soon to a record shop near you.

"For real?" a guy asks the man from *Showtime*.

He looked shocked. Would a fight promoter fib?

"Absolutely," he insists. "Confidentially [at a fight?]," he adds, "we've been told that Tyson is going to come in to a new and spectacular ringwalk."

"To be heard one time only," he adds.

Sort of like Peter McNeeley.

Every heavyweight title fight has its own particular brand of craziness. You come to expect it. What sets this fight apart, the thing that has been all but forgotten in the hype, is that this isn't a title fight at all. It's a guy who hasn't fought for four years, the last three of them in prison, going in against a guy whose 36-1 record includes victories over the halt, the ancient and the nearly blind. Go figure.

Maybe it's got that pit-of-the-stomach wonder that sends non-race people to their television sets every year to watch the Indy 500, and made a television event out of Evel Knievel's bid to jet over the Snake River Canyon. Maybe they want to be there in case Tyson crashes and burns.

Maybe some of them still feel that Tyson was railroaded, that the rape of Desiree Washington never happened. How else do you explain Jose Sulaiman, president of the World Boxing Council that has sanctioned this card, standing at the podium, looking over at Tyson and saying: "Mike, justice will be restored on Saturday night."

There is no logic to it. But then, for the fight Gypsies, there doesn't have to be.

"What are you doing?" the No Mas lady asks as her friend paws through her purse. "I tell you, they'll be cheaper later."

"Yes, but the programs may be sold out," says her friend, and plunks down her $15.

ONLY IN AMERICA ...

August 19, 1995

"I have out-performed every promoter in the history of mankind, I have broken every record, and the only records I have left to break are mine."

— Don King, August 16, 1995

LAS VEGAS — There is one Don King record he never mentions anymore, nor do any of the minions who surround him. You will not find it in the eight-page bio that came with the media package for the Mike Tyson-Peter McNeeley fight, that King-produced monument to curiosity over logic.

The record is in the files of the Ohio Penitentiary, where King did four hard years for manslaughter, 1966 through 1969. He was running a large part of the numbers racket in Cleveland, and killed one of his runners in a fistfight, later described as a stomping.

Maybe that's why Mike Tyson went back to him this year when other promoters were scrapping for a piece of his comeback: one ex-con trusting another. If so, it is a tenuous connection at best. Compared to what King endured, Tyson's three years for rape in the Indiana Youth Centre were a walk in the park.

To hear King discuss it you have to dredge up files from 1975, when seemingly out of nowhere this bombastic black man with the electric-shock haircut described as "cotton candy rescued from a coal chute" was suddenly boxing's new power broker, the man about to give the world Muhammad Ali and Joe Frazier in the Thrilla in Manila.

Reports from Indiana suggest that Tyson enjoyed everything from extra visitations, phone and recreational privileges to sexual liaisons and an affair with a female staff drug counsellor. King spoke of the six-by-12 cell where they made you wash out the toilet bowl, and the days of perpetual darkness in the Hole with only bread and water and a Bible used as a pillow and read by what light slithered through the cracks.

He was a bad man, Don King. Some say he still is. On October 1 he faces a federal indictment on nine counts of wire fraud. In 1985 he was charged with income-tax evasion, and found innocent. In 1963 he shot a man to death but claimed self-defence and was never charged.

He is 64 years old. The hair is gray. He has high blood pressure. The man who wore tuxedos the way other men wear shirts spends more time now in all-black or all-white outfits closer in design to sweatsuits, the shirt hanging loose to blur the lines of an expanding paunch.

But the mouth still works. Lord, but it works ...

"In America, they give you the opportunity to practise your trade and use your skills, and in spite of and irregardless of what they say, the doomsdayers, naysayers and critics, you continue to persevere and achieve."

— Don King, August 16, 1995

Don King is bullish on America. The country and his love for it are the bedrock upon which every speech is based.

Cynics who've seen the act a hundred times say there should be a four-letter word between the bull and the ish. A book just out attacking the man and his methods uses his pet expression as its title: *Only in America, the Life and Crimes of Don King*. He writes it off as the petty grumblings of lesser men and lets the words roll on, as relentless as the tide.

"A lot of my friends that was on board with me jumped ship because in the error of their ways they said a leopard never changes his spots. So they always had trepidation about me," he says. "But when it comes to America, that's what it's all about. They all want to see me go away, but there's more that want to see me stay. But I love you all [the media]. I love your personalities, but I don't have to love your ways."

He throws in a mangled Greek quotation, this man who gave the world such words as "trickeration" and "insinuendo" and spoke this week of a fighter who had "risen from the bowels of the ghetto seeking fame, fortune and effluence", then forgives his media transgressors.

"You are all great human beings. You do your thing the way you want to do it, let me do my thing the way I want to do it, and let the American people be the judge."

They love him. They sneer at his butchering of the language, they tell each other that he is a crook and probably guilty of all the things he's accused of and more. But they run to him for quotes or pictures or sound bites. They cover the circus, and he is the guy in the centre ring ...

"George Gershwin wrote 'Rhapsody in Blue', but he couldn't have done it without the black keys." — Don King, August 16, 1975

He has done about 30 minutes now, this man who had no seat at the 34-seat podium because, what the hell, he'd be at the mike or pacing anyway. His fight speech has included references to Jim Thorpe, Ray Charles, Aretha Franklin ("I want a little respect"), Cary Grant, Dorothy and the Tin Man and George Armstrong Custer.

He has mangled the heritage and home of Joe Hipp, the American Indian who fought Bruce Seldon for the WBC heavyweight title ("From the Dakota territory ... the Blackfoot tribe in Ya-keema up in the Seattle area. Dakota territory"). But always he returns to the theme of every speech: his work for Black Americans.

"I create jobs!" he hollers. "Jobs! Jobs! Jobs! We're not looking for handouts. We go out into the vineyards carving out of the niche of destiny whatever we can for ourselves and our families and for a better quality of life, not on our hands and knees being subordinate, but standing up equal, looking you in the eye, man to man.

"We [Black Americans] go to colleges, we put up our fists, we holler 'Black Power!' and scream about Black studies — and we deal White! White managers are the rule, not the exception.

"If a man is hungry and you give him a fish, he'll be hungry tomorrow. But if you teach him how to fish he can expand on his menu so he has a better variety of food. I teach — and I have a great crop of students who have graduated *summa cum laude*.

"I serve the Master, Mike Tyson," he shouts. "Where are the rest of the athletes, the entertainers, the sliders and the gliders, the singers and the crooners who would go out and help their community by helping their own? Mike Tyson did that!"

They are laughing now. This isn't a fight card, this is a Happening, an Event — and isn't Tyson lucky to have him? It's easy being Samson when you can use the jawbone of an ass ...

Showman or con man? Patriot or pitchman? Fighter for Black rights, or Black dollars? He'll never tell. But there is one quote, attributed to him by Jack Newfield, author of the new King book, that might offer a clue to the calculator working behind the smile: "I've decided, no interviews for your book. The day your book comes out, I want to be able to call a press conference and tell the whole damned world, that damned white boy didn't have the decency to speak to this poor nigger."

The greatest promoter in the history of mankind smiles and waves. He has pulled off the greatest fight scam of them all. Was this a great country, or what ...?

SUCKER PUNCH

August 20, 1995

LAS VEGAS — Good morning, suckers.

You there at ringside, who paid the $1,500 for your seat. You up in the rafters who paid $100. All you millions out there on six continents who paid $40 or $50 to get the pay-TV telecast.

You were had. The fight mob picked your pockets as cleanly as Johnny the Dip.

Or maybe it wasn't the fight mob. Maybe it was the McNeeley mob.

Whatever. At 1:29 of the first round, with Peter McNeeley already downed twice by Mike Tyson but obviously unhurt, McNeeley's cornerman Vinny Vecchione jumped into the ring. Cornermen aren't allowed to step into the ring. Automatically, the fight was over, ended on a disqualification. The joke of the week became a reality: The national anthem, at 2:36, DID last longer than the fight.

The Nevada State Athletic Commission will look at the tape and perhaps launch an investigation. But this is the same commission that refused to deal with the original cause for doubt: Why was this fight allowed to happen in the first place?

"It was my decision," Vecchione said of his leap that stopped the fight. "It was the speed more than the power. This is a young man who's only 26 and will have a heavyweight title fight a few years down the road. I stopped it. It was my call."

"I came to fight, I fought, I got beat. That's it and that's that. I was satisfied with my performance," said McNeeley, who picked up $540,000 U.S. for the 89 seconds' work. "I landed some, I took some, but I've been hit harder by my sparring partners."

Was he upset with Vecchione for stopping the fight?

"No!" he shouted. "I love this guy. He's been like a father to me."

Thus the months of speculation over what kind of Mike Tyson would step into the ring after three years in prison and four without a fight go essentially unanswered. In this much ballyhooed first fight that reportedly drew the biggest viewing audience ever, he barely had to break a sweat.

"He came right at me. I didn't have time to anticipate anything. I just used my instincts and started punching," Tyson said.

His instincts were good enough to put the swarming McNeeley on the deck in the first 10 seconds. McNeeley was bouncing through the mandatory eight count on that one. On the second, although he took a solid right hand, it appeared that he tripped over Tyson's feet or he might have been able to stay erect.

Among the mystified was referee Mills Lane.

"He's been knocked down a couple of times and the three-knock-down rule was in effect, but he looked ready to keep fighting," he said. "Why the guy stepped in I don't know."

McNeeley's version of the second knockdown went like this: "He swung and missed ... I slipped on the rope and twisted my knee. He hit me again. Uppercut? It was so goddamn fast I don't know what it was.

"I was confused. I thought [the stop] might have been the three-knockdown rule, which shows you how confused I was."

A defiant promoter Don King praised McNeeley.

"He's a warrior," he said. "He walked the walk and talked the talk. He came here to fight and he did. He was fighting at the end and the fight was stopped because of the love between him and the people in his corner."

Tyson was asked to rate McNeeley.

"I've beat people with bigger reputations quicker," he said. "Don't ask me. I'm just a fighter trying to get better."

It could be argued by some that Tyson kept his promise to "win spectacularly." But against an unschooled brawler whose 36-1 record came at the expense of nobodies, the nearly blind and men who hadn't fought for years before he met them, what did he prove?

Tyson looked as though he could still punch, but he missed as many as he landed. The rust of four years had no chance to flake away. The Mike Tyson of today is the Mike Tyson of yesterday, but $25,000,000 richer.

Just what Team Tyson has in store for the hottest commodity in boxing is unsure at the moment.

Last night's bout, the first for the 29-year-old Tyson since June 28, 1991, when he beat Donovan "Razor" Ruddock, was the $25,000,000 down payment in a six-fight deal with *Showtime* that could eventually bring in several times that figure. If he wins the heavyweight title, the figure goes over the moon.

It is now a matter of who and when.

King insists that Tyson will fight at the MGM Grand again November 4, going head-to-head with the Riddick Bowe-Evander Holyfield bout on the same night down the road at Caesars Palace. Probable opponent: Buster Mathis Jr. But that's less about fighting than about a power struggle between rival promoters and pay-TV networks. Tyson ("I make the decisions now. Me!") hungers to regain the crown and may feel he's ready for a bigger step toward it than Mathis would represent. And, after the McNeeley fiasco, would the fight mob pay to see him fight anyone but a contender or a champ?

George Foreman? No way. Even for boxing, the limits were reached here last night.

COVER AND CLINCH

February 11, 1997

Four days after a tear-stained and confused Oliver McCall broke down in the ring against Lennox Lewis, professional boxing is still going about the business of covering its ass.

The Nevada State Athletic Commission says it tested McCall for drugs and HIV before the fight, so it's not to blame. ("Well, boys, we know he's in drug rehab and maybe a few of the logs are rolling off the truck, but he peed clean and he ain't about to give anybody AIDS, so what's not to licence?")

Promoter Dino Duva says he and his mob pleaded with Don King weeks before the fight to get a substitute for McCall, so they're not to blame. McCall is in King's stable, and King would put Butterbean in with Mother Teresa if it drew. As McCall waited to run into the ring — wearing a wing-nut grimace even then — there was King behind him yelling, "One more time! One more time!"

"I believe he had a nervous breakdown and maybe it was a reaction to the way he was living outside the ring," shrugged Jose Sulaiman, president of the World Boxing Council and, one suspects, the Don King fan club.

The psychiatrist who evaluated him the morning after says his mental state is fine, but recommended psychiatric treatment. Is that "fine" as in "normal" or "fine" as in "For a guy who walked around the ring with tears in his eyes and refused to fight, he seems okay to me."

How many clues did they need, these people who decide who's fit to step into the ring and compete in the only sport in the world where the objective is to render another man unconscious?

Oliver McCall was on his third stint of drug rehab — while he was training for the Lewis fight. He was arrested twice last summer for drug possession, charged with vandalism and resisting arrest in November for throwing a Christmas tree in a hotel lobby in Nashville, and he arrived in Las Vegas for the fight accompanied by a drug counsellor. All of this was public knowledge.

And the men who govern the fight game looked at one another and basically said: "This is a rematch for a vacant title. Lewis is gonna be one of our big-buck pay-TV guys, and McCall beat him last time out. Hey, he looks fine to me."

It would be so easy to give it the old Sulaiman shrug and laugh off Oliver McCall. There is no shortage of ammunition.

Walking around the ring with his back turned to Lewis was, he says, part of his fight plan to tire him out. "Kind of like Ali's rope-a-dope," he said. He was half right — the dope half. Lewis was sitting on his stool while McCall wandered the ring. ("Boy, old Lennox, he fallin' right into my trap.")

The referee, he says, simply didn't understand his plan. The fight should never have been stopped. He wants a rematch, and he'll give his purse to charity. He's going back into training. Just you wait ...

It was the stuff of stand-up comics.

"So Custer says, 'Men, we'll surround these Indians who outnumber us about 200 to one, we'll let them shoot us until they run out of bullets, and then ...' "

Except for the tears.

Oliver McCall says now that they were tears of frustration because he couldn't land on Lewis as he'd planned. One look at the fight tape exposes the lie. The face of Oliver McCall was the face of a man in torment, his mind walking roads no one else could see.

George Foreman knew, sitting there at ringside doing colour commentary. "After the second round," he said, "all I wanted to do was go up there and give him a big hug and say, 'It's all right, Oliver, it's gonna be all right.' "

It's not gonna be all right. Oliver McCall is finished as a boxer. His battle with drugs and personal demons will be fought without the support of the one part of his life that, until now, made him special. And the people who let it happen will shrug, and continue the search for fresh meat.

SUMMIT MEETING

June 25, 1997

LAS VEGAS — Jimmy "The Weasel" Fratriano, a former hit man who grew so loquacious in custody that the FBI had to hide him in maximum security lest his Mafia brethren purchase his silence with an ice pick, was always puzzled by one aspect of this city of gambling and glitz.

"I dunno why nuttin' grows there," he said. "We planted enough stiffs to fertilize anything."

The Weasel was right about the vegetation but dead wrong about the cash crops.

Hotels grow here, each generation bigger and tackier and more ersatz-opulent than the yesterday wonders demolished to make room. Casinos flourish under artificial light in stadium-sized caverns devoid of fresh air and clocks, where slot machines have moved from pull handles to push-buttons lest the tourists' elbows give out as they pump in coin after coin.

And, once or twice a year when the fight mob gathers for a heavyweight title bout, hype grows here — hype based on speculation and odds and the anticipation of watching two multimillionaire warriors try to pound each other to jelly, all overlaid with the faint, sweet smell of con.

On the parking lot next to the 16,331-seat arena that sits like a pimple on the backside of the MGM Grand has risen a huge white tent. It is here that the sporting media gather daily, awaiting the Evander Holyfield-Mike Tyson rematch, the fight that is supposed to settle the burning question of whether Holyfield's stunning 11th-round win here November 9 was a dazzling display by a man who started as a 25-1 underdog, or a case of Tyson believing the tales of his own invincibility after demolishing sacrificial lambs like Peter McNeeley as part of his post-prison rehabilitation.

Tyson has trained in secret, emerging briefly for a press conference in the home of promoter Don King at which he claimed the fighter with whom he most identified was Sonny Liston, who also had his troubles with the law and died in a hotel room in what police delicately called "suspicious circumstances."

Holyfield has chosen a different road, training in private but coming daily to the tent to spar and answer questions while gospel music blares incessantly in the background with tent-revival fervour and the decibel level of rap. The real work is already done, but the media ritual must be observed.

It's pretty tame stuff. Holyfield puts his faith in the Lord and His plan for him, whatever it may be. Tyson has eased up on the me-and-Allah-and-Chairman-Mao theme that has been woven through his post-prison tune-ups, speaking more of his family and his faith that the real Mike Tyson will show up on Saturday and scrub away the blot of last November.

Neither man can or would answer the question that has generated a $35,000,000 payday for Holyfield and $30,000,000 for Tyson, the question that has sold every seat — from a top of $1,500 to a bleacher at $200 — and created a pay-TV climate the promoters say could be the biggest of them all: Can Tyson find a way under or around that darting, daunting left jab that prevented him from getting inside where he likes to work?

In an effort to find an answer he has made his peace with Richie Giachetti, his trainer when he was mugging the heavyweight division at will. Giachetti, it is hoped, will re-hone the tools he needs to get under and inside, and to avoid some of the cumulative punishment dealt by Holyfield in the first fight.

If he can do it well enough to win, the inevitable rubber match will make this one seem like the payoff on a nickel slot. Which is why some insist that's the way it will be. The Weasel was wrong about nothing growing here. Cynicism grows just fine.

THE POWERS THAT BE

June 27, 1997

LAS VEGAS — Fight week in Vegas, and the shills are alive with the sound of music.

In the camp of Iron Mike Tyson, who now marches on the path of Islam and opens every interview with a soft-spoken commitment to Allah, it is the bap-bap-bap, don't-gimme-no-crap of Black America rap. But when Evander Holyfield works, he toils to the pounding beat of Gospel — revival-meeting stuff with the key-thumping fervour of backwoods church piano, long on inspirational chorus, heavy on the Hallelujahs, and laced with the shouts of the preacher man promising better days to come.

Saturday night, in a basement arena of a bread-and-circuses casino in a city built on gambling, drinking and the scenic wonders of semi-naked flesh, these two servants of a Greater Power will try to pound each other into road kill.

In a sporting world where too many athletes tend to find God just after the cops find them ("Ah did it! Yes! I stole them things, your honour! That shoebox full of co-caine was MINE! But I seen the light, judge! Honest!"), it is difficult not to view these shenanigans with a certain cynicism.

It is particularly difficult in the land of Evander Holyfield and his wife of eight months, Dr. Janice Itson.

Without even looking at the records, says Ms. Itson — herself a medical internist — she knew that the medics had misdiagnosed Holyfield's alleged heart condition in 1994, the one that was supposed to keep him from fighting ever again.

"I knew in prayer," she said. "And it turned out it WAS [a misdiagnosis]."

She knew when it was time for Holyfield to begin training for this second Tyson bout because God told her "during a walk to the store."

She knew when the fight date was set for March that it wasn't going to happen. She even phoned Holyfield and told him to quit training and come home — which he did — because the fight wouldn't happen in March, it would happen in June.

When Don King set it for May, she didn't waver. It would be in June. And, after Tyson suffered a cut eyebrow in training it was, indeed, set for June 28.

"He [God] wanted him to fight in June," she says. "We just try to live by the Lord in everything we do, even the timing of the fight. Because God has a purpose for the timing and everything else."

That purpose, she says, is for her husband to successfully defend his heavyweight crown. God has told her. "You hear God, and God promises you victory. And I think that when you've got that assurance, the outcome [is settled]."

A query about the possibility of a Tyson victory throws her for a second. Then: "No, no. I can't answer that because that's not going to happen. He will win ... he WILL win!"

Holyfield, while totally committed to his beliefs, has what seems a more rational approach: That the Lord has given him the talent and the ability to work and to learn. "The only time bad things happen," he says, "is when I don't do the work."

But Tyson is working too, his Islamic convictions apparently every bit as firm. The bookies, a bottom-line lot, have him at 2-1 now and figure he'll still be favoured, although at lower odds, come fight time. If the Greater Power factor has a place in their equation it is in the old story of the two boxers of equal religious fervour, crossing themselves just before the bell.

An old Irish-Catholic priest was sitting at ringside.

"Does that help?" a man asked.

"Only if he can fight, my son," he answered. "Only if he can fight."

FAITH, AND IT'S A MIRACLE

June 28, 1997

LAS VEGAS — There lives in boxing legend a fighter known as Phainting Phil Scott, who once fell to the canvas under such questionable impetus that someone in the crowd screamed, "Did he fall, or was he pushed?"

Phainting Phil, meet Missing Mitch.

Mitch Halpern, who was supposed to referee the Mike Tyson-Evander Holyfield heavyweight title fight — a prestigious plum for which he would be paid $10,000 — decided late Thursday night that he didn't want the job. He phoned the Nevada State Athletic Commission, pulled the pin, and will be replaced by the veteran Mills Lane.

The chronology is at the very least intriguing.

At 6 p.m. Thursday, after a one-hour delay in which they basically stood around staring at one another, the commission held a public meeting to rule on a protest by Team Tyson asking that Halpern be replaced because the reappearance in the ring of this man who'd stopped the first Tyson-Holyfield fight in the 11th round could be potentially distracting and maybe even downright damaging to the tender psyche of poor little Iron Mike.

The five commission members heard testimony, called up lawyers, had minutes read, fumed, fussed and hunched their shoulders, confirming a long-held suspicion that if they'd been running D-Day we'd all be speaking German.

Sixty-five minutes later, they told Team Tyson to go pound sand. By a vote of 4 to 1, Mitch Halpern was their guy. Halpern was delighted. He appreciated the confidence of the commission, he said. No, he certainly wouldn't let the protest affect his performance. "I have a job to do, and I'm going to concentrate on doing it."

His feelings were dutifully reported in the morning prints, by which time they had been obliterated by onrushing events.

It seems that some time after the meeting, Halpern went to the Sporting House to work out — and during that workout it came to him that he "should not be the focus" of Holyfield-Tyson II.

"He thought long and hard about the situation at hand," said commission spokesman Marc Ratner in a hastily produced press release, "and he felt he shouldn't be the focus of one of the greatest sporting events in the history of the sport. He called me and said he felt very strongly that he should step aside, so that the focus is squarely on the two fighters."

Gee. What a guy, that Mitch Halpern.

The Tyson camp doesn't want him, the Holyfield camp says he's fine but they would go along with Mills Lane just to expedite matters, old Mitch goes for a workout — and Pow! It comes to him that maybe he should say to hell with the 10 grand and get out of the way so 16,331 people in the MGM Grand and all those millions in the pay-TV audience can concentrate on Tyson and Holyfield instead of poking each other and saying things like: "Migawd, Martha! That's Mitch Halpern!"

"You know, Fred, I think you're right! But who are those two guys in there with him?"

So where are we?

Well, Team Tyson gets its wish. There's a new referee. Iron Mike Tyson's much discussed and supposedly suspect psyche will not have to wrestle with the spectre of Mitch Halpern.

But wait! Evander Holyfield LOVES Mills Lane! He once called him "my referee." Will this strengthen his sense of inner peace? If Mike finds out, will it trigger inner doubt? A sense of isolation? The heartbreak of psoriasis?

Stay tuned. Soon they get to hit each other. May the better id win.

THE REAL MEAL DEAL

June 29, 1997

LAS VEGAS — And so, after all the hype, it will go down as the first heavyweight title fight in history where one of the shots should have been tetanus and the champion won by an ear.

And maybe, in the end, it did answer the week-long question about the psyche of Iron Mike Tyson. Maybe the guy IS nuts. Or maybe he was just hungry. If that's the case, it may turn out to be a $30,000,000 snack — $15,000,000 for biting the right ear of Evander "The Real Meal" Holyfield, $15,000,000 for coming back for seconds on the left.

When a man is disqualified for biting his opponent on both ears, as referee Mills Lane disqualified Tyson at the end of the third round, he surely must forfeit his purse. It also raises some question as to whether he will ever fight again.

I hope they have great videotape. I hope they were close enough with those new jillion-dollar cameras to chronicle it fang by fang. For without the evidence of their own eyes, who will ever believe what happened here at the MGM Grand?

Title fights are settled with fists, not teeth. They do not end with the champion standing in the corner having his ear power-washed and the challenger raging in the other corner like a pit bull who's slipped his collar. This was supposed to be a fight for the ages, not the comic pages.

Take it bite-by-bite.

They're clinching, as they've done through the first two rounds. Suddenly, Holyfield rocks back and jumps into the air in rage. A line of blood shows under his right ear.

Lane signals time out while he considers the possibility that one of his fighters has been bitten. Tyson, tired of waiting, rushes over and shoves Holyfield from behind into the ropes.

Lane restores order. They pound away at each other. It is shaping up as a fight they should move out into the alley where they can use garbage cans and lead pipes. Maybe it's going to be a classic after all.

And then — another clinch, and another bite, this time on the other ear.

The bell goes. The round is over. Confusion reigns.

Lane goes to Holyfield's corner, takes a look, and signals disqualification. The Sound and the Fury has become the Fanged and the Famished. Fights break out in the ring. Tyson wants everybody — anybody.

Tyson's entourage leaves. Somebody in the stands spits. Somebody else throws water. All hell breaks loose. Security troops land on the guy and haul him away. The crowd of 16,331 is stunned to near silence. And millions of pay-TV customers are left thinking that if they were going to watch someone eat, they should have used the $49.95 to order pizza.

And now the whole mess falls into the hands of the Nevada State Athletic Commission, the World Boxing Association and possibly the Campaign Against Hunger.

One thing you can take to the bank: There'll be no rubber meal. Evander Holyfield is a religious and forgiving man, but he has but two ears to give to his profession, and he gave them both last night.

Where does this leave boxing? Looking for another contender — Michael Moorer, perhaps, or Andrew Golota, who was ahead of Riddick Bowe in two fights before losing for hitting him down where Nellie wore the beads.

A better question might be where it leaves Mike Tyson. When he promised all week that the old Iron Mike would return, we thought he meant the fighter. We didn't expect him to reach further back and resurrect the thug.

Chapter Five

SOFA, SO GOOD

We've all heard about the pinch of garlic, the dose of salt, the ounce of prevention and the pound of cure. The big one is missing: A doze of baseball.

This is not to knock the game that is the lifelong passion of millions and the October pastime of so many millions more. It's just that after years of beating my head into walls (with maximum hairline damage) I have finally come to understand what these people mean about the game's subtle rhythms.

They are the rhythms of gently heaving chests as the devoted fan drifts off to the Land of Nod while watching some millionaire foul off nine consecutive pitches before striking out.

They are the soft exhalations of breath in time to the soothing sound of Jim Kaat explaining in 25,000 words or less why Rickey Henderson isn't taking his usual long lead off first as the White Sox fret themselves into puddles wondering when he's going to take off.

They are the reassuring drone of statistics proving that more left-handed Toronto Blue Jays have had success hitting the split-finger fastball on Wednesdays in the Central time zone than on Thursdays during road trips to the Pacific, and that the Chicago White Sox have gone without a World Series title longer than any other major-league team except the Cubs.

They are the delicate sounds of sunflower seeds landing on dugout floors as players pttui! between pitches, and the scritch-scritch-scritch, perhaps imagined, of fingernail on itch.

Put them all together — Pttui! Scritch! "Was that a hanging curve, Tim, or a fastball that got away?" Zzzzzzz! "Check the rotation on that back-door curve!" Pttui! Scritch! Scritch! — and you have both the essence of the game and the secret to watching it: To be properly appreciated, baseball requires a great sofa.

Preferably it should be placed at proper visual distance from a big-screen TV and within reaching distance of something cool, and come with a punchable cushion to place across the armrest where you're going to plant your head. Throw in a bag of potato chips and maybe a smaller pillow at the other end so you can get your feet a tad higher than the rest of your body, and you're set for the latest chapter of the burning question to be settled in the Illinois sunshine: Can Canada's team of hired Americans beat Chicago's?

Lie back and let those subtle rhythms flow over you. Feel your eyelids grow heavy as you listen to the Alphabet Lullaby ("ERA ... RBI ... You will sl-e-e-p by-and-by-eye ..."). Let your thoughts drift to the days of pick-up games and vacant lots and summers that lasted forever ...

WHAZZAT?

Oh! It's the play-by-play guy. He raised his voice. Something must have happened. Not to worry. I'll catch it on this replay. And this one ... and this one ... and ...

See what I mean? A beautiful game, baseball. Especially the home games, the games where you stay at home. You stretch out, you snooze, and you never miss anything because the announcer always wakes you up in time to watch the replay.

And don't let anyone tell you baseball isn't educational. Why, just yesterday I found out that ALC doesn't stand for a labour union. So keep those subtle rhythms coming, guys. I can use the sleep.

ODE TO BOBBY-JO

June 13, 1974

Little League Baseball Inc. rules that girls can play on its teams because of "the changing social climate." — News item

Where I grew up the only game the girls didn't play was doctor, and it wasn't because they weren't asked.

Mercifully saved from the clutches of organization, we played co-ed baseball, football and, on a good day, wrestling. Football was always tackle because we'd been warned we mustn't touch. Unaware of any changing social climate, we sneeringly let girls in for the best of all possible reasons. We didn't have enough boys.

It was a mistake, an error far more traumatic than your first pimple or the day your voice broke while proving your manhood by singing 37 verses of "North Atlantic Squadron." We discovered the enormity the day Bobby-Jo Woodman threw a perfect strike from second base and cut off the tying run at the plate.

Girls 12 and under are better athletes than boys. They run faster, they get their reflexes faster and, until the day they develop unsightly bumps, can out-do most boys at any sport you'd care to name. Bobby-Jo could even spit farther.

It takes a girl a few years to mature to the point where she throws a ball like a 70-year-old beating off a masher with her purse. Through the eight-to-12 Little League years they just rear back and fire. That's why Little League is wrong to integrate. They'll blow the psyches of thousands of little kids, all of them boys.

The announcement was made in Williamsport, Connecticut, by Peter J. McGovern, board chairman and CEO of Little League Inc., who sounds like a jerk. Mr. McGovern, whose organization made the move of its own free will just as soon as it found out the courts were about to do it for them, says things like "The board believes that its concern and reaction to the recent intrusion of the administrative affairs of Little League by various self-interest groups was justified, since they have opted to ignore the purviews of constitutional law and have breached, as well as demanded, abrogation of the rights of others."

We had a kid once who talked that much. Fat Artie McWilliams sat on his face.

Peter J. McGovern, who was maybe never a kid, also says girls "would have to prove equal competency in baseball skills, physical endowments and other attributes scaled as a basis for team selection." Bobby-Jo was 10 when she was our second-baseman, and as far as physical attributes went we knew she was a girl because she told us.

To change the rules so girls can get in, Peter J. McGovern, who sounds like he'd be big in Sport Canada, says his league "will petition the House of Representatives judiciary committee to introduce legislation to amend Little League's federal charter under which it has operated since 1964." We had our own rules committee. Somebody said, "Can she hit?" and if she could she was in. Took 10 seconds. But then, we were only kids. I wonder if Fat Artie has any big-butt friends in Williamsport?

I don't like the idea of co-ed leagues. At anything past puberty it's a cop-out because they're making room only for a token gifted few. It would make far more sense to set up corresponding age-group leagues in every kids' sport going, and make sure that the financing, coaching and park allocation is strictly 50-50. Why does it take some high-priced badger and a federal charter just to say "Play Ball!"? But in Little League it doesn't matter. From eight to 12, girls are just boys who talk funny.

There will be, Little League insists, big problems with integration. Let us take them one by one:

1. Hair. Right away you'll notice the difference. Girls' hair is much too short.

2. Washroom facilities. Big deal. You show me a 10-year-old kid who wants to wash. As for separate johns, what's good enough for us is good enough for them. You cross your legs, get in one more inning, then run home. If you don't make it, you're charged with an error.

3. Physical injury. True. In times of stress, Bobby-Jo used to bite a lot. Happily, it was a habit she retained in later years.

PUT 'EM IN A BOX, TIE 'EM WITH A RIBBON ...

February 28, 1992

The Sporting News *will eliminate baseball box scores to make room for additional sports coverage.* — News item

Personally, I always figured box scores were a plot by the optometrists to promote eyestrain. Or maybe they were IQ tests: Anyone caught reading one flunked.

Incredible things, box scores. Almost as dumb as the people who read them. Names shortened by apostrophes so they'll fit. Endless numbers strung out in type the size of ant dung, laid out in columns that reduce typesetters to gibbering idiots.

And for what? So that on an October morning a Detroit Tigers fan can leap out of bed to learn that someone named Frymn who apparently belongs to the SS had four abs, no rs, one h and a bi.

I can just see him at the breakfast table, sports page dipping into his peanut butter, Tigers cap set sideways on his head in LOCK position so's it shouldn't block out the light.

"Hey, honey, we lose big to the Orioles last night. Whtker 2b got two hs and an r, but nobody else did squat. They oughta ditch that guy Brgmn 1b. Two abs and all the rest zeroes. And hey, leggo my Eggo!"

It has taken *The Sporting News* only 116 years to figure out that people who think that way are not buying their copy on the way to MIT or a Mensa meeting. That's when it ran the first box scores — in its first edition back in the spring of 1886, a century or so before people began writing about the game as though it were something mystical instead of a bunch of guys standing around trying to hit a ball with a stick.

When kids do that it's called recess. When grown men do it, it's called the National Pastime. Go figure.

In simpler times when I worked for the broadsheet paper down the hall, we ran line scores, not box scores. The theory was simple: They saved space we could then use for real sports stories with words and syllables and everything, yet still had enough WPs and LPs and HRs in them to satisfy the typical baseball fan without being long enough (say, six lines) to confuse him.

(You think I jest? One of my jobs was to underline the WP and the LP so the printer would put them in dark type to save the readers the strain of figuring out what the letters meant.)

Oh, there was pressure to run the full box scores. Baseball fans would phone and say things like "Me and my friends at the pub want you should run the box scores or maybe you shouldn't start your car." But we resisted, because we had no space.

Then I moved to the *Province*, we went tabloid, which meant we had less space per page — and suddenly we were running full box scores.

"Lots of interest out there," I was told. "They're really popular."

Sure, there was — but shouldn't we be running them in crayon?

Still, we weren't as bad as *The Sporting News*. At least the box scores we ran were one day old. (Okay, two days.) The ones *The Sporting News* ran were a week old. There were people out there reading tiny little numbers that told them that Cminiti 3b had 4 ab for Houston against Atlanta last Thursday.

These people need help. *The Sporting News* — the "Bible of baseball", lest we forget — has seen the light. It is moving to save their eyeballs and what's left of their sanity. It will no longer run box scores.

As a responsible daily, I believe it's our duty to follow suit, and I have every faith that my beloved sports editor will agree. If he ever finishes oiling his glove.

DAY OF THE BARBER

December 29, 1992

We had this TV set, a Crosley Super-V, 16 inches, black and white, the only one in the rooming house, which made my mom and me something of a power because even the landlord couldn't watch unless we said so.

There'd be a knock on the door, every Tuesday night, I think it was, and there he'd be with his wife and maybe a kid or two, ready to watch *Life of Riley*. Sometimes, just for the hell of it, I'd say no, we were watching *Name That Tune*.

It was so long ago I hadn't yet learned to loathe baseball.

Reception wasn't what you'd call super. Cable hadn't been invented, the house was only two storeys high, and we'd bought the bargain-special antenna because the best one cost six dollars more. Sometimes the picture got so foggy it was like watching radio. We only knew the Lone Ranger was coming over the hill because we could hear the thundering hoofbeats of the great horse Silver.

It made it perfect to watch Sal Maglie go against Don Larsen in the fifth game of the 1956 World Series, the Dodgers vs the Hated Yankees.

Colour TV would have spoiled it. Today's colour-co-ordinated, hi-I'm-Sal-what's-your-sign? uniforms full of over-exposed, under-talented millionaires tippy-toeing over artificial grass would have turned them into a bunch of clowns three weeks early for Halloween. The Hated Yankees wore white and the visiting Dodgers wore grey as the Good Lord intended, and it was a street fight from Pitch One.

Larsen looked okay, for a Hated Yankee. Clean and neat and determined not to get shelled out in this one as he had in losing a 13-8 thriller in Game Two.

Maglie looked like he had friends named Vito and Marvin the Torch who for a hundred bucks would drop over to your house and build you a vacant lot. He was all loan-shark eyes and a five-o'clock shadow already working on next week. "The Barber," they called him, because when he was ticked off he'd throw something that would scare the bristles off a batter's chin. And he was always ticked off.

I knew these things because by that time I was working for my first newspaper and had discovered that if you got to the office before the boss you could open all the envelopes containing the Red Smith and Jimmy Cannon columns. They didn't write all this baseball-as-metaphor-for-life stuff that puts my stomach on permanent puke. They told you about the people playing it, and they told me a lot about Sal Maglie.

They told me the reason he always looked peed off with life was that in 1947, after he'd gone 5-4 in 13 games as a rookie with the New York Giants, they refused to raise his $6,000 salary and he got so mad he told baseball to screw the reserve clause and jumped to the Mexican League. He did four years there before the majors revoked his lifetime ban.

They had taken bread from his table and money from his wallet. He couldn't blow them up or make them part of a freeway project, so he put their faces on every guy who stepped to the plate.

Today I wouldn't watch an entire baseball game on a bet. But I watched that one, Larsen and Maglie going at it like they'd be there forever if forever was what it took.

Everybody remembers Larsen threw the perfect game and the Yankees won 2-0. What I remember is that Maglie faced the Hated Yankees of Mantle and Berra and Howard and Martin and Bauer and held them to five hits over nine innings. He lost, but it took perfection to beat him.

The Barber died the other day. He was 75 years old. When they face him in heaven, they'd better not dig in.

THE PHILTHY PHILLIES

October 15, 1993

We could be watching history here: the first World Series ever picketed by *GQ*, boycotted by Gillette, and shut down by the Board of Health.

This isn't Toronto vs Philadelphia; it's Ritchie Rich vs the Bowery Boys, Team Squeaky vs Team Grunge, Charlie Brown vs Pigpen. In Toronto, fans holler at the Jays to take it downtown. In Philly, they yell, "Take it down-wind!"

Did you *see* those guys while they were knocking off Atlanta? Pot-bellied, double-chinned, wild-haired, stubble-cheeked, knuckle-dragging, pantleg-ripped — and that was just John Kruk. On this team, he's the trend-setter. It's the only Series in history where the plate umpire should be reaching into his pocket and tossing out a new bar of soap.

There are guys on the Phillies who look like they're entering the Hoyt Wilhelm look-alike contest. Is that a waddle, or did the earth move? And then there is Mitch Williams, who'll probably make an extra $1,000,000 or so in endorsements because they call him the Wild Thing, and he is. On any given day, old Mitch is gonna beat some team. You just never know whether it's yours or his.

Bring the Jays to church, they'd sing in the choir. Bring the Phillies, and they'd barricade themselves in the bell tower with the sopranos.

The Jays are clean-cut, combed, curried and tucked in, shrewd young millionaire businessmen who take their uniforms home in hand-stitched briefcases and probably only signed the glowering Dave Stewart to protect their stock portfolios. The Phillies are the street gang on the corner who'd take them.

The Jays have people like Paul Molitor, who use three- and four-syllable words and talk about life after baseball. The Phillies have people for whom the two-syllable word would cause hernias. In good restaurants, the Jays would lean to port or sherry. The Phillies would ask for a giraffe of wine.

In short, the Jays are the movies, the Phillies the new reality. Or have you not noticed that in today's sporting arena the Look of the '90s is Sweat-Stained Mugger?

I'm not sure when it started, but the next time you look at an NHL telecast, check the faces. There may be a talent inequity in the NHL, but there's a 26-way tie in stubble. The mugger-types, the Marty McSorleys et al, skate around wearing 18-hour beards and maniacal grins straight out of Smiling Zack. For them, it's supposed to be intimidating. The stubble also serves to slow the flow of blood.

But even the role-model types, the Gretzkys and Lemieuxs and Yzermans, come into the games looking like they're between razor endorsements. Throw in the natural sweat and adrenaline rush of combat and every team in the NHL looks like the Dirty Half-Dozen. And then, in case you haven't got the message, they spit.

It's not that they're dirty by nature. If athletes stopped showering we could solve the world water shortage. Win or lose, the post-game dressing rooms are alive with the hiss of the shower, the rub of deodorant bars, and the whir of a dozen blow-dryers. The fingernails may scrape the dirt, but the cuticles will be shaped and clean.

Like it or not, on ice, field or floor, grubby is everything, and may always be. They're too old, and too rich, to be sent to the bathroom and ordered to clean up before they'll be allowed to go out to play.

"PLEASE, SIR, I WANT SOME MORE ..."

December 28, 1995

Once upon a time in the kingdom of Toronto, where the sacred bird was a Blue Jay whose nest had a retractable roof and a bar and rooms with windows through which, upon occasion, visitors could be seen doing exotic things to one another, there lived a poor little boy named Roberto who loved to hit balls with sticks.

It wasn't Roberto's only game. He could also catch balls hit by other people with sticks. He could play both these games so well that soon word of his magic spread throughout the land — indeed, to the very boundaries of the Ontario universe — and the people in their hundreds of thousands mounted their cars and their trucks and their trains and their buses for the pilgrimage to Toronto for a glimpse of the wondrous boy who could strike a ball with a stick as often as one time in three or four.

As Roberto's fame spread, the people in the kingdom of Toronto grew fearful, and showered him with gifts to keep him happy so that he would not stray outside their walls. They gave him gold. They gave him silver. They gave him fruit-juice commercials. And Roberto smiled and took the gifts and said how wonderful it was to live in a kingdom like Toronto when other, less fortunate little boys had to play with sticks in places like — yecch! — Baltimore.

And then one day, Roberto had a Wonderful Thought.

Sticking his glove in his hip pocket, he screwed up his courage and knocked upon the door of the Evil Team Owner. "Please, sir," he said. "I want some more."

"More what?" thundered the Owner.

"More gold," said Roberto, his voice quavering. "I have been hitting balls and catching balls for you for a long time now — three, sometimes four hours a day, seven months of the year, which leaves me only — let's see: 12 minus seven, carry the one — Five! That's it: Five months to spend my money and relax on the beach and live better than you. And tell me this: Who else you got who can time it so he spits and scratches himself just as the TV camera comes in for the close-up? I got skills, man!

"So," he concluded, "I want more gold, or I gonna go hit balls with sticks somewhere else."

"How much gold?" asked the Evil Owner, his voice cracking.

"Twenty-one million dollars," said Roberto. "Seven million a year for how many that goes into 21. Plus $4,000,000 for signing the contract, because look at all the letters I got to deal with in the Roberto alone, never mind my last name."

"How about $5,000,000 per year?" pleaded the Evil Owner. "These are tough times in the kingdom. Even the royal belt has to be tightened. Take one for the team, Roberto. Make do on the five mil! Brown bag it to lunch, or something."

"No," said Roberto. And, climbing into his Mercedes, he began the arduous trip from kingdom to kingdom, searching in vain for someone who would pay him $25,000,000 to hit balls with sticks for them.

Supplies dwindled. The paté grew mouldy. The caviar turned. His gold supply dwindled. One fateful night, alone in his five-star tent in a strange kingdom far away from his beloved Toronto, he was reduced to drinking room-service wine served from a bottle with a screw-on top.

Crushed, he picked up the phone and made the call he'd sworn he'd never make.

The next day, in the land of Baltimore, he picked up the pen and, for a mere $2,000,000, signed his entire name to a paper that indentured him to another bird called an Oriole, for whom he would hit balls with sticks and catch balls hit by other people with sticks for three years — and all for a paltry $12,000,000.

But as he signed, he made a silent vow that he would fight his way out of this poverty, that somewhere, somehow, he would find another kingdom where they truly appreciated a boy who could hit a ball with a stick.

In the meantime, if things got a little tough at Christmas, there was always the Food Bank. "I wonder," he thought, "if they serve Dom Perignon with the turkey ..."

LIFE IN THE BIGS

August 11, 1992

The last time Jack Clark opened his American Express card bill the total read $55,955. Maybe Karl Malden is wrong. Maybe you *should* leave home without it.

In Clark's case, he also should leave his Visa ($19,820.78), his Nordstrom department stores card ($37,000), every other piece of plastic that allows him to buy on credit, and all business cards from automobile dealers or real estate agents, lest he feel the urge to buy his 19th car or second mansion. As urgent as it now seems, he shouldn't even have his head read unless the shrink takes only cash.

Weekend word that Clark — who is paid $16,250 per game by the Boston Red Sox to hit a ball with a stick and so far has done it once in every five attempts — has managed to pile up $6,700,000 in debts no doubt struck a responsive chord with the North American working stiff. Hey, who hasn't gone a little plastic crazy once in a while and bought a third pair of shoes, or said to hell with it and sprung for a second round for the boys after bowling?

But there are a few fundamental differences between Clark and a guy like, say, Fred Schwartz of the Coquitlam Schwartzes, who still drives the Nash Metropolitan to Public Works to pick up the jack-hammer and spend another day playing hell with his kidneys.

When Fred figures the Metropolitan has had it he'll check out the used-car lot looking for something where he can handle the payments.

When Jack Clark wanted a car, he bought 18 of them, including a 1990 Ferrari F-40 for $717,000, three Mercedes Benzes ($103,000 to $142,948), seven older classics and a racing team.

When Fred uses his credit cards he gets twitchy if he can't clear them every month and avoid the interest. If he misses a payment or two he gets letters containing the banking equivalent of threats to break his kneecaps.

When Jack Clark misses a payment nobody says anything. How else would Visa, Nordstrom's and AMEX let him get into them for better than 112 grand?

When Fred buys, Fred pays. Maybe not right away, but as soon as he can. When the bills pile up, he sweats and worries and starts asking for extra shifts down at the Works.

When Jack Clark buys, he doesn't pay. When the bills pile up, he declares bankruptcy and walks away free as a bird.

And you know the amazing part? Instead of calling him a bill-dodging bum in the process of blowing two-thirds of a three-year contract worth more than $8,700,000, agents and lawyers and accountants are rallying round spewing pap about how tough it is to be an athlete, and how nobody ever explained to the poor guy about putting any away for the years after baseball.

You know what they would do with Fred Schwartz if he ran up heavy bills?

The bank eventually would foreclose on the mortgage and take the house. The credit-card people would turn the whole thing over to a collection agency. Depending upon where he bought the car, he'd have it seized by law or lose it to a repo man.

Fred could declare bankruptcy. But he wouldn't. He'd have to live with himself afterward. Jack Clark has no problem. He's bankrupt. And next year, when the rest of the contract kicks in, he'll make $2,900,000. After all, he's a big leaguer.

IT *IS* WHETHER YOU WIN OR LOSE

June 6, 1993

It was an interesting exercise: Read the *Time* magazine piece on the game played by the ancient Maya while watching replays of Nolan Ryan applying a series of noogies to the skull of Robin Ventura.

The shots of the Texas-Chicago game were offered as evidence of the growing tendency toward violence in baseball. But hey — nobody got killed. They're just lucky they weren't playing in the old Mayan league where, according to *Time* researchers, they took their games rather seriously: "Human sacrifice frequently provided the grisly finale of a game: either the defeated players were decapitated and their heads possibly used as balls, or they were tortured to death when the winners trussed up their bodies into human spheres and bounced them down pyramid steps."

Admittedly, the Maya were not playing baseball. They couldn't have been. "The solid rubber ball was kept in constant motion in the air," says *Time*. Regular viewers know that constant motion has as much relationship to baseball as hula hooping to ant farming. If it wasn't for replays there'd be hardly any motion at all. That's why TSN shows 10,000 games per week: they provide so many lulls for commercials.

Actually, no one knows quite what the Maya were playing. One of the objectives apparently was to put the solid rubber ball — or a loser's head — through a hole in a solid wall. Which, come to think of it, might discourage the drive down the lane, not to mention the slam dunk.

But as little as we know about the game, it's obvious the Maya had some sound organizational ideas that the leaders in today's troubled mega-sports might be wise to consider.

Take, for instance, this business of using the heads of the losers as the game ball. On the surface, a tad tacky. But it's cost-efficient, it eliminates the supply problem, and if a ball goes into the stands you can almost count on it being thrown back.

Once the initial queasiness passed, pitchers would love it. Think what a good junkballer could do if he could quit groping for seams and simply stick two fingers in the nostrils or get a good grip on one ear.

Tired of carpet-baggers like David Cone and Rickey Henderson, hawking their talents from team to team and city to city in search of maximum bucks? How much player movement would there be when a switch to a weak franchise could mean one bad game and a few weeks of being trussed up into a sphere and bounced up and down the pyramid steps until your skin wore off?

Scholars are still working on an accurate translation of the Mayan language, but to date there is no recorded instance of player strikes, autograph sessions at so much per signature, or gold-filled rooms for untested Mayan rookies whose heads wouldn't even make decent game balls until the zits cleared.

Best of all, they've found no Mayan trading cards. It figures. In that league, holding still for a head shot could be injurious to your health.

TERMINOLOGY GAP

October 19, 1993

Several zillion studies have been done over the years trying to fathom the unfathomables of baseball.

When a pitcher throws a curve ball, does it?

By what wizardry of mathematics did Abner Doubleday — or Alexander Cartwright, or whoever — come up with just the right distance between the bases, short enough to give the batter a fighting chance to beat out a slow roller, but long enough to give an infielder with a gunner arm enough time to make it a race?

Why 90 feet? Why not 84 or 92? Why the extra six inches on the 60 feet from mound to plate? Why is there a mound, anyway? Did old Abner remember how great it felt getting a little high the night before?

Think about it as you watch the ever-so-misnamed "World" Series. Here's old Abner, sitting around one day considering this ball-toss game played in infinite variation since the day some caveman invented the beanball. He decides what the game needs is one set of rules for everyone, so he writes some down.

"Let's see ... we'll make them run, oh, say, 90 feet from one point to the next. But we won't call them points, we'll call them bases, like hide-and-seek. And we'll put the thrower 60 feet away — no, 60 feet, six inches, for luck — and stand him up on a hill to give the man who has to catch it a better view, in case the thrower happens to have split his finger on an axe or something and the ball is harder to catch.

"Now, where to put the bases. In a straight line? No, if a batter hit a ball far enough to allow him to reach all four of them, he'd have to walk 360 feet just to get back to his team. 'Course, if they ever get around to inventing television that would allow great commercial breaks, but ... nah! A square is better. Better yet — a diamond! Give it a touch of class. Besides, 'Baseball Square' sounds like a home for aging athletes.

"Now, how many swings should the batsman have? Two sounds good. That allows for one mistake. If he hasn't figured out how to hit it by then, to hell with him. No, better make it three. Some of these guys aren't too bright. Come to think of it, better put a point on the plate the thrower has to throw it over, so the batsman will know where to look."

All in all, a pretty fair organizational job for old Abner. But he was a little weak on terminology.

Why is it called a "strike" when the ball isn't struck at all? Why didn't he call it a "miss"?

Why is it "foul" to strike a ball and send it out of the field of play? The man tried his best. He didn't cheat. He just didn't get it done. Why pick on him? Why not call them "miss" and "near-miss"?

Why is it called a "home run"? The man who hits the ball out of the park doesn't run home. He stays for the rest of the game. He doesn't run at all. He just trots around the bases so he can get back to the dugout and get high-fived, belly-butted and hugged and have tobacco juice slobbered over him by his exuberant teammates.

Actually, I think history has done Abner a disservice. It seems obvious he intended to call the home run a "walk" and the base-on-balls a "trot" — because that's what they do when they get a base-on-balls: They trot.

If nothing else, the change in terminology would do wonders for the play-by-play broadcast.

"Two out, three-and-two on Molitor ... the pitch ... and Molitor drives it deep to centre ... this baby is GONE! Paul Molitor has walked! Well, Jim Kaat, this could be all for Curt Schilling. How do you explain this mediocre effort by the Phillies' ace?"

"Well, Greg, he looked pretty good early. But you just can't win this game when you come down with the trots ..."

THE RIPPER AND THE ROCK

September 7, 1995

One of the presents Cal Ripken Jr. received after playing in his 2,131st consecutive major-league baseball game was a 2,131-pound granite rock. Just like that, the world had a new definition of "Gee, you really shouldn't have."

The wire stories don't say just who presented him with the rock, which had 2,131 etched on the front. Perhaps it was his Baltimore teammates, who figured the solid mahogany pool table wasn't enough. Maybe it was the visiting California Angels, on the theory that he might get a hernia lifting it.

It matters not. Someone did it, for there it sat in Camden Yards, this two-ton-plus monument to dogged persistence, baseball immortality, and the warped sense of humour of whoever dreamed it up.

So what does he do with it? How does he get it to wherever he puts it?

"Hello, Federal Express? You know those envelopes you use for your guaranteed overnight anywhere-in-the-world delivery — how big do those things run, exactly?

"I see ... you'll send a boy over with an assortment, seal it up here, and he'll take it. Listen, has his bike got a carrier?"

Because all eyes were on Ripken during the ceremony, we are not blessed with footage showing the look on the face of Mrs. Ripken as she eyed the monument that must somehow find a place in the family home. Her thoughts might also have been illuminating ...

"Jeez! We spend all summer getting the rocks out of the front yard, and now this. Where are we supposed to put it, in the den next to the TV? I can't wait to call home. 'Yes, Mom, Cal got a mahogany pool table and a Waterford crystal vase, and a Paul Picot watch and a Chevy Tahoe truck and, oh yes, a two-ton rock with numbers on the front. Hello ... hello ...' What's that? Smile for the cameras? Yeah, right ..."

There's also the matter of baseball ritual and its passion for statistics. Technically, the record will fall again and again until Ripken quits or misses a game. One inning from now, the rock will be obsolete. What's he supposed to do, add a pebble a game?

You could see where that might tick off frau Ripken, who's been given the short end of the stick in this thing from the beginning. ("So the big baseball hero goes to work every day, puts in four whole hours, and it's a big endurance deal. Let him stay home with the rug-rats for 2,131 consecutive days and see what endurance really is.") She feeds him, she does his clothes, and now he's tracking rocks into the house. And he's going to the Hall of Fame. Where are those National Organization of Women types when you really need them?

That's the thing about really big ugly gifts. Small ones, you give to someone who you know has no taste. Big ones, you have to keep. There's no smiling and shipping this thing off to the next Hadassah bargain table. People come to the house, what's the first thing they're going to want to see? The rock. What are you supposed to say? "Sorry, it's in the wash"?

Really big ugly gifts, particularly the ones from the big days in your life like when you recite the Ten Commandments and win the porcelain cherub or play your 2,131st consecutive baseball game, have to stay in the family. They are handed from generation to generation, whether the generations want them or not.

Someday, as life continues its never-ending cycle and Cal takes his place at shortstop on that big diamond in the sky, it will be time to pass the rock down to a new generation of Ripkens, to show his children and pass on the story of their grandad, the major-league baseball star.

Poor sucker had better own a fork lift.

NATIONAL PASTIME

October 3, 1996

Given Roberto Alomar's critically savaged revival of Great Expectorations and a major-league response proving that the game's balls are all on the field, it seemed an opportune moment for our annual look at the Great American Pastime.

Big mistake.

Baseball remains as it's been for years: a sport minus leader, rudder and guts; a sport of crybaby millionaires who live by their own rules, whine their way to the courts when things go wrong, and think the words "I just wanna play baseball" are an eraser that can wipe clean any slate, no matter how badly they've besmirched it.

It has never been my sport, this game in which perfection is defined as nine innings in which one team does nothing and announcers paid to provide colour and information babble non-stop but don't dare tell you what's happening lest they bring down some jinx on the guy working on the no-hitter or perfect game.

Baseball writers, each believing deep down that he is another Hemingway, churn out miles of copy about this game whose most dramatic play involves one guy hitting a ball out of the park and trotting around the bases while nine other guys stand around looking disgusted. And when you suggest that a 1-0 game may not be the pinnacle of athletic perfection, they sigh theatrically, tell you you don't appreciate the game's subtle nuances, then turn and crank out five more paragraphs about the way the golden sunlight turns the infield grass a glowing emerald.

Ah, the nuances ...

"Well, Joe, Bobby's looking down at his lineup. He could be considering bringing in the righthander to face the lefthanded hitter."

"Well, yes, but there's always the chance that he knows the Indians know that's what he's thinking, so if he does that, they'll pinch-hit a righty, which might then force the Orioles to go to the bullpen again and counter with a lefthander."

"That's right, Joe. But it could be that Bobby has anticipated their thinking that way, and he's just got the righthander warming up to make them think he's going to when that's not his plan at all ..."

Or the discussion between two guys who are parked three storeys up in the press box and 100 feet back, over whether a pitch was a fork ball, a split-finger fast ball, a knuckler or a curve that hung, as though they're in a position to have any idea.

And, worst of all, the inevitable portrait of baseball as a metaphor for life.

If that be true, then Roberto Alomar has proved that life is in sorry shape. Because Alomar, who spat in umpire John Hirschbeck's face in a fit of pique and used the death of the umpire's eight-year-old son as an aspersion on his judgment, is no better than third on the list of those who must share the blame for the whole sorry episode.

Before the despicable Roberto, with his token why-the-hell-do-I-have-to-do-this apology, and his cynical after-the-fact donation to the fund for research into the rare brain disease that claimed Hirschbeck's child, you have to place major-league baseball itself, which slapped his wrist with a five-game suspension, then okayed the appeal that allowed him to keep playing.

And now there is a new leader: the Major League Players Association.

On Wednesday the association convinced Roberto Alomar to withdraw his bid for a hearing on Friday. That way, the whole thing can be delayed until the beginning of next season, when a five-game hit is nothing more than an extra week's vacation.

Alomar spat on an umpire. The association spat on the game. And it, too, will go scot-free. Let's see the nuance floggers rhapsodize about that.

THE PATIENTS OF JOBE

January 23, 1996

"Tommy John pointed to his left elbow and said 'Fix this.'
"I said 'Tommy, it's never been done before.'
"He just looked at me, pointed to the elbow again and said 'Fix it.' Tommy John was one stubborn, stubborn man." — Dr. Frank Jobe

LOS ANGELES — If you were making a western, Frank Jobe would be Old Doc Somebody, getting down from a buggy he's driven for 50 miles to set a broken arm or deliver a calf and get paid off in chickens and preserves.

He has the white hair, the dark suit, the soft whispery voice that could soothe the fear from a trembling child or convince an expectant father that he should go somewhere and boil water because everything is going to be fine. His office would be a back room of his house — the one with the shingle hanging from the porch that says "Doc Jobe". Spencer Tracy could have played him, or Barry Fitzgerald.

He does not look like a man who made medical history. House calls, sure, but never history. Yet the walls of his tiny office in the Kerlan-Jobe Orthopedic Clinic are covered with signed pictures of men whose careers he's saved, extended or put back on course: Wilt Chamberlain, Jerry West, Jim McMahon, Jerry Pate, Paul Azinger, Ivan Lendl ... so many others, their pictures rotated by his secretary because there's nowhere near enough wall.

Orel Hersheiser's is a permanent fixture. It was Jobe who rebuilt the shoulder of his pitching arm and essentially rescued his career. Doug Flutie's likely will be there one day. It was Jobe who re-attached the flexor tendon to the elbow of his throwing arm.

And Tommy John. His picture they could hang with cement ...

Frank Jobe is an arm-and-shoulder guy. The Kerlan-Jobe Clinic he opened with noted orthopedic specialist Robert Kerlan in 1965 now has 16 doctors, including three who concentrate on the spine (and made the call that kept Wayne Gretzky OUT of surgery and in the exercise and medication program that brought him back to hockey), one who works on feet, another on hands. Sports medicine is big business, which draws a smile from Jobe, who once described himself and his fellow orthopedists as "the bag ladies of medicine, the ones who put out the lights and locked up."

Doctors in other fields shook their heads at the idea of men of medicine dealing exclusively with jocks. The proliferation of professional sport and the fitness explosion changed all that. "Now," says Jobe, "they'd kill to have my job."

And why not? The clinic cares for the hockey Kings and Mighty Ducks, the baseball Angels and Dodgers, the basketball Lakers, all the teams at the University of Southern California and the PGA golf tour. Jobe handles golf and the Dodgers (who treat his judgment so highly that they don't sign a pitcher until he's examined him and rated the arm and shoulder as sound). When you love baseball as he does, what better place than the ball park to do a little post-op visitation?

There is this, though: Frank Jobe doesn't go to watch teams as much as to see how his work is holding up. "We'll be watching a game together," says son Cameron, "and he'll say, 'Look at that guy's arm. I worked on it a couple of months ago. Look how well it's doing.' "

Not a bad life for a 70-year-old vanilla ice-cream addict, son of a country postman and farmer, who joined the army at 18 as a medical records clerk "without much sense of direction as far as my life was concerned."

The war taught him a few things, including that he could run a lot faster than he'd ever known. When his platoon was surrounded and captured by German troops, he and a buddy used the noise and confusion to dart off down a hill and jump in the back of an oncoming truck. But there was another, more important lesson.

Watching the field doctors at work, he was fascinated by their skill and the way they saved lives under near-impossible conditions. The doctors in turn took a liking to the kid, and urged him to go to school when he got out. The GI Bill and school loans provided the funds, and he was an MD, doing three years as a general practitioner, making the house calls and putting in the impossible hours that go with the shingle.

That part of it hasn't changed. Frank Jobe still does perhaps a dozen operations per week, goes to Dodgers games in season — but leaves early because he has to be up to make his rounds. "I got into this business to help people," he says. The period at the end is understood. Here endeth the discussion about slowing down.

The clinic and Frank Jobe were doing fine in the days before Tommy John walked into his office with his throwing arm basically hanging from his elbow by one frayed tendon and asked to have it fixed. The techniques Jobe used to do it are routine today, but what he attempted back then had never been tried before. It worked. Boy, did it work. And life for Frank Jobe would never be the same.

When Tommy John ruptured the medial collateral ligament of his left elbow throwing a sinker to Hal Breeden of the Montreal Expos in Dodger Stadium in the third inning that July 17 night in 1974, he was 13-3, the best start in his career. He was 31 years old, at the height of his power, and he was finished. One pitch, and goodbye career.

Eighteen months later he was back, throwing and winning. Before surgery he had won 124 games. He was to win 164 more. As a Yankee, an Angel, an Athletic and a Yankee again he pitched until he was 46 years old. Before surgery he'd never been in a playoff or a World Series. Post surgery? Six playoffs and three Series. He wasn't the old Tommy John. He was better. "I know they had to give Tommy John a new arm," said a disgruntled Pete Rose. "But did they have to give him Koufax's?"

There have been a lot of arms and shoulders since for Frank Jobe. Techniques have changed, equipment has improved, he has polished his own approach. Repetition has brought speed that has made him something of a legend. There's little wasted movement, says son Christopher, himself an orthopedic surgeon. "It's a little bit like doing the hula. Everything he does means something. It looks like he's going slowly, but it's actually going very fast."

Jobe shrugs off the accolade. "Repetition and touch," he says. "You get to where you can feel what's wrong, when the suture should be given a little twist so it goes through the hole cleanly. The other thing is, I don't flip-flop. I know what I want to do going in."

You might say that. The Hersheiser surgery that triggered so many magazine articles, endless medical diagrams and enough discussion to fuel talk shows for a year was done in 45 minutes flat.

Hersheiser's injury was the result of overuse of the shoulder and elbow that snapped off that devastating curve ball. The pounding of some 800 innings of major-league pitching had stretched the casing, or capsule, of the shoulder so badly that the strain pulled the arm bone partially out of the socket.

Jobe and his team slit open the capsule at the front of the shoulder joint and tightened its tough, fibrous tissue by overlapping and stitching the incision's edges into a doubly thick band. They then strengthened the entire structure by anchoring sutures ("They actually have little toggle bolts on the end now") in the bone of the shoulder socket. The operation was not new. Jobe himself had done it more than 30 times. But this was the first time it had been done on a pitcher. Some questioned how the repairs would stand up. Six years later, Hersheiser is still providing the answer.

The Tommy John surgery was something else — jungle country, some doctors call it: the business of going in not knowing for certain where the tigers are. It was two operations, not one.

First, he removed the palmaris longus tendon — which stretches from below the palm of the hand halfway up the arm — from John's right arm. "It's not something that's essential to use the hand," Jobe says.

Tendons attach muscle to bone, as opposed to ligaments, which connect bone to bone. Jobe took the removed tendon and transplanted it to John's left elbow, lacing the tendon through holes drilled in the elbow. Presto: the tendon in effect became a ligament, and John was halfway to becoming a lethal weapon.

Then came the hard part. In a second operation, Jobe transferred John's inflamed ulnar nerve from behind the left elbow to a position in front of the joint, thereby curtailing the inflammation which had resulted in the pitcher losing the ability to manipulate the pitching hand.

The 18 months of post-operative therapy weren't easy but, as Jobe says, Tommy John was a stubborn man who wanted to get back to throwing baseballs. He was 33 years old when he returned, a pitcher who'd never won more than 16 games in a season. With the new gun strapped to his shoulder he had three 20-game seasons and won 80 over a four-year stretch. For students of pitching, and students of orthopedic surgery, he was a joy to behold. The career stretched on and on. Sometimes it seemed he would pitch forever. Tommy John almost believed he could.

On the event of his 40th birthday, a reporter mentioned that it was a day when most pitchers were long gone from the hill.

"Well," he replied, "I'm 40, but my arm is only nine. And the little devil is getting smarter by the minute."

For which he could thank the white-haired doc sitting in the stands, licking a vanilla ice-cream cone and waiting to see his wonder at work. Dodger Stadium on game night — and it counted as a house call. Old Doc Somebody never had it so good.

Chapter Six

SKATEGATE

I've been known to invent characters: Billy-Joe Lardbutt, the football player who thinks softball is a physical condition; Fred Schwartz, who runs a jackhammer, loves hockey and can't find the price of a game ticket; his wife, Martha, whose answer to the story of Marathon was "Beware of Greeks wearing shifts"; Herm the Sperm ("Herm's the name and spermin's my game!"), who volunteered to make daily donations to the sperm bank as long as they serve cookies.

I could never have invented Skategate.

A comic-opera plot to whack a figure skater across the knee so another skater could win the U.S. championship? The FBI swarming over Detroit to investigate a mugging? A set of thugs who make Abbott and Costello look like Mensa material? And in the end, the biggest TV ratings in the history of the sport, after which the skater with the whacked knee goes off to Disneyland and becomes a millionaire? Nobody would buy that.

But there really was, and is, a Tonya Harding, unlikely though it seemed. There really was a Nancy Kerrigan and a Gang That Couldn't Think Straight. The columns almost wrote themselves. As my friend Nick the Matchmaker used to say when he was backing a sure thing: "Jimmy, it's like shootin' fish wit' an axe ..."

PLAIN JANE

January 20, 1994

Pretend for a moment that she wasn't Nancy Kerrigan and she wasn't defending the U.S. figure-skating championship. Her name was Jane Plain, and when the guy stepped out of the shadows and slammed her across the knee with the steel bar, she was on her way to her assembly-line job at the widget factory.

Would it have made headlines in Detroit, where the parking lot outside Joe Louis Arena has to be floodlit or you might not make it to your car, and if you do get there it might not have wheels? In a major American city where muggings are the *assault du jour,* would it have made the papers at all?

Would the FBI have been involved? Would a federal law-enforcement agency with no logical jurisdiction in what was essentially another street crime have arrived with its computerized photo-enhancement equipment to try and pull the phantom attacker's face from a muzzy amateur camera shot?

Would there have been press conferences in which the head of various law-enforcement agencies pledged that the attacker would be brought to justice? Would the head of Widgets 'R' Us International have said, "Jane Plain was about to try for a position that's now been taken by someone else, but we're going to let her share it"?

Would there have been days of time-consuming police work as far away as Portland, Oregon, to try to pull the net on a one-time mugger from Detroit when the victim, shaken and distraught for two or three days, was back to work in less than a week?

No way. Timing, celebrity and the terrifying prospect that there might be a copy-cat assassin out there emulating the wacko who knifed Monica Seles made the Nancy Kerrigan story a world-wide sensation. It was treated accordingly by a nation that, for all its might, had been unable to protect one of its athletes from an assault right there in the rink on the eve of its most important skating event.

Jane Plain would get a case file number and questioning from an over-worked police department that deals with a dozen such muggings every day. Shortly thereafter, her file would work its way from pending to open to dead. Nothing against old Jane, but widget-making is not a medal event.

I will make you a bet about the Nancy Kerrigan story: It will generate a book and at least one prime-time network-TV dramatization. If she wins Olympic gold, make that two or three books, two network specials and maybe a movie.

This is not to suggest that the law should have laid back. The cold, mindless brutality of planning and executing an attack of this nature — apparently to push a competitor forward for a better chance at the estimated $5,000,000 or more in endorsements that comes with Olympic gold — is enough to chill the blood.

But it's turned soap opera.

The bodyguard and the estranged husband of the skater who went on to the American title with Ms. Kerrigan sidelined, both charged in the plot? The skater herself going 10 hours with the FBI, then emerging to announce that although she still believes he had nothing to do with the attack, she thinks it's best that she and the former husband — divorced but living together — should part company so she can concentrate on the Olympics?

It took the LA earthquake to shift the Nancy Kerrigan story from the front page. It will return. The supermarket tabs may run it forever. All it lacks is Michael Jackson. For now.

Pared of the glitz and avarice, what happened in Detroit that day was another assault with a club, metal and high-tech retractable, but nonetheless a club. Apparently they have the people who planned it and the man who did it. Book 'em, Dano. We've got to get to the widget factory.

TOUGH ACT TO FOLLOW

February 13, 1994

Forget Tonya's televised tears, Nancy's nobbled knee and the lobotomized loonies of the Gang That Couldn't Think Straight. The International Figure Skating Association has a real problem.

What does it do for an encore?

Come 1998, how does it match the ghoulish, cartoonish and ultimately foolish events of Skategate, which have given the women's singles a lock on the biggest skating audience in history? What happens if, God forbid, all the American entrants do in '98 is *skate*?

Consider for a moment what might have happened had Jeff and the Gillooligans not plotted to put the slug on Nancy Kerrigan's knee to give their entrant, the rough-edged, combative Tonya

Harding, a better shot at the U.S. title and the cash fountain that comes with Olympian gold:

*Someone — maybe Nancy, maybe Tonya, maybe not — would have won the U.S. women's title, made the cover of *Sports Illustrated*, and taken her place in a U.S. Olympic squad only slightly smaller than some emerging nations.

*Americans would have cheered. Europeans would have yawned. Canadians would have checked the hockey schedules.

*The finals would have drawn the usual large TV audience of people who love it when some ex-skater says, "OOOH! She gave up on the triple, and her left foot was a little slow coming down when she lutzed her wallbanger!"

*Winners would have cried for happy, losers for sad. And then the cameras, every drop recorded for posterity, would have moved on to the next event.

The Gillooligans changed all that. With a single stroke of that collapsible metal rod, a Fairy Goonfather named Shane ("Sure, I used my own name to rent the getaway car") Stant changed a simple skating event into a soap opera and a million-dollar industry.

Would Nancy have had three insta-books written about her without that bang on the knee? Would Tonya's dewy eyes and quivering lower lip close-up been worth the $300,000 or so she got from the *Inside Edition* television people?

Would three of the four major networks be planning dramatic specials? Would the world — not just the figure-skating world, but the soap-opera world, the heaving-bosom, torn-bodice, two-hanky, tear-jerk, romance-novel world, the supermarket, trash-tabloid-peeking world of Oprah and Geraldo — be glued to TV sets in such stupendous numbers that Skategate out-drew live coverage of the Los Angeles earthquake?

But this was no average person. This was a possible figure-skating champion. And so a city that greets murders with a shrug while fretting over the state of the Red Wings, Tigers and Pistons rallied the forces of justice and finally cornered a gang without the brains to play follow-the-dots.

The world cheered. If nothing else, it had learned a valuable life theorem: The amount of force exerted in pursuit of a mugger and the public interest therein is in direct proportion to the identity of the muggee.

Who said sport isn't educational?

INTELLIGENCE TEST

February 16, 1994

Really, now, one must object to the blatantly sexist "Are you a Tonya Person?" quiz run on these pages.

Nancy and Tonya. Tonya and Nancy. Two references to her "ex-bodyguard" without so much as a mention of Shawn Eckhardt's name. Of estranged husband and freestyle plea-bargaining champion Jeff Gillooly and the alleged hit team of Shane Stant and Derrick Smith, not a single word. On this evidence, figure skating's greatest crime since the men began dressing like begonias was all Bonnie, no Clyde.

Credit where credit is due, I say. Herewith, The Gang That Couldn't Think Straight Intelligence Test:

1. Shawn Eckhardt's method of finding a hit man was to ask people whether they'd be interested in taking the job for X dollars.

2. Once the hitter was found (allegedly the aforementioned Mr. Stant), the conspirators discussed the game plan on the telephone. Apparently fearing that one of them might forget some of the key details ("Like, who's this dame we're supposed to slug again?"), someone taped the call.

3. Eckhardt felt moved to tell someone. Well, wouldn't you? ("Hey, guess what we're gonna do this week? We're gonna smack that Nancy Kerrigan across the knee so she can't skate no more.") The person he chose was a minister.

4. "Let's make it look like a mugging and robbery attempt," someone said. Great idea. So where do they put the smack on Ms. Kerrigan? In the skating rink, as she's coming off the ice. Would she be carrying any money on her? Would she be carrying a purse? So how will it look like a robbery? Oh, yeah ...

5. Having done the dirty deed, the assailant Gets Rid of the Weapon, a key move in any great crime. He gets rid of it in the dumpster behind the rink. ("They'll never think of looking for it there!") Strangely enough, the police find it. There are fingerprints. ("Hey, you bring the gloves?" "Me bring the gloves? I thought you were bringin' 'em!")

6. "Imagine that! A mugging — and in Detroit," cry the local police. "Who'd ever have believed it? This looks like a job for the FBI!" Shortly thereafter, Messrs. Eckhardt, Stant and Smith are in custody.

7. Too young to remember Jimmy Cagney movies ("You ain't gettin' nuttin' outa me, copper!") they take the high road to repentance by saying they're sorry and apparently ratting on Gillooly. (Hey, what are friends for?)

8. All parties, including Ms. Harding, are grilled by police. Gillooly rats on Ms. Harding, claiming she was in on the plan all along and gave final approval. He only ratted on her, he insists, after the police showed him her statement in which she'd ratted on him first. Her disloyalty shakes him. Had they not promised not to rat on each other? Boy, you just can't trust anyone these days.

9. Gillooly, facing seven racketeering charges, plea-bargains his way down to one by providing police with details of the Master Plan and implicating Ms. Harding.

His contribution to the hearing is one word: "Guilty." Through his lawyer, he also says that Ms. Harding shouldn't be allowed to skate for her country in the Winter Olympics. Those who've been keeping track recall that getting Ms. Harding into the Olympics was the objective of the whole exercise. Of course, that was before they got caught.

10. At last report, all four men were out on bail. Police aren't worried about them trying to run. On their record so far, they'd just get lost.

THIS LOOKS LIKE A JOB FOR ROY ROGERS

April 24, 1994

I tell you, they're a-stompin' and a-whoopin' in Nashville today. The word is flashin' 'cross the American west faster'n a Pony Express hoss with the trots: Tonya Harding is a-gonna be a country singer. The west ain't bin this excited since Roy stuffed Trigger.

Yessir, it seems like Tonya was kinda settin' 'round the campfire at Spike Lee's place t'other day when she just started in a-singin' for no reason at all, 'cept maybe to scare away the re-porters. And dagnabit if old Spike didn't say sumthin' like, "Hey, this little filly can flat-out sing!"

Anyhow, 'cordin' to the newspaper, he finds her one of them business ty-coons who ponys up $981,000 so's she can make herself a record and a video and get herself some publicity that don't involve smackin' anyone. And just like that she's goin' off to Nashville, long as the marshals in Oregon let her out'n the state, which they'll prob'ly be happier 'n a hog in a mud bath to do, considerin' all that Skategate stuff.

Fact is, the Nashville cats on 16th Avenue are already workin' up new arrangements on some of your Golden Oldie, former-pick-hit-of-the-week blasts from the past they figure would be natchrals for her day-bue, and down at Club Dance they've already figured out the new dance craze, the Tonya. It's kinda like a square dance, only when one couple comes sashayin' under the arches, one of the cowpokes in the line leaps out and kicks her one in the knee. They're tryin' for Billy Ray Cyrus on the vocal, which goes sumthin' like:

Please bruise my knee,
My itsy-bitsy knee.
I just don't think you understand
If you don't bruise my knee,
My itsy-bitsy knee,
I'll never make big bucks from Disneyland.

The way the Nashville folks got it figured, Tonya's the kinda talent that can make your cross-over hits, singin' either country or pop, 'cause hers is the kind of message that can be brought across without words, 'specially if you happen to be totin' somethin' heavy. They got some of the songs picked out already.

"Knees Up, Mother Brown" might be the first cut off the album to go single, although there's a lotta support for the old Ames Brothers thing, "It Only Hurts for a Little While." Myself, I lean more to the classics like "My Boyfriend's Back and You're Gonna Be in Trouble," or maybe something simple like "Sh-Boom." It's a flat cinch that "Catch a Falling Star" has to be in there somewhere, and the Elvis crowd will eat up Tonya's Nancy Kerrigan impression on "Don't Be Cruel." The Jordanaires are just itchin' to do the background.

Word is that Tonya wants to do a special tribute to the guys in the gang that planned the knee job, but just can't make up her mind between "Who's Sorry Now?" and "Unchained Melody." But the one for young figure skaters all over the world is what you call your no-brainer. She's gonna do "It's All in the Game," and they guarantee there won't be a dry eye in the house. But she's flat said no to suggestions that, considerin' how much money the Kerrigan girl's made out of Skategate, she should try to get her for a doo-et on "Nancy With the Laughing Face."

It all kinda makes you think, don't it? Like, every time I see Tonya's picture I start thinkin', "I wonder if Roy's got any of that stuffin' left over?"

O.J., CAN YOU SEE ...?

December 30, 1994

To truly sum up 1994 in sports, we need only remember that its two biggest stories were the world's slowest drag race (Ford Bronco division) and a $2,000,000 bruise on the knee.

Stanley Cup, Grey Cup, Super Bowl, hockey lockouts, baseball strikes, Winter Olympics, the death of a Colombian soccer player gunned down because he put the ball in his own net during a World Cup game while trying to avert what would have been a certain goal anyway — none of these things came anywhere near capturing North America's imagination as did Skategate and, later, O.J. Simpson's sedate, police-escorted parade along California's freeway system with his buddy at the wheel and O.J. in the back seat with a gun to his own head.

An estimated 95,000,000 television viewers glued themselves to that one — impressive, but nowhere near the 126,600,000 who tuned in for the women's figure-skating short program at the Winter Olympics to see whether Nancy Kerrigan would beat Tonya Harding or scratch her eyes out. Only five shows in television history had a higher rating: the final episode of *M*A*S*H*, the *Dallas* 'Who Shot J.R.?' episode, *Roots*, and three Super Bowls.

It was tough, picking one over the other as sports story of the year. The decision went to Skategate, if only because it produced a better joke.

The O.J. pursuit triggered a final, mock Hertz commercial: O.J., jumping luggage, dodging little old ladies yelling "Go, O.J.!" and saying, "When I need a getaway car, I've got no time to stand in lineups. With Hertz, I know that Bronco will be gassed up and ready when I get off the plane ..."

Skategate produced an entire song, written and produced by a California deejay and sung in a great English accent to the tune of the Beatles' "Bang-Bang, Maxwell's Silver Hammer":

Nancy went away,
To Detroit to skate that day,
Tonya got annoyed.
She was worried Nancy would win the go.
Oh-oh-oh.

Then Jeff Gillooly,
Who loved his Tonya truly,
Wanted to impress,
So he planned to take out our brave Nancy,
Hee-hee-hee.

Though Tonya had got wind of this plan,
It happened anyway.
Bang-bang Tonya's Lillehammer
Came down upon her leg.
Bang-bang Tonya's Lillehammer
Could not strike her dead.
Lill-e-hamm-er! Bonk-bonk-bonk-bonk-bonk!

Maybe it was the irony of it that got to me. Because when it was all over — when the FBI had finished swooping in, and the possible torn knee had been diagnosed as a bruise, and the Gang That Couldn't Think Straight was in custody and the two TV specials had been aired and Tonya had blown a skate at the Olympics and a little Ukrainian orphan named Oksana Bajul had taken gold from the clutches of Nancy and the American public-relations machine — Nancy Kerrigan made about $2,000,000 from her ordeal and went to Disneyland.

Chances are it's a trip O.J. will never get to make. But don't count on it.

* * *

POST SCRIPT ...

February 13, 1997

On the evening of February 12, 1997, Tonya Harding phoned police to say she had been abducted outside her home, but escaped when she drove her pickup truck into a tree and fled.

When last we left our heroine, Tonya had been shot down in her bid to skate for Norway, Spike Lee's promise to make her a country music star hadn't worked out, and she'd turned down an offer to be a pro wrestler in Japan. But now, a mere 10 days before she is to launch her comeback with a three-minute exhibition February 22 in Reno, at a time when she's been put out of the public mind like labour pains and the ozone layer, Tonya Harding gets kidnapped!

Nobody sees the guy but her, and she doesn't see him well enough to describe him to police as anything but bushy-haired.

He's making her drive him to a town 30 minutes away. To divert his attention, she drives into a tree. That'll do it, all right. While he's diverted she runs away, calls her boyfriend, and they call the police. She is not hurt. "Tonya's resting safely," her agent says — and no, it will not interfere with her skating comeback February 22 in Reno.

Gee, isn't it funny how things work out? If Tonya hadn't been kidnapped, her figure-skating comeback — did we mention it's on February 22 in Reno? — might have passed by unnoticed. Now everybody knows about it. Faith, and it's a miracle.

No doubt the Oregon police are hot on the trail of clues to the identity of the bushy-haired fugitive ("Tonya, are you POSITIVE he didn't have one arm?"), lest he make another attempt between now and her skating comeback February 22 in Reno. But they won't waste time looking for members of the old Skategate mob, the Gang That Couldn't Think Straight. On past performance they couldn't find Tonya. Or Oregon.

Ms. Harding had reported another late-night assault in 1994, called police again a year later to say she was trailing a man who'd been stalking her, and a year after that got a restraining order against her estranged second husband, saying he'd threatened her and kicked in the bathroom door.

Then she more or less faded away. Until Wednesday, when she got kidnapped. But fret not, it won't stop her comeback February 22 in Reno. There's no business like show business.

Chapter Seven

RADICAL, EH?

My first year covering Canadian football I wandered into the B.C. Lions' dressing room in old Empire Stadium unannounced and uninvited. They wrapped me in athletic bandage, ran a noose under my armpits, hoisted me to the rafters, tied it off, and left me dangling there while they went out for practice. How can you not love a team like that?

Today, a reporter handled that way would rush to his lawyer, as did the Boston *Globe*'s Lisa Olson after one of the New England Patriots waved a protruding portion of his anatomy in her face. ("Why didn't she just bring up a knee?" wondered my wife, the former Plymouth Brethren.) But that was 1966, and I was getting paid to write about a game I'd loved since I was 13 years old. So I took the only possible course of action: After that, I knocked.

Canadian football is wild and wonderful and woefully mismanaged. By the time you read this, it may be dead, at the very least on the usual life support. Television, the westward sweep of the NHL, major-league baseball in Toronto and Montreal, pro basketball in Toronto and Vancouver, have all contributed to the near-demise of a league that survives almost in spite of itself.

Each season it offers new reasons for the paying customers to turn away: expansion to the U.S., carpetbagging American owners in Canada with no understanding or respect for a game and a league that were in business before the NFL (Jim Speros, owner of the Baltimore franchise, arrived in Montreal to negotiate a move there trailed by a flunky carrying the Grey Cup in a green garbage bag), lack of leadership at the top, lack of money everywhere else.

But the game is better than the one they play to the south. Three-down football is more exciting than four-down. The Grey Cup game is always better than the Super Bowl. Lui Passaglia, the man with more points than anyone in professional football, got them all as a B.C. Lion.

It's never easy, explaining the CFL to strangers. Prior to the re-entry of Montreal in 1996, it went something like this: "Well, we've got eight teams, four in the east and four in the west, except that one of the ones in the west actually plays in the east, and two of them are named Roughriders, one two-word and one one-word."

My first football hero, in the first game I ever saw live, was Indian Jack Jacobs in Winnipeg's Osborne Stadium, where a kid could sneak in over the roof and under the power wires that could fry you at a touch. It held 5,000 people, tops, the end zones were only five yards deep and the field was 10 yards short because that was all they could squeeze in.

The parks are bigger now, and more empty than full. But the game is still there, still wonderful, still fighting for its existence. Three downs at a time, not four.

DANNY RAY

October 3, 1996

My friend Danny Ray Kepley went into Canadian football's Hall of Fame, still without confessing whether or not he really bit off that guy's ear.

The affair of the missing lobe came in the oft-troubled retirement years, after the medical problems and before the broadcasting career, when he went through the not-uncommon trauma of life after jockdom. He hit the trauma with the same force he'd hit everything else, and one of the pieces that allegedly came off during a misunderstanding in a bar was a chunk of his opponent's ear.

"Well, maybe a little bit of the tip," he conceded one night after a broadcast. "And it might have been an accident."

Today's Danny Ray is one of those Dorian Gray types who looks younger now than he did in his decade at middle linebacker for the Edmonton Eskimos. You hardly notice the hearing aids, made necessary by a stubborn refusal to go to hospital when an infection was still treatable. Single guys want to troll him through the singles bars in hope of catching the ones he throws back. He has built a solid career as CBC colour commentator, and when he pulls on the blazer he looks like one of those people in the TV commercials who just sold you a house, or maybe a bridge.

But the Danny Ray I remember best is the other one, best personified during a play in 1982, when he played the entire season with a torn left shoulder. If he hit a man straight on, he was fine. If he had to arm-tackle him, the shoulder would pop out and the arm hang there like a spaghetti strand until he popped it back in.

He'd just made a tackle in front of the Edmonton bench. Coach Hugh Campbell, who knew about the shoulder, saw him trying to pop it back and tried to grab him to bring him off.

Danny Ray stepped over the sidelines and glared at him.

"What the hell do you WANT?" he screamed.

Campbell looked at him. "You're okay," he said finally. "Get back in there."

Campbell understood two things: that Kepley wouldn't play if he thought he was hurting the team, and that his career was based on the theory that pain is a matter of mind over matter: If you don't mind the pain, it doesn't matter.

You can get arguments about the greatest linebacker ever to play in the CFL. Given the new pass-happy offence, the wide-open spaces of the Canadian game, more telecasts, better isolated cameras and a proliferation of quick, mid-size players deemed too small to play in the NFL, there is no shortage of current candidates.

But those who've watched the game for a long time narrow the choice to two: Wayne "Thumper" Harris, eight-time all-Canadian and a western all-star in every one of the 11 seasons he played (1961-72) for the Calgary Stampeders, or Danny Ray Kepley. The argument inevitably ends with the assertion that, even today, there isn't a coach in the league who wouldn't kill to have the loser.

Harris was quietly deadly. Legend insists that his pre-game ritual included emptying tins of tape rolls and using the tape to attach the tins to his arms. Kepley was louder, on and off the field. The Eskimos were family, and he considered it his role to bring recalcitrant family members into line.

At one training camp some 20 years ago he decided a rookie wasn't doing his part in holding the tackling dummies, volunteering his body for skeleton drills, and basically running his butt off. So one night he went to the rookie's dormitory room and knocked on the door.

Actually, it was 3 a.m. and he didn't knock on the door, he kicked it in.

Before the rookie could get off the bed, Kepley had flipped on the light, grabbed a water glass, smashed it on the edge of the dresser, straddled the kid's chest, pulled his head back by the hair and begun gently stroking the jagged glass across his exposed throat.

There was no danger. It caused just enough of a scratch to get enough blood on Kepley's fingers to show the kid. He then explained that, as a veteran, he didn't appreciate the rookie's deportment on the practice field, and suggested that it had best change the next day.

The kid never did make the team. But boy, did he work at it.

There are all kinds of stories like that. The danger in telling too many of them is that they might obscure the fact that Danny Ray was one of the greatest players, never mind the position, ever to grace Canadian football.

But let me tell you one more.

We were working on a book, sitting in my living room on opposite sides of a coffee table, the tape recorder between us, discussing the jocks-for-God movement. My head was down as I made backup notes.

"It's okay," I conceded, "but sometimes I think athletes find God right after the cops find them."

I heard a shuffling noise. Danny Ray had come off the couch into what looked like a three-point stance. There was a snarl on his lips. He looked ready to come over the coffee table.

I remembered the rookie and the broken water glass.

"But maybe not," I concluded weakly.

"Damn straight," said Danny Ray Kepley. In life, as in football, the man competes.

POSITION FILLED

November 23, 1996

HAMILTON — It's a tricky word, "greatest", and naturally it was being thrown around with abandon here as Doug Flutie, the tiny perfect quarterback, graciously accepted his fourth outstanding player award in five years.

Nothing wrong with that, as long as you broaden the definition with "greatest modern-day", "greatest of the '90s" or even "greatest thing to happen to Canadian football since they heated the press box in Saskatchewan". In B.C., in Calgary and now in Toronto, Flutie has been little short of marvellous. Had he not missed seven games last season he'd probably be riding a five-year run.

But in the days preceding this latest foregone-conclusion coronation — and even during the season — commentators have been suggesting that when it comes to the Canadian Football League, Flutie should now be considered "the greatest player of all time".

Sorry. That position has already been filled.

It belongs to a drawling, jug-eared, hunch-shouldered, semi-bowlegged assassin named Jack Dickerson Parker, and until someone else comes along who plays four positions well enough to be an all-star at any of them and kicks field goals on the side there is no earthly reason why he should not continue to fill it.

It's not Flutie's fault. As a quarterback he's done everything anyone could humanly ask.

But he has yet to play both offence and defence. He hasn't won three Grey Cups, although No. 2 could come Sunday, or made eight straight all-star teams, let alone made them at various times at quarterback, running back and defensive back, or become one hell of a receiver when pressed into service, or produced perhaps the all-time finest one-line defence of the British people: "Any country that invented Beefeater cain't be all bad."

He hasn't led his team to three straight Grey Cups, as Parker led the Edmonton Eskimos in 1954-55-56 over luckless Montreal.

In the first, Parker played offensive and defensive halfback, and scooped up a late fumble by Montreal's Chuck Hunsinger to cart it 84 yards into the end zone in the game that first truly burned the national final into the national psyche. When Bernie Faloney left after the one season, Parker slid over to quarterback — or running back, when coach Frank "Pop" Ivy felt moved by whim or circumstance to insert Canadian Don Getty at QB and let Parker wreak his particular brand of havoc elsewhere.

There used to be arguments over what was Parker's best position on offence — quarterback or halfback. The New York Giants, who had the Mississippi State phenom locked away until the Eskimos' brass dumped $10,000 on his hotel-room bed ("I swear I 'bout fainted"), had him pencilled in as a receiver.

CFL coaches, however, had no doubts. They wanted to see him anywhere but quarterback because at quarterback he handled the ball on every play. Nobody ever ad-libbed better than Parker, although Flutie could give him a run.

Like Flutie, Parker had other attributes. He didn't play guitar, but giving him a deck of cards was like handing Capone an extra gun. His brother, Fred, wasn't an athlete like Darren Flutie, but he was competitive. Parker still has a hairline scar from the night a football argument ended with Fred firing a bullet pass with the telephone.

Different times, of course, and a different game. Greatness is produced by being the best of your era, its rules and its circumstance. Comparisons are for bull sessions and Grey Cup Week, when the memories flow like fine old wine and the old stories are buffed to a new lustre with the re-telling.

Normally, you would not read them here. But in these wobbly, uncertain times for Canadian football, when even a game like this one with its Fluties, its Plesses and its Pinballs cannot totally erase the worry of tomorrow, there is comfort in recalling that we did, indeed, have a wondrous yesterday.

"IT'S WHAT I DO ..."

November 22, 1996

HAMILTON — We've had some goes over the years, Don Matthews and I.

He believed I got him fired in B.C. in 1987. I denied it, but said it was a great idea. Things kind of went downhill from there.

No matter where he went — and he's been on more highways than road kill — the feud bubbled merrily on. Sports dinners, charity dinners, media interviews — if there was a function where both of us spoke, we'd use at least part of the time to carve each other.

He once said that if he walked across the water to rescue a drowning man and left his dog on the shore, the head on my column would read "Matthews' Dog Can't Swim!" I replied that he was the only coach in football whose cap had a message on the front: "Surgeon General Warns Contents Can Cause Drowsiness."

Yesterday, we just talked.

For a change, I wasn't smart-ass. For a change, he didn't dodge. And out of it came the philosophy — and the personal cost — that has driven him, this time with the Argonauts, to yet another Grey Cup game and a coaching record that arguably marks him as the greatest in the history of Canadian football.

There are seven Grey Cup rings in 10 tries to show for the road trip that's wound from an Oregon high school to Edmonton, to B.C., back to Edmonton, on to Toronto, to a one-year pit stop in Orlando in the WLAF, to Saskatchewan, to Baltimore and now back to Toronto. There are also four failed marriages.

"There's no question that the same reasons I've sometimes had success have cost me failures in other parts of my life," he admits. "Other people have been able to juggle it better. But coaching consumes me. Even when I'm not at the office, I'm at the office."

Earlier, someone had asked him how he'd enjoyed his two years in Baltimore, where he lost one Grey Cup final and won the next. The reply carried its own unspoken sadness: "I have a life that revolves around 15-3 ... playoffs ... those things," he said. "I don't know how much coaches enjoy their surroundings. I get pretty involved with what I do ..."

The answer trailed off. How do you explain an obsession to the un-obsessed?

Everywhere he's gone, the players have performed for him. A lot of guff has been written that it's because he treats them like men. More likely it's because his record (147-71-1, league and playoffs) says he'll put money in their pockets if they do things his way, and because they recognize that obsession in him. Bottom line, only line: Don Matthews wants to win.

He may go clear to retirement without anyone truly knowing him. How do you pigeonhole a man who won a Grey Cup in Toronto, fled to Orlando, and after one season suddenly climbed on his Harley and rocketed away? "He said he had to find himself," then-wife Kathy said later.

Whatever he is, whatever he found, Matthews has been his own architect. If the life and the success have had pockets of emptiness, well, that's the price you pay.

"My choice, yes," he admits. Then: "Well ... I don't know if I had a choice. It's how I am.

"I guess if I had a choice I wouldn't be as consumed. But what I like about it is, I'm still consumed. I think some people start out that way and it fades. They get other priorities. My priorities are still on the sidelines, coaching a football team. I'm the general manager here, but that's a title. I'm a coach. That's where the adrenaline comes. It's what I do."

It's said his record has caught the eye of some NFL owners. If it's true, he'll go. Pure ego, if nothing else, will drive him to accept the challenges of the biggest league. There, surrounded by the NFL basic plethora of assistants, he could step back and, at 57, take another stab at that other kind of life and stability that but for brief interludes has somehow eluded his grasp.

He could. But maybe, to Don Matthews, the price would be too high.

JOSHUA

November 1, 1993

His name is Joshua, and he is three.

On nights when his Daddy works at home instead of out of town, Joshua gets to go to the office with him. He sits and watches him work, and when the job is done he takes his hand and walks with him to the place where he gets out of his work clothes.

Joshua sits there quietly next to his Daddy, wondering, maybe, why it's taking him so long. If *he* took that long to dress in the morning, Mom would tell him to get a move on. But people keep stopping him to poke the microphone-things and the camera-things at him and ask him the same questions, over and over again.

Through all the questions and the noise and the people swarming around, Joshua says not a word. It's late, and he's tired, and he's waiting for his Daddy to finish so they can go get Mom and go home.

His name is Joshua, and he is three. He doesn't know about roll-outs and slants and fly patterns and blocking assignments and the mental "Thousand-one, thousand-two, thousand ..." that is all the time his Daddy has before he hits the artificial turf really hard and his ribs hurt or his shoulder pops and he hears the ugly sound of 35,000 wolves in full cry.

All he knows is that this is where Daddy works, and Daddy is the greatest football player in the world ...

Danny Barrett brings his son, Joshua, to every home game the B.C. Lions play. He calls him "my perspective". When things have just gone badly, as they have so often lately, he can look down at the small figure next to him and feel his universe jolt back into orbit. When Joshua smiles, the microphones and the cameras and the notepads disappear and he is not Danny Barrett, quarterback, anymore. He is Daddy, and life is good.

A curious and terrible thing has happened to Danny Barrett this season, an incomprehensible, festering something that burst and spewed its poison in a 54-14 loss to the Edmonton Eskimos. The customers weren't just booing him anymore. They were waiting for him to fail.

He expected the boos. He's a quarterback. Booing is part of the package. As Doug Flutie's replacement he's been two incompletions away from booing in every home game he's played. But that was just frustration. This is something else.

The good games, the record-setting 601 passing yards against the Argonauts, the comeback in Ottawa — all old news, tossed aside and forgotten during a half-season in which he has struggled along with the rest of a team turned old and tired. They want Danny McManus as their starting quarterback. Danny Barrett they just want gone.

He has never mentioned it. Not once. No one has to tell him he's going through a bad patch, or that as the quarterback he is the focal point win or lose, or that he's getting the big bucks to win. He has never questioned the customers' right to boo.

But there is something different about this. The booing that rolled down on him as he trotted off the field at half-time had an ugliness to it that took it beyond football into a personal attack.

Maybe it would be best if the Lions didn't win this bush-league squabble over who gets the semi-final at home. If there's a way out of this, maybe the path starts in Edmonton. On the road, the blessed road, the boos are for somebody else ...

His name is Joshua, and he is three. If he was six or seven he would know about the boos and the losses and endure the jeers and insults at school, and feel the sting of tears. But he is three. And his Daddy is the greatest football player in the world.

FROGGIE SEE, FROGGIE DO

August 12, 1994

He is the old frog dozing on the lily pad, seemingly oblivious to the swift young flies as they dance past him in the sunshine. They are having so much fun they fail to notice that those ancient eyes aren't quite closed ...

For 11 seasons Less Browne has been out there on the corner, playing defence in the loneliest spot on earth. He has watched the brash young receivers come and go. Some have gone past him into his end zone. On occasion, he has been beaten upon like a drum. But along the way he has probably cut more receivers than the men who coached them.

He is 35 years old — young enough, if you happen to be a tree. But to the young fast guns coming into the league, 35-year-old cornerbacks are sent by God to be humiliated. "Hit me," they say in the huddle. "I can beat him ..."

The young fly darts closer to the sleepy old frog, hanging in the air, daring him to wake up. The frog is motionless. But if the fly could peer through those slitted lids, he would see the eyes begin to glow ...

It is early in the second half, Toronto Argonauts leading the B.C. Lions 32-24. The Lions have just wasted a magnificent one-handed catch by Ray Alexander at the Argo seven-yard line. The Argos have the ball back, and here comes a fine young receiver named Eric Drage, out wide against Less Browne.

Mike Kerrigan drops back and lofts the ball toward Drage. Once, earlier, Browne has bitten on the pump fake. This time he is with Drage step-for-step. Timing it perfectly, he cuts in front of him at the last second, goes high, and comes down with the interception at the Toronto 34.

Out by the lily pad, the little fly moves closer for one last look at the sleepy old frog. ZOT! The tongue flashes out. "Urp!" says the old frog — and settles back in the sunlight to wait for dessert ...

To understand the importance of Less Browne's sixth interception of the season, you need only look at the plays that followed it.

The Lions scored on that possession. Then they held the Argos on downs — and Browne blocked the punt. Two plays later, Darren Flutie made a dazzling one-handed catch behind Keita Crespina for a touchdown. Now the Lions were up 37-32.

In the fourth quarter they held them again on a third-down gamble, and drove for another major. Another interception, this time by safety Tom Europe, and Mike Trevathan took a pass from Kent Austin and ran out of the coverage for the touchdown that put it out of reach.

Now, you can say that a lot of good things came together for the Lions, that Austin and his receivers are slowly but surely getting on the same page, that the defence is toughening up, that Alexander and Trevathan and Flutie had huge games, that Cory Philpott continued to make people forget Jon Volpe. You can note that Austin discovered Merv Fernandez, and that the promise of that combination was there to be seen and gleefully filed under "Just wait!"

But every game needs a trigger. Before Browne's interception, the Lions had failed to convert two and come away with nothing. Then the old man gave them the kickstart, and they were away.

Oh, yes: In the fourth quarter, when Kerrigan was forced to play catch-up, he sent Paul Masotti deep. When the ball arrived, the guy who came down with it was Browne.

The old frog sat back on the lily pad. Dessert had arrived on schedule. As usual, it tasted just fine.

YOU GOTTA HAVE HEART

July 31, 1992

Sonny Homer is mildly claustrophobic, throws up on airplanes, played 10 years of pro football with one kidney and has a heart that now contains eight bypasses and one metal valve. If he was a used car, he'd be sitting in a scrap heap somewhere compressed into a foot-square metal block.

Instead, he is recuperating at home from the last operation three weeks ago — the one that put the five bypasses in to go with the three he had in 1973 — taking blood-thinners, and debating the relative merits of a pig valve vs the metal one that went in with the latest five detours.

"Metal is more trouble because it causes stuff that means you have to take the thinners," he says. "But the pig valve lasts only five years and the metal is lifetime.

"However the hell long that is ..."

Lawrence "Sonny" Homer is 55 years old, a B.C. Lions' receiver from 1958 through 1968, a Vancouver kid who ran so fast he seemed to float over the grass without disturbing a blade. He might have been even faster if he hadn't had to lug that extra pad around, the one that covered the only kidney he had left.

He had the surgery after his rookie year. He'd been squeezed between a tackle and a running back in his senior year at Grey's Harbor Junior College and emerged with one kidney squished to the thickness of a 50-cent piece. The doctors removed it and said he was nuts to play pro ball. Get hit just the right way at just the wrong time, they said, and you could run out of kidneys. "Right," he said, and played 10 more years.

The playing was the easy part. Getting there was something else. Sonny hated to fly. His stomach hated it even more. These days, he'd be selling monogrammed NIKE barf bags. Those days, he just threw up.

The claustrophobia became public knowledge on a road trip to Winnipeg, where he was trapped between floors in a stalled elevator loaded with Lions' linemen. Sonny began to freak. Fortunately, his buddy Jerry Bradley was on the floor above to talk him through it.

Bradley leaned into the shaft.

"Homer!" he called. "You're gonna DIE, Homer! You're gonna be trapped down there until you run out of air!"

"You sunnuvabitch," Homer screamed. "I get outa here, I'll show you who's gonna die!"

It took about 30 minutes, Bradley maintaining a running commentary on Homer's life expectancy. When power was restored, Homer burst out in pursuit of Bradley, who says to this day he only did it to take Sonny's mind off his problems.

But then, as now, Sonny never much stopped to realize he had any problems. He just played — and smoked, maybe a pack a day. The first bypass operation didn't convince him to quit, but five bypasses have now done what three could not. He's been a non-smoker for three entire weeks. Eight hours on an operating table ("It was scheduled for 5 1/2, but they hit scar tissue") does tend to get your attention and shuffle your priorities. He dreams of cigarettes now, but dreams contain no nicotine, and he has other things to keep him busy.

The first is a projected walk around the block, and two blocks the week after that, and so on. "Don't worry about it," he says. "I wouldn't have much resale value on the car lot, but the motor's still running."

And hey — if he needs encouragement, he can always call Jerry Bradley.

RIDER PRIDE

November 16, 1995

The cynics insist that the Grey Cup game should never have been awarded to Regina, where the snow blows and the winds howl and the chill factor can freeze the balls off a Christmas tree. The cynics have never heard the voice of Taylor Field.

It's not an easy thing to do, listening to a building. You have to cock your ear for the creaks and the groans of shifting timbers or settling concrete, and open your mind to the voices of players and coaches who've come and gone. Do that, and the walls will tell you stories ...

There was the afternoon in 1970 when the snow was blowing and the wind was doing its worst, so malevolently cross-field that Calgary's Larry Robinson, lined up for a last-second field goal with his team trailing 14-12 in the deciding game of the western final, actually had to kick the ball away from the goalposts.

Robinson kicked, and the crowd went dead silent — so silent that one man's voice echoed across the park: Roger Kramer, the huge Stampeder offensive tackle, shaking his fist and screaming into the wind: "Bend, you sonofabitch! Bend!"

The ball listened, bent left, and dropped through the uprights for a 15-14 win. The Riders had gone 14-2, Ron Lancaster would win the Schenley as the league's outstanding player — but the Stamps were going to the Grey Cup.

The crowd went home stunned. But they would be back. In Saskatchewan — not just Regina, but all of Saskatchewan — they always come back. In Saskatchewan you are not merely *for* the team, you are *of* the team. Sandy Archer, the Riders' trainer from 1951 through 1980, remembers one game against Hamilton when the rain came down so hard that all the towels were soaked and there was no way of keeping the kicker's shoe dry. A fan noticed the problem, came out of the stands, peeled off his angora sweater, and wrapped it around the kicking shoe. "The guy kicks the field goal," Archer says, "and we win 5-3."

Archer's first year was also the rookie season for a quarterback named Glenn Dobbs, lured out of a two-year retirement as an answer to the hated Indian Jack Jacobs in Winnipeg. He'd been a college all-American at Tulsa, an all-pro with the Los Angeles Dons in the old All-American Conference. The man was a star. "I went to my first practice," he recalled years later, "and they handed me a bucket of paint and a brush. The Riders' job that day was to paint the Taylor Field fence."

He stayed two years and loved it as the city loved him. Saskatchewan issued vanity licence-plate holders labelling the province as "Dobberville". The battles with Jacobs were classics. Taylor Field had itself another legend.

Not that there was ever a shortage. This was a team that had its offices and dressing room at the city race track, dressed there and bused to the stadium on game days, and had to beware of oncoming horses as they crossed the track to practice in the infield. For years the only heat in the dressing room was provided by a pot-bellied stove. But even then there was tradition: a support beam in the middle of the room was festooned with the name tapes ripped from the helmets of players cut or released over the seasons. Sometimes they'd add the name of a hotshot rookie, just to watch him turn green.

Once, when trainer Dale Laird had a heated argument with coach John Payne over dressing-room territory, Laird hid the footballs for an afternoon game, which didn't start until they found replacements. Laird was also a key figure in the development of a country-western record: Tim Roth on guitar and vocals, Nolan Bailey on drum, and gigantic Clyde Brock singing and pounding a wrench on a steel pipe. The title was to be the combined weight of the three players, but Laird's dog wandered into the cover picture, so they added his weight and called it 800 Pounds of West Country Rock.

More than anything, the Riders are a team that makes do, a team that became the green and white in 1948 because a team director found two sets of nylon jerseys in a surplus store in Chicago and couldn't resist the bargain; a team that exchanged tickets for wheat in a year when times were tough in Saskatchewan; a team that survived for years on the funds from civic dinners, in a province where employers used to give their help one day off if they bought a season ticket.

In those years, Taylor Field has grown from an 8,000 capacity to the 55,000-plus for the Grey Cup game, thanks to those cold metal scaffolding temporary seats. Last October 14 they did a dry run with the new seats — and drew 55,438. Somebody figured that on that day, not counting Regina and Saskatoon, Taylor Field was the largest community in Saskatchewan.

The cynics have it backward. Saskatchewan isn't lucky it has the Grey Cup game. Canadian football is lucky it has Saskatchewan.

LANGUAGE BARRIER

July 11, 1996

It is no secret that in the minds of many professional athletes the word "mother" ends with a hyphen.

No, wait: not ends, exactly. The hyphen is more of a bridge to another word, the combination then taking on a meaning that has no connection whatever with mom, affection, Chevrolet or apple pie.

While students of the language remain uncertain of the hybrid word's origin, historians have traced it back as far as 1873 to the southwest corner of Arizona, where a U.S. cavalry private, assured by his sergeant that there were no Indians for miles around, stepped outside the fort, where arrows made him an instant pincushion.

Falling back inside, he glared at the sergeant.

"You muh ...!" he groaned. "You muh ...!"

And thus did the city of Yuma get its name.

All of which is a roundabout way of noting that mother has fallen into disrepute yet again. This time, the blame falls on the Canadian Football League.

A bunch of Nervous Nellies upset at some aspects of the league's Radically Canadian ad campaign — to wit, the T-shirt bearing the message Our Balls Are Bigger — are approaching cardiac arrest over phase two, a shirt informing the world that CFL players are Tough Mothers.

"First balls, now mothers," they bleat. "Where will it end? Stamp out these smutty T-shirts before our young women reject motherhood and our young men go blind!"

Psssst! Folks! Yeah, you there, with the blue noses. Got a bulletin for you: *The kids know about the hyphen. They don't care!*

What they see is a cool new line of sports gear with slogans across the front that might shock a parent or two — which, of course, is another neat reason to be wearing one.

What the parents should be seeing, particularly those who've followed the CFL's historically stumbling course through the marketplace, is a campaign that's catchy and innovative and has every chance of giving the league a shot at a new fan base it ultimately must tap if it is to survive.

This is the league whose idea of marketing in the past has been to get a connection with a greengrocer and bill meaningless pre-season exhibition games as a fight for the coveted Salad Bowl.

This is the league so weighed down by an inferiority complex by that bigger league and lesser game to the south that its theme song should be "I Surrender, Dear."

This is the league we've pleaded with for 30 years to stop apologizing for the differences in our game and start boasting about them, to quit genuflecting in front of the Super Bowl and start reminding people that the Grey Cup was a football tradition for better than half a century before the NFL's big-deal trophy was a gleam in Pete Rozelle's eye.

And now, finally, it's come out swinging instead of begging for crumbs, going for a chunk of the clothing and paraphernalia market that has been worth billions to the NBA, the NFL and even the NHL — quality stuff, as good as any out there — and people are bitching?

Tacky? Of course it's tacky.

Off-colour? Not unless the dye runs. And it won't.

Look around. Check out the messages on T-shirts these days. Double-entendre is not a football formation, it's a fact of life.

Some of it goes too far. But I would rather see a kid in a shirt that said CFL Players Are Tough Mothers than in some I've seen that said Kill Whitey, or Screw the World or (Bleep) the Olympics.

What we have here is a nifty campaign that is having an impact. People are talking about it, and thus about Canadian football — the league, not the collapse. When was the last time that happened?

Those who fear that their children's moral fibre will melt at the first touch of a new CFL T-shirt, golf shirt, sweatshirt or cap have the answer in their wallets. The merchandise — more's the pity — is available only by credit-card mail-order through toll-free numbers. You don't want it in the house, don't let your kid have your card.

But think about it first.

What's the greater worry: that your kid wears slightly risqué gear that brags about a Canadian game and Canadian sports heroes, or that he grows up worshipping at the shrine of American jock millionaires and believing that when it comes to sports, Canadian is an eight-letter word for bush?

TOO GOOD TO DIE

November 25, 1996

HAMILTON — Were you watching, Canada? Did you see this incredible, blizzard-blown monument to the game our neglect and indifference have left on life support?

Were you watching Doug Flutie, he of the tiny hands and the lion-hearted cockiness, running for the key first downs, chucking that infuriating underhand, overhand, sidearm, everywhichway pitch again and again and again with Edmonton Eskimos' defenders inches and milliseconds away from turning the play into nothing?

Were you watching, America? Did you turn away from the NFL colossus to peek at ESPN and see a Grey Cup game that, year after year, makes your Super Bowl look like a pick-up game on a corner lot?

Do you see now, in Vancouver and Ottawa and Montreal, why this three-down, chilblained chunk of Canadiana deserves a chance to live?

Tell me the last Super Bowl when, in one quarter, the lead changed hands five times, 41 points went up on the board — and the defences were still playing brilliantly. When did you last see a game played on an ice floe, with frozen stadium workers clearing the yard stripes with brooms, in which the players didn't so much adjust to the conditions as ignore them?

And when did you see a quarterback — Elway, Montana, Unitas, Stabler, Marino — perform a better magic act than Flutie, the game's best quarterback of the decade, the half-century and maybe ever, yet still regarded by some coming into this game as a man with something to prove?

What kind of a game was it? Try this: At 7:34 of the second quarter, Danny McManus hit Jim Sandusky with a 75-yard touchdown pass that gave the Eskimos a 16-13 lead — and didn't get on the field again until there were only 35 seconds left in the half. In that space, three touchdowns were scored, two by the Argos on time-consuming drives that were like arrows in Eskimo hearts, and one on a 91-yard kick-off return by Gizmo Williams.

You ever see that in a Super Bowl?

Okay, it was a brutal call that allowed the Argos to keep the ball and kick the field goal that put them up 36-30. Flutie fumbled on third-and-inches, the Eskimos clearly got the ball to stop the drive, and the officials said the ball was dead. But when the media tried to get coach Ron Lancaster to rant in the dressing room as he appeared to be doing on the sidelines, he would have none of it.

"Too good a football game to talk about that," he said. "Two good teams, great game. That's what matters."

As for Flutie, if he didn't stuff a snowball down the throats of those who said he couldn't play in winter weather, there is no hope for them.

It takes more than cockiness to throw that inside pitch when the wind is blowing and the feet are slipping and the ball is hard enough for curling. It takes timing, precision and the sublime confidence of a superb athlete who believes with every fibre of his being that his teams never lose, they just run out of time to win.

His stats tell part of it, but only part. Thirteen rushes for 98 yards is impressive, but figures can't tell you how many of those runs were for first downs that kept drives alive. Thirty-five pass attempts, 22 completions for 302 yards looks good, but it wasn't so much the passes as when they were thrown, and how many were those little dump-offs that can be six the other way if you don't get it right.

He had a lot of support, particularly from the apparently indestructible Robert Drummond. And, of course, the field-goal kicking of Mike Vanderjagt — and when was the last time a Canadian kicker DIDN'T win the Grey Cup game?

This game, this 43-37 showcase, did not save Canadian football. The danger is that too many people will think it did, because somehow the season always ends with this 60-minute dip into euphoria.

What it SHOULD have done is prove to the fence-sitters that this is one thread in our national fabric that cannot be allowed to unravel.

If they were watching. And if they still care.

VINCE WHO?

January 23, 1997

If we are to believe the yards of newsprint drivel being pumped out of New Orleans, the ghost of Vince Lombardi hovers over the Green Bay Packers as they prepare to do unto the New England Patriots in America's monument to wretched excess, the Super Bowl.

It's nonsense, of course. It's been 30 years since Lombardi's Packers won the first Super Bowl game, and then the second. Most of the current Packers weren't even born. Are you telling me that in these money-hungry, drug-abuse, wife-beating, heat-packing, smack-a-hooker, gang-banging days of professional football, the current Packers feel any affinity for a cliché-creating autocrat coach who's been dead for better than a quarter-century?

Can't you just hear them in the final pre-game huddle? "All right! Let's get out there and kick some mother-bleepin' ass for good ol' Vince!"

As a coach in the '90s NFL, Lombardi wouldn't have lasted a month. Time, unions and cynicism have long since spiked his guns.

He couldn't deal with agents the way he did in 1964 when his all-pro centre, Jim Ringo, sent in two to represent him in contract negotiations. Lombardi excused himself for a moment to make a phone call, then said, "Gentlemen, you are dealing with the wrong man. Mr. Ringo is now the property of the Philadelphia Eagles."

Imagine the gales of laughter today if old Vince tried to inspire his players with lines like:

"No one is ever hurt. Hurt is in the mind."

("Oh, yeah? Lessee you take one upside the head from some mutha tryin' to scramble your brains.")

"There's nothing that stokes the mind like hate."

("Right on. And what I hate most is listenin' to this crap.")

"If you aren't fired by enthusiasm, you'll be fired with enthusiasm."

("Read my contract, bro. I got me a no-cut, no-trade.")

"Winning is not everything — but making the effort to win is."

("Oh, yeah? We don't win this one, see how fast they fire YO ass.")

"Winning isn't everything, it's the only thing."

("Hey, you stealin'! Dumb-ass thing isn't yours. Red Sanders made that up when he was at Vanderbilt. You ever heard of plagiarism, man?")

In Lombardi's day it was big news when he fined Max McGee $500 for breaking curfew and said, "The next time it will be $1,000. And if you find anything worth $1,000, let me know and I may go with you." Today the fines are limited by the collective-bargaining agreement, and usually refunded as part of the next negotiation.

He could build his legend, and have it embellished through the years, because time and circumstance allowed him to be a tyrant and because his Packers won those first two showdowns after the war with the AFL. In today's Super Bowl climate, where hype is everything, TV commercials run $40,000 per minute, the coach is less a coach than a millionaire media personality and the pre-game, post-game and half-time spectacles are so all-engulfing that the game itself becomes a bothersome interruption, Vincent Thomas Lombardi would die of concussion from batting his head against too many walls.

Paul Hornung, who was there in the big years, tells this story of the way things were run in Lombardi's day: "One night after a long, cold, difficult day, Lombardi came home and tumbled into bed. 'God,' his wife said, 'your feet are cold.' And Lombardi answered, 'Around the house, dear, you may call me Vince.' "

DEAR ED: DROP DEAD

January 28, 1997

It's always a sad thing when a hero falls, particularly in a big game like the Super Bowl.

But one of mine did at half-time of the Packers-Patriots game, and frankly that about does it with me for Ed McMahon and maybe even Dick Clark, although rumour has it that he's been dead for years and keeps on ticking only through the courtesy of the Energizer Bunny and the mortician who's got the Lenin account.

On Sunday, Ed — well, not him, but a guy representing him — gave the $100,000 down payment of the $10,000,000 first prize in the Publishers Clearing House contest to a woman named Beata Sankiewicz of Sudbury, Ontario. Well, nothing personal, Beata, but take a hike. That money is mine.

Every few months I'd get this envelope with kindly old Ed's face on it and my name in big black letters saying how well things were breaking for me. First I was in the barrel. Then I was in the finals. Then it said they'd present me with a cheque for $10,000,000.

Okay, there was a flyspeck underneath that turned out to be an "if", and a bunch of other crap about buying magazines. But the way I figured it, once Ed gave me the $10,000,000 I'd buy as many magazines as he wanted. What could be fairer than that?

Besides, we're talking Ed McMahon here, the guy who was once named as one of the most trusted faces in America. Ed McMahon, such a bright guy that he spent years on the *Tonight Show* laughing at Johnny Carson's jokes before he even told them. Ed McMahon, who played W.C. Fields on stage and sometimes off. Ed McMahon, who married a chick younger than some of his underwear.

America believes in Ed McMahon the way my mother used to believe in Walter Cronkite when he was covering the early space shots. One time when Cronkite announced that NASA had postponed a moon launch she yelled at me from the living room. "Walter's called off the moon shot," she said. That's faith, and that's precisely the kind of trust I put in Ed McMahon.

So there was that face on the envelope, laughing the famous laugh and telling me I was going to be the big winner, splashing it across the envelope in black type the size the tabloids use for Madonna, Michael, UFOs and the nose close-ups proving beyond a shadow of a doubt that Wayne Gretzky is actually Princess Diana.

When Ed McMahon laughs, who looks at the fine print?

I was going to win $10,000,000. I was going to get all of it, because unlike America, Canada does not tax lottery winnings. And Brett Favre thought HE was having a Super Sunday.

Sure enough, there was a knock on the door at half-time.

"You ever coming up for air?" my wife asked. "That thing's been on longer than the O.J. trial."

And then came the news about Beata Sankiewicz, and how she cried when she got the money. Big deal. I did, too.

How could you do this, Ed? What did she have on you — negatives of you and Dick and his battery recharger? Tape recordings of a night when you were doing W.C. and said that on the *Tonight Show*, you were the funny one?

That was my money, Ed. I already spent some of it on a new computer. I had plans, man. I was going to pay Damon Allen's salary, and buy Esa Tikkanen's contract so I could fire his ass. Now what?

Don't write to me again, Ed. And by the way: Stuff your magazines.

Chapter Eight

DECALS ON THE SUITCASE

Every so often someone wants to know why I don't get out of the playpen and do some Serious Writing. Politics, maybe. Editorials. Novels. It's simple: The trips are too good.

Serious Writing gets you trips to your own basement where the computer lives and it's quiet and you can think Deep Thoughts about the ozone layer and OPEC and why the O. J. verdict is an argument against ever again asking 12 people to reach a unanimous decision about anything.

Politics? I live in Vancouver. The government meets in Victoria. Play my cards right and I can go on a 90-minute ferry ride. And back. Whoopee. Federal politics? Listen, anybody wants to bring this country down, go blow up the bridge between Ottawa and Hull, Quebec. A week, tops, and the nation's capital dies of boredom.

Editorials? The stress of writing three- or four-paragraph pieces — sometimes two or three times a week — that have to sound so pompous that you live in fear one might accidentally get by-lined? No thank you. Novels? Only sex novels sell, and all the good positions have been used.

No, I'll stay in the playpen, thank you. Ernest Hemingway was a sports writer. So was Paul Gallico, and Jimmy Breslin, and Damon Runyon, who wrote *Guys and Dolls*, and gave us Harry the Horse, Nathan Detroit and Nicely-Nicely. Jim Murray stayed in the sports department. So did Red Smith, the greatest of them all. On my best day I couldn't run with them, but at least I can say I'm in the same dodge.

But mostly, it's the trips.

Stay in the dodge long enough and they start sending you not just out of town, but out of country. I've been to Olympic Games in Japan, soccer's World Cup in Italy, the Aquatic Games in Belgrade and Cali, the first Canada-Russia hockey series in Moscow — too many countries to count.

It isn't for everyone. ("The trouble with this city," said one of the Team Canada hockey stalwarts during pre-tournament training in Stockholm during the '72 series, "is the same thing you're gonna notice about a lot of your European cities. Too many old buildings.") But to travel around the world, expenses paid, and sit in the best seats in the house for the major sporting events of the year; to watch our greatest athletes, amateur and pro, perform against the world — and get *paid* to be there? What's not to love?

We've probably seen the best of it. The Olympics are unwieldy and unnecessary and corrupt and cannot last much longer. The hate-mongers and the wing-nuts have discovered the world stage that international sport provides, and how simple it is to kill and maim your way into the spotlight. Satellite television puts the spectacles in your living room, complete with replays and wrap-around sound. Things do not look good for my frequent-flyer points.

But they've been great times — great, funny, scary and sometimes terrifying times. You have not lived until you're standing in a dark and dirty stadium washroom in El Salvador about to give yourself an insulin injection, and three soldiers burst in and find you standing there with a syringe in your hand.

And if the party ends, well, nobody can steal the memories ...

PERCY, HARRY — AND BEN

September 30, 1988

The word "tragedy" is much abused as the net of truth tightens inexorably around Ben Johnson and his grubby entourage. Consider the cards fate dealt his predecessors, and ask yourselves how tragic, really, is the story of this man who had it all and threw much of it away.

Much, but not all. Not when he has the money he'd made before the steroid scandal. Not when he can still sell his notoriety, and has moved to do so with gold-medal swiftness.

The Canadian people who supported him will not hear Ben Johnson's story first. That privilege, if that be the word, has been sold to *Stern*, the West German magazine widely considered to be Europe's answer to the *National Enquirer*. When in doubt, go for the bucks.

I wonder how Percy Williams would feel about that, or Harry Jerome?

By the only true measuring stick — performance on the day — Percy Williams was the greatest of Canada's three star-crossed world-champion sprinters. In 1928, an unknown from Vancouver, he went to the Olympic Games in Amsterdam and won gold at both 100 and 200 metres.

There were no government support teams then, no big dollars for travel or equipment or allowances — or coaches. Bob Brown, the old baseball man, paid Percy's way to the Canadian championships in Hamilton in 1927. His coach and mentor, Bob Grainger, got there that year and the next for the Olympic trials by working in the CPR dining car. To get to Amsterdam he worked on a cattle boat, arriving three days before Percy's events.

Would Ben's entourage have done that, I wonder? Would they feel that strongly about him if the big bucks weren't out there for the taking?

Percy Williams should have had it all. But he tore a thigh muscle at the British Empire Games in 1930. Had the damage been repaired then, he'd have recovered fully. But the Canadian team didn't have a doctor, and though he did compete in the '32 Olympics, Percy Williams was effectively finished as a world-class runner.

He never attended another meet. As the years passed he became something of a recluse, spurning the banquets and the honours that came his way. And in 1982, the arthritis in his knees and ankles causing him terrible pain, he climbed into his bathtub with a shotgun, and took his own life.

A few days later Harry Jerome, his successor as Canada's world-champion sprinter, suffered a brain seizure and died at 42, a man who never made the big money and lived the last 20 years of his life under the horribly inaccurate and unfair tag of the guy who seized up in the big ones.

Here was a man who'd tied the world 100-metre record at 19, and over the next decade had more world-class sprint performances than any runner in history, including gold medals at the '66 Commonwealth Games and the '67 Pan-Ams.

But we expected more. When he pulled up lame in the 100-metre semi-final at the Olympics in Rome and fled in tears rather than explain about the pulled hamstring muscle, the whispers began. When he did it again in the final at the Commonwealth Games in Perth, the whispers turned to snickers. Never mind that he'd torn the big muscle in the front of his left thigh, leaving a gap so huge he could insert his fist. He hadn't won as expected. Ergo: He'd choked.

He took a year off, came back in 1964 to tie the world 100-metre record again, and won bronze in Tokyo. Considering the injury and the comeback, that bronze medal rated more than a dozen golds. But again, he hadn't won.

Jerome lived under that undeserved tag for much of his shortened life. Like Williams, he paid a terrible price for his turn on the world stage. If Ben Johnson's story is a tragedy, what is theirs?

TIPS FOR THE TRAVELLING MAN

June 22, 1990

ROME — The first thing you learn about travelling to the World Cup is that there are a lot of things the travel pages don't tell you.

So, as a public service before the second (i.e. REAL) round of the world's greatest sporting event, let me give you a few tips if you are planning a European vacation:

1. Sell your house. If you live in Shaughnessy, this should give you enough working capital to cover two weeks in Italy.

2. Get heavily into dieting. A month on crackers and water should do it. Otherwise you may feel compelled to eat three meals a day here, which will seriously deplete the money from the house and possibly shorten your vacation by a week.

You think I jest? There's an imitation McDonald's down the street from the convent where I'm living. (My travel agent booked me into a convent, the Sisters of the Sacred Families, where the sisters take in roomers and the bathroom is down the hall. He knows a swinger when he sees one.) You can get an imitation Big Mac and a glass of mineral water — *con fizzy*, as we say in Italy — for only $6.50 Canadian.

3. Before you come to Italy, try to see Switzerland, where the legendary mountains are almost as high as the bill for lunch. If the Canadian government is serious about killing off the national debt, the solution is easy: Nationalize the restaurants and charge Swiss prices.

4. Take a crash course in Italian. It's no picnic trying to find your way around town when every word you see looks like a new kind of pasta.

5. Bring books, or forget about reading. A pocket novel marked $6.95 Canadian sells here for just under $13 Canadian.

6. If you don't speak Italian, it will be helpful to learn a few key words like "Avanti", which appears on the traffic lights when they are green and means "Walk". Unless, of course, you're an Italian driver, in which case it means "Target". In Rome, the land where "Uppa yu tailpipe" is less a curse than a way of life, crosswalks are to drivers what game preserves are to poachers.

7. Take the bus a lot. It's the best way to see the city, and the most fun, because it is based on the honour system. You buy your bus ticket in any store on the block. When you get on the bus, you stick the ticket in a machine that stamps it. Nobody seems to care whether you do or not and nobody ever asks to see your ticket.

8. If you must drive, let your wife (or husband) do it. I always do because (a) she's a better driver than I am, and (b) she knows North from South, which is particularly handy when you're driving in through the mountains from Switzerland and don't want to reach Rome by way of Czechoslovakia.

"Thank you! Thank you, oh world traveller," I can hear you saying. "But what about the World Cup?"

Oh, yeah.

Well, I decided to skip the first round, which is a lot like the NHL regular season and in the final games leads to suspicions that some teams with second-round berths already clinched are doing a little manoeuvering to avoid meeting certain other teams in the first match once the going gets serious.

Mostly I watched them on TV from the convent (black and white set, *con rabbit ears)* or sat on the balcony sipping fizzy water and listening to Italian home play-by-play.

The way it works is, every time Italy scores a goal, horns blow on the streets and cheers pour out of apartment windows opened against the heat. Every time the other guys score, there is a city-wide groan and some words that require no translation. So far there have been more cheers than groans, so Italy is doing okay.

Now we get serious. It's almost playoff time, my wife is leaving for Paris and Amsterdam, I can say "mineral water" in Italian, and I know how to ride the bus. Bye for now. Or, as we say in Italy, "Bobby Lenarduzzi!"

ROAR OF THE BLACK LION

June 24, 1990

NAPLES — Look up to the west of Sao Paolo stadium and you saw the glory that was old Naples. Look down on the pitch and you saw the glory that was Old Roger.

Move over, Naples. On this night, at this moment, it was Old Roger in a walk. Or maybe in the ecstatic, triumphant hop-skip-and-jump after the second goal of his personal decimation of Colombia's national soccer side — the twin thunderbolts that did unto the Colombians as his previous two had done unto Romania in the first round of soccer's and perhaps sport's greatest show.

Of all the stories that have been written in World Cups past — be they the dazzling feet of Paolo Rossi or the legendary Hand of God of Diego Maradona — surely there has never been one more unlikely than this.

A second-round match between a Cameroons team that had looked so terrible in the African championships that goalie Thomas N'Kono snorted that "There's no point even going to the World Cup if we're going to play like this," and a Colombian side that had been disbanded seven months ago after a referee was shot and killed in what was either a drug-war hit or a betting scandal, depending upon which of the two official stories you believe.

And the Cameroons trot onto the big stage all giggly and excited, upset Argentina for openers, and go on to win their group. In a land where better than 50% of the populace lists its chief religious belief as witch-doctoring and several practitioners have offered to get behind the team with something considerably more potent than moral support, what's to get excited?

And then there was, is, and remains Roger Milla, whose name is actually Miller, but who uses Milla for soccer purposes because it sounds more African and besides, it keeps drunks from staggering over and asking him to sing "King of the Road."

Old Roger is 38. When he left the national side three years ago, distraught over the death of his mother, his nation built a statue, threw a hell of a farewell party, and waved goodbye. Old Roger went off to an island called Recepcion somewhere in the Indian Ocean and played amateur soccer.

When his team called him back late in this up-down season a lot of people objected. What bothered Milla most was that some of the loudest critics were his teammates. "But I was an old Army horse," he said. "I heard my country call."

He isn't a starter. His critics still insist he's not fully in condition. But when he comes onto the field, something wonderful happens. Not always — but often enough to level the Romanians and do in the Colombians and lift the Black Lions into territory no African team has seen before: The third round of the World Cup.

And suddenly, soccer and senior citizens everywhere have a new hero: Old Roger, the Old Engine That Still Can. If he lacks the stature of a Maradona, he also lacks his arrogance. If his offensive gifts are not as enormous as those of many of the magicians who roam this tournament, so much the better. He is a people's hero, and if the Black Lions fade away in the next round — and with four players out through suspensions many insist that must happen — well, he's given the game a touch of the fun it has on less opulent pitches with so much less at stake.

As you watch Argentina play Brazil and hear the description of this alleged collision of the colossi, remember Naples. Remember that there in the middle of the millions of dollars worth of electronics that carried the match to untold millions around the world; there before a world soccer press that decries the power and pressure game that has invaded the sport, and pulls secretly or publicly for the Black Lions to weave their spell at least one more time, there were jungle drums from another time, pounding out a savage rhythm that built to a joyous crescendo as Milla scored twice in the second half of overtime.

Forget the money and the spectacle and the sheer magnitude of the World Cup. Forget that the Americans want to redesign the game to North American standards in 1994 with four quarters and the trappings of major-league baseball and NFL football.

Remember, instead, the close-up look at the face of Old Roger as he faced the drums and the flags and the dancers and threw his arms aloft with the pure joy of it.

Hoist a glass to Old Roger. And, just in case, hoist another to the witch doctor. This thing is too great to stop now.

WARM-UP IS EVERYTHING

February 21, 1992

I have an idea: Let's make a rule that on the opening day of every Olympic Games, winter and summer, every covering newspaper must run the following front-page story under a headline in the biggest type that will fit:

OLYMPIC ATHLETES LIKE SEX!

OSLO — According to a survey conducted by the International Olympic Committee, every athlete in the current Olympiad says he/she has the same interest in sex as non-competitors.

While opinions varied on whether or not the act of love-making should take place (a) in the hours before the event, (b) immediately after the event or (c) all of the above and as often as possible, the unanimous opinion was that boys will be boys, girls will be girls, and since the activity is (a) enjoyable, (b) physiologically stimulating and (c) better than sitting in your room reading the Wit and Wisdom of Juan Antonio Samaranch, they plan to follow their natural instincts on every possible occasion.

Given this overwhelming support of sex as a participant sport, the IOC should submit a motion at its next Congress that the motto of the Olympic Games be changed from "Swifter, Higher, Stronger" to "Faster, Harder, Yes! Yes! Yes! More! More! Oooooh!"

You see all the trouble it would save?

With the sex question out of the way early we wouldn't be biting our nails today wondering whether Kerrin Lee-Gartner did or did not get a 120-second jump-start from husband Max on the morning of the day she won the women's downhill at Meribel.

A Swiss paper ran what it claimed were quotes from Lee-Gartner: "Beside me [in bed] my husband Max opened my eyes with a warm-up under the covers. We made good vibrations for the race. That was enough to be in good shape." The paper then added "One hundred and 20 seconds later, the quickie was over. A quickie is very good. Longer sex is bad for condition."

Upon her arrival in Canada, Lee-Gartner said she was embarrassed by the story and had never spoken to the Swiss reporter who wrote it. But since she didn't actually deny the event itself, we are left to mind-boggling speculation.

Had we run my Games-opening sex story, the Lee-Gartner story wouldn't have caused a ripple. We might even have been mature enough to think that a married couple in a romantic chalet in the mountains of France might have awakened on medal morning with a Really Good Idea. And that either way, it was nobody's business but theirs.

As to the advisability of sex before competition, it is a question that has plagued scholars for centuries.

Believers trust in the words of golf commentator Ben Wright, who once wrote of a colleague who took a shot off his five-handicap while on honeymoon, and Babe Ruth to the desk clerk: "Tell her to come right on up." Doubters lean to Casey Stengel to the New York Yankees: "You gotta learn that if you don't get it by midnight, chances are you ain't gonna get it; and if you do, it ain't worth it."

Every athlete has his or her own ideas on the subject. But because they are athletes, they're not silly enough to ignore the possibility that they might be wrong. Actually, they probably hope they never will find out for certain. In this case, the result isn't nearly as interesting as the research.

GOING FOR THE PARSLEY

July 14, 1992

Leaders of the G-7 took time out from saving the world to save the Olympic Games.

"Let the Yugoslavians compete," they thundered in a letter to IOC president Juan Samaranch, "but not as Yugoslavians. Put white vests on them with no identifying marks and have them compete under the IOC flag. If they win, play the IOC anthem."

Brilliant. That way when they march into the stadium — the only athletes wearing plain white vests — everyone can point and shout, "Look, Ma! There's the Yugoslavians!"

Personally, I preferred the old Group of Seven, who pretty much stood around all day painting pictures and not bothering anyone. But the decision on the Yugoslavian Question — quickly adopted by the IOC — does prove that it's time to offer my own personal solution to the problems that regularly beset these gatherings of the world's highest-paid amateurs in the spirit of sportsmanship, competition and sneaker endorsements:

The Buck-Naked Olympics.

This is not an original concept. The first Olympians competed that way all the time, wrestling, racing and jumping about clad in nothing but sweat and glory.

Not for them, fights over sneaker trademarks and togas covered with everything from "Flavius Spears — the Winning Edge" to "Caesar's Sandals — Where the Arch meets the Apia". They competed for glory and wreaths made from home-grown veggies:

olive at Olympia, laurel at Delphi, fresh parsley (and later pine) at Corinth and dried parsley at Nemea. (That alone would clean things up. Can you honestly picture Carl Lewis or Flo-Jo talking to the local scribe: "That's right, Octavius, I'm going for the parsley"?)

Of course, the original Games were as crooked as the current. The victors, supposedly competing as individuals, would receive ample rewards from their home states: cash, estates, theatre tickets and extravagant homecoming processions. Some city-states even bought athletes, hoping to benefit from their skills. In the fifth century B.C. one Astylos of Croton, a double winner from the south of Italy, changed his national allegiance to Syracuse (in Sicily) between Olympiads. One of the reasons the original Games were cancelled was the suspicion that some of the competitors were using drugs.

But if the crimes were similar, the punishments were far more severe. States caught breaking the rules paid stiff fines used to build statues of Zeus, set up at Olympia as a permanent warning to potential cheaters. The unofficial record of six statues was held by Kallipos of Athens, who bribed his opponents in the pentathlon.

Then as now there were suspensions and boycotts. When his own country was banned from the Games, a Spartan named Lichas entered his horse in the chariot race claiming to be a Theban. He won the race but was caught and horsewhipped. In retaliation, the Spartans invaded Olympia.

So, as the honest athletes line up and the sponsors and agents circle like vultures and the cheaters offer silent prayers that their urine samples will slip past the testing devices, be reassured: The times are no worse now than they were in the beginning and ever shall be. All, of course, in the name of sport.

CONDOM

October 28, 1993

No doubt you are as relieved as I at word that the 1994 Victoria Commonwealth Games now have their own official condom.

Ortho Pharmaceutical recently began distributing its Ortho Shields — "Official Condom, Victoria 94" — complete with a Games logo on the package. Okay, so the Games don't open until August, but you know what the coaches say: "Practise, practise, practise. You'll never get anywhere unless you do your reps."

Until now, this may have presented a problem to a generation raised on the theory that if Nike isn't giving it away it ain't worth having. The shoe people who tell us to "Just Do It" have never bothered to add that, in matters of the heart or libido, it is wise to enter the event wearing something besides really spiffy shoes.

Now Ortho has provided the answer as part of its $25,000-to-$200,000 payment in cash and product — the range set by the Games Society to qualify for "Proud Sponsor" status. (Slogans leap to mind: "Be Proud. Wear Ortho.") Ortho's offerings include condoms and muscle relaxants (now that's what you call covering both ends of the market) plus, for those who may have been caught short of one or the other, pregnancy-test kits.

Given that boys will be boys, girls will be girls, and we are throwing a few hundred of the world's healthiest and most competitive young people together in one big, happy village, the approach makes nothing but sense. There is, however, one teensy potential problem.

Games bylaws state that the host country must provide a complete pharmacy in the village. Again, common sense. Trainers, doctors and athletes have more important things to do than go searching for local drugstores, and prescriptions filled out by foreign doctors may not be worth squat. Thus, the Games provides doctors with prescription pads for the village pharmacy, and the process is so closely monitored that, in the words of Games spokesperson Amy Hart, "if an athlete wants an aspirin tablet, he'll have to get a prescription."

So what happens if boy meets girl, the windows steam up, the guy is trying to play it like Omar Sharif, and ...

"Uh, excuse me a minute, okay? Got to go see the doc for a prescription. I need a ... a ... *aspirin*! That's it: an *aspirin*!" That's not Omar; that's Gomer.

Word of the condom caper has drawn one irate call to Ms. Hart, pointing out that nothing was mentioned in the release about abstinence. No doubt there will be more. The problem with abstinence is that, given the marketplace, it's such a tough sell. How do you package nothing?

Face it: We live in a world where you market or die. That's why there is an official Games potato chip, an official Games drink, and an official Games clothing line soon to be announced. Our athletes are the cream of our physical crop. It's only logical that Ortho would want to tie its condom to a star. Particularly one that's proud.

SOCCER-TO-ME ...

March 13, 1994

Switzerland's World Cup soccer team has been ordered to stay celibate from June 7 until they win the cup or are eliminated, which would be June 26 at the earliest.

"I want my players to concentrate totally on football with all their strength," says coach Roy Hodgson. Like Italy's Azeglio Vicini heading into the last World Cup, he wants nothing stiffening but a grim resolve. Obviously, there is a language barrier. The Swiss are neutral, Roy, not neuter.

Sex and the pursuit thereof has always been a bit of a mystery to national coaches, most of whom are former players who've somehow forgotten the dedication with which they used to pursue it themselves.

Truly, it is amazing. They spend an entire career on the road with the lads. They know all the tricks, all the pubs, all the established haunts of Europe's Football Annies. Then, when they're too old to pull on the boots, someone hands them a whistle and says, "You're now the coach." Bam! Instant Pope.

Besides, there's not a lick of evidence showing that games in the bedroom have any ill effects on performance on the pitch. To the contrary, the Bible itself tells us that the bridegroom emerges from the bedchamber like a runner to a race. When you're sitting alone in your hotel room with the sounds of girlish laughter drifting in from the pub, whose word are you going to take — Hodgson's, or Gideon's?

Some coaches have it figured out. Casey Stengel, the noted Yankees' manager, always said it wasn't the sex that tired you, it was the pursuit of it. Mind you, Casey also thought syntax was a tip for the hooker.

All of the research, pro and con, runs smack into the brick wall of human nature. Besides, the coaches have no leverage. Not in something as big as the World Cup.

Suppose the Maradona of the '90s is caught flat-footed and buck naked by his coach, fumbling to get his key into the lock while a bevy of giggling and impatient beauties hop up and down at his side. What can the coach do about it?

Suspend him? Not likely. The coach would be overruled by his own football association and quite possibly lynched by his fans. The tabloids would have a field day. Maradona Scores — But Not for Us. He'd be back in the lineup before the coach quit bouncing. This is the World Cup. It matters not how you score in the bedroom as long as you score on the pitch. Get the winning goal in the final and the women who don't throw themselves at your feet will be thrown there by their boyfriends.

Personally, I've always believed that the coaches are going at this backwards. If they really want their players to abstain, they should appeal to their wives and girlfriends.

Pay their fare and accommodation for the World Cup trip. Encourage them to stand by their man no matter where he may be, all expenses paid. In exchange, all they have to do is follow one simple, patriotic rule and prove what great soccer fans they are:

"Give your all for the team — don't give your all for the team!"

IT'S TUTU MUCH

February 23, 1995

Aside from the split infinitive, what is wrong with the following sentence? "Canada failed to even qualify a skier for the ballet final."

It appeared on the sports pages as part of what read like a disaster story out of Kirchberg, Austria, where — oh, say it isn't so — this country proved dismally short in the areas of aerials and moguls. Truly, we are a nation in decline.

The worst part, according to a quote from coach Peter Judge, "is that there are no excuses. They had enough time to rest, enough time to prepare. I don't know what it is."

Exactly. I don't know what it is, either.

Why are Canadian skiers taking up ballet? Does Mikhail Baryshnikov slalom? Did Rudolf Nureyev ever enter the downhill? Are we soon to be blessed with the sight of Edi Podivinsky, his skis encased in the world's largest ballet slippers, gallumphing his way across the stage in *Swan Lake*? Will TSN soon show us Brian Stemmle shivering his way through the downhill in helmet and tutu — or, given the climate, a threethree?

Call me old-fashioned, but the words "skiing" and "ballet" seem mutually exclusive. Skiing is skiing. Ballet is ballet. (You can't fool a trained reporter.) You do not combine them for the same reason you do not make ham and jam sandwiches. Taken separately they are of great merit. Taken together they make a lousy sandwich and draw you strange looks at the deli.

Yet, there we are in Austria, competing our buns off in the world freestyle skiing championships in Kirchberg, where we are obviously in some sort of crisis situation because, among other things, one Darcy Downs of Manotick, Ontario, fifth in the overall ballet standings, placed "a disastrous 21st." Mark me down as shocked.

Canadians are supposed to do well in freestyle skiing. It fits in so well with our penchant for finding sports in which only a few countries compete and gathering medals until the rest of the world catches on. If this keeps up, Sport Canada soon will have to form a committee to prepare a White Paper to determine how we have fallen into the freestyle-skiing gap, and arrange several European tours to study the training methods in the countries that have passed us by. Given the inherent dangers — Sport Canada members faced with the prospect of expeditions to foreign climes have been known to throw out backs and shoulders in leaping up to volunteer as *chef de mission* — we certainly wouldn't want that.

Yet, there is no avoiding the fact that we failed miserably in Kirchberg. Which raises the question: Who cares?

Freestyle skiing requires strength, athleticism, agility, courage and judgment. A total disregard of the benefits of keeping all bodily parts in good repair can also be a boon. But what triggered this sudden need to invent new sports? We didn't have enough already?

TSN, that collecting pool for the sporting bizarre, has shown us skateboarders, and people who strap on skateboards and ski-dive from high altitudes to see whether they can hit the earth skating. Snowboarders demand equal time on the hills. Skiers aim for moguls and build their own when they can't find any while their ballet brethren slam poles into the snow and pivot and leap like Nijinsky — not the ballet guy, the horse.

It's as though people gather in focus groups to see what recreational hijinks they can push to the status of recognized sport. They arrange competitions with people in, say, Blaine, which makes it an international event, and before long they're representing their country in a sport it knows nothing about.

We can but wish our skiing balleters well. Meanwhile, we await a new contender for the spectator dollar, log-rolling ballet. You put piranha in the pool, smear the loggers with gravy, and the guy who lasts longest ...

A-ONE AND A-TWO AND ...

April 5, 1995

Ballroom dancing and surfing granted provisional recognition as Olympic Games events. — News item, *The Province*

"Good afternoon, ladies and gentlemen. This emergency meeting of the Canadian Olympic Association to discuss the critical ballroom-dancing issue will now come to order.

"As you know, both ballroom dancing and surfing have been given provisional status in the Olympic Games, meaning that it is only a matter of time before they become medal events. Upon hearing the news, as is our policy, your executive immediately called for White Paper, Green Paper and Blue Paper investigations and a series of progress meetings on the Riviera and the Costa del Sol. The Chair will now hear the report by the ballroom-dance committee."

"Thank you, Mr. Chairman. Your committee has toured the dance centres of the world in an attempt to rate possible competing countries. We even took wives and/or girlfriends along in order to properly assess dance-floor facilities and compare them with our own. You'll find our expenses under Appendix A.

"Our findings are as follows: Spain is going to kick our butts in the tango. If Cuba is allowed to compete, we can pretty much write off the samba. The lambada is a possibility because it died off so quickly most countries don't even know it exists. The down side is that it's so steamy there'd be no TV and at the end of the event the couples would have to be hosed down and separated."

"Are you suggesting that we do not bother flooring a team in the dance events?"

"To the contrary, Mr. Chairman. It would be unfair to deprive some of our members of the right to those expenses-paid trips in supervisory positions."

"Not to mention the competitors themselves."

"Yeah, right. Them, too. No, sir, the trick is not to skip the competition, but to limit ourselves to events where we feel we have the best medal opportunities. For example, the Viennese waltz competition. Austria has a lock on the gold, but given that the people of this country have been waltzed around the block by assorted governments for the past 30 years, the committee feels we should be able to come up with a Canadian couple or two who've come to enjoy it. Silver would be iffy, but bronze is a definite possibility. And a bronze to go with our gold ..."

"Excuse me? What gold?"

"The gold medal we win in the one dance that Canadians do better than anyone in the world. In fact, we may be the only people in the world who do it at all."

"You mean ...?"

"That's right: the bird-dance. The bird-dance is our ticket to Olympic gold."

"Explain."

"Mr. Chairman, how many times have you gone to hockey games or watched them on TV and heard that stupid song with the buck-buck-buck-buck at the end of it, and watched people stand up and flap their arms like chickens to keep time? In Edmonton, it's practically the Oilers' national anthem.

"You give me a few hundred thousand dollars and some airline passes and I'll form a committee that will scour the coliseum for the best bird-dancers in Edmonton. We'll take them to Hawaii for extensive conditioning in the sand and surf — which I myself will supervise on a daily basis — and by the time the Olympiad of the Year 2000 is upon us we will be ready to bird-dance our way to glory!

"I've taken the liberty of moving ahead with this project, Mr. Chairman. Our bird-dance coach will be that fine Canadian and mascot extraordinaire, Ted Giannoulas of Windsor, Ontario, also known as The Chicken. Our medical support team is in training even as we speak, memorizing the official statement in the event of any sort of inadvertent stimulant usage: 'I didn't know those Odor-Eaters were loaded. She should have read the label.' In short, Canada stands ready to dance!"

"Uh, thank you. But don't you think your preparations are, well, bizarre?"

"Mr. Chairman, they've made ballroom dancing an Olympic event. Don't talk to me about bizarre."

A PRICE TOO HIGH

August 1, 1996

You could argue that construction of the pipe bombs that exploded in Atlanta began in 1936, when the newsreel cameras cranked out footage of the strutting Adolf Hitler's message of hate from the

Olympic Games in Berlin, and rushed it to planes to be flown out and shown to the world a few days later.

Or maybe it was in 1968 in Mexico City, where John Carlos and Tommie Smith stood on the podium with their arms raised in the Black Power salute, and the television cameras were there to capture the moment live. Or 1972 in Munich, where jock reporters became instant war correspondents as Israeli athletes and officials died under terrorist attack.

In a world blessed or cursed with instant communication, any event big enough to draw world-wide live coverage becomes a world-wide stage.

Any terrorist with an agenda, any zealot who believes that dying is a sure-fire route to heaven if you take a few hundred non-believers with you, any twisted nobody with a grudge and a desire to get back at the world that's ignored him, can buy his moment of glory as simply as dialling up the how-to-build-a-pipe-bomb page on the Internet.

In case some of them didn't know that, the bomb expert on CNN told them. Building a pipe bomb is easy, he said. You can find out how on the Net. And the timer? A cheap alarm clock, even a wrist watch. You can buy magazines that show you how to make them, he said, how to detonate them, and even where to place them for maximum destructive power.

"Thank you for coming down," the anchorperson said.

"My pleasure," he replied.

The message from Atlanta is not that security was lax. It wasn't. The message was that Atlanta is not the end of it, that while you might be able to protect the Olympic Village and the venues, you cannot protect the entire city in which the event is being held.

So maybe the answer is to curtain off the stage, or at least down-size it.

Build one Olympic Games site to be used over and over again. Build it on an island. No stadiums, no spectators, just one big TV sound stage surrounded by armed troops. Let the world watch from its living rooms, where it's safe.

Or, more realistically, split the Olympics by sport into separate venues countries apart. Better yet, gas them.

The old Olympic celebration of amateurism is a joke. The Games of the '80s and '90s are little more than an excuse for bigger and more expensive TV commercials. Do you think NBC paid $546,000,000 for exclusive rights in Atlanta — and a total of $3,500,000,000 for the rights to six of the next seven Olympiads —

because it likes sport? The Olympics have become a vehicle to push product, like sitcoms or talk shows or the Super Bowl.

They're nice, and they can be thrilling, but we don't need them. The beauty and meaning of athletics is in the striving. Every sport has its world championships. Let them be the goal. The competitors will be the same. Only the size of the stages will change — and perhaps, in the shrinking, become a less tempting target for those who view them through the cross-hairs of insanity.

The hard truth is that death and destruction in sport will not likely end with Atlanta. Another international border has fallen. Terrorism has crossed the ocean at last — in Oklahoma City, on TWA flight 800, and now in a city park in Georgia, where the bitter lesson already learned in other parts of the world has finally hit home:

There is no perfect security. You cannot stop mindless terrorism. All you can do is react to it, clear the area, and zip up the body bags. Show me the sports event worth that risk.

CREDIBILITY GAP

August 8, 1996

There's only one thing wrong with the idea of 100-metre champion Donovan Bailey taking on 200-metre champion Michael Johnson in a split-the-difference match race over 150 metres to see who really is the world's fastest human.

It doesn't go far enough.

Why set anything as arbitrary as 150 metres? Why not Bailey over two feet in a match race against a Mississippi jumping frog?

("Well, Steve Ovett, how do you see this race between our great Canadian world-record holder, Donovan Bailey, and the American entry, uh, Warts?"

"I've got to go with the frog on this one, Brian. Donovan's never been quick off the blocks, and that looks suspiciously like a pile of dead flies over the finish line.")

How about Michael Johnson over 60 metres against a jaguar? And if you want real excitement, sprinkle him with goat's blood and give him a 10-yard head start.

("Steve, a lot of people are backing the jaguar over the world champion in this one. You watched the heats leading up to this final. What's your take on this battle that has the sporting world, not to mention the SPCA, agog?"

"The jaguar looked particularly strong all day, Brian, particularly against that rather chunky entry from the U.S., the late Fats Walker, although its time would have been much better if it hadn't paused just before the finish line to belch.")

Either of the above contests makes as much sense as a Bailey-Johnson "showdown". This thing is a scam, a promotional toe in the water to see if the television networks will bite, a flyer that has produced world-wide coverage without costing the scammers a sou.

And before you say it couldn't happen, remember Bobby Riggs.

Bobby Riggs was the 1939 Wimbledon singles champion turned sports hustler. In 1972 he began a carefully calculated campaign by denouncing women's tennis as pit-a-pat and suggesting that even at his advanced years he could beat the best woman player of the day. Australia's Margaret Court took the bait. So did American network television. And when Riggs completely psyched her out and beat her easily, television bit again.

This time it was Riggs vs Billie Jean King in a two-hour, world-televised match from a Houston Astrodome full of Beautiful People. King took him apart, but there was big prize money at stake, the ratings were huge, and this match that everyone knew was a joke drew a crowd of 34,700, the biggest ever to watch a tennis match before or since.

The stories we're reading this week are just the first beats of the drum. If there is a sniff from television — the cultural wonderland that brings you *American Gladiators, Baywatch* and *Geraldo* — agents for the two sprinters will sit down and start talking numbers. If the numbers fit, the race will go on.

Don't think of it as track; think of it as WWF wrestling. Everyone who attends admits it's probably fixed — but they scrap for ringside seats, holler when the hair is pulled, pull for the goodie and sneer at the baddie.

Scamming is not new to sports. Jesse Owens ran against a racehorse. So did Vancouver's Percy Williams. They did it for money. Throw a few million apiece into the pot and so will Bailey and Johnson. In sport, as in life, only the dollar values change.

SIXTY-TWO YARDS TO GLORY

May 18, 1997

In the late 1940s, a local sporting scribe named Duke McLeod and a few of his *Vancouver Sun* newsroom buddies marched off to Stanley Park to set a world track record. It was 3 a.m., and they'd had a few.

With as much precision as could be managed in pitch dark, they measured off exactly 62 yards from the spot where the Duke was sort of standing. A rope was stretched across the finish line and a stop-watch produced.

Given their condition it was probably just as well no one had a gun. But someone yelled "Go!" and here came the Duke, lurching pell-mell to glory.

His time has been lost with the ages, but if the old Canadian Amateur Athletic Union files are ever unearthed it will be there, because Duke and the boys wrote letters claiming the world record for the 62-yard dash. For some reason, the claim was rejected.

Flash forward a half-century. Welcome to Duke II: the 150-metre match race in Toronto between Donovan Bailey and Michael Johnson.

All right, there are a few differences. For one thing, the participants will be cold sober. The loser gets $500,000, the winner $1,500,000. (The Duke accepted a drink or two but dared not take money, lest it endanger his amateur standing.) There'll be live television and at least a modicum of world-wide interest.

But that's about it. Duke II, like Duke I, is a manufactured event over an unrecognized distance to answer a question no one asked.

Until the promoters came along, no one in track and field wondered who was the world's fastest man. It was a given: the title went to the man who held the world record over 100 metres and that was Donovan Bailey, 9.84 seconds, Atlanta Olympics. End of story.

But Michael Johnson had run the second half of his world-record 200 metres in Atlanta in 9.20. Never mind that he'd had a running start, or that with the same advantage in his finishing 100 of the 400 relay Bailey was clocked in 8.95 — inquiring minds would want to know: who really IS the world's fastest man, anyway?

Now, if Michael Johnson was from Kenya or Uganda or Korea, there'd be no question, no match race, no half-mil each just for showing up. Sponsors and TV execs would be in terminal yawn.

But Michael Johnson is an American, and in the fertile mind of a California-based hypster named Jim Butler, that made all the difference. The known universe (i.e., the 50 American states) would demand to see this fastest-man business settled once and for all. More importantly, they'd pay money to see it.

So, operating on the First Commandment of Public Relations ("You want a spontaneous demonstration, you gotta organize it") he proposed a split-the-difference showdown over 150 metres. And the drums began to beat.

They were still beating here as Bailey prepared for an appearance in the Harry Jerome Track Classic. Only now the pitch has changed.

No more long-distance insult-swapping. No more chest-beating, I'll-kick-his-ass repartee. To the chagrin of promoters, both runners have admitted that the result won't settle the burning fastest-man question. A new approach was needed. So now the race is being held "to give more exposure to the sport" and "raise the level of interest" in track and field. Nowhere in the interviews I heard was anyone crass enough to mention the money.

It is an ersatz event worthy of nothing more than a Styrofoam medal and a passing wonderment at the gullibility of man. But it will be televised world-wide and it will rake in millions.

Poor Duke. Before he lurched to the park, he should have called the CBC.

Chapter Nine

KIDS AND OTHER PETS

Maybe it's because, as manager of a soccer team of 11-year-olds, I once watched us lose to a black Labrador. OUR black Labrador. The team mascot.

One of our kids had somehow managed to lift a ball over the head of the goalie as he rushed out to stop a breakaway. The ball was rolled toward the empty net. Just as it was about to cross the line, Pep the Wonder Dog rushed out and stopped it. While our kids rushed over to berate the dog the referee handed the ball to the goalie, who kicked it downfield. The other guys scored. We lost 1-0. Pep, who had never run onto the field before, never did it again.

Or maybe it was a few years earlier when a team of six-year-olds played a big game on a gravel schoolyard and scored just before the ref blew the whistle.

"You won!" I said. "Way to go!"

The kid who'd scored looked at me.

"Does that mean we have to quit?" he asked.

He had to be kidding. He wasn't. So I yelled at the other coach and we sent them back out for another half-hour. I'm not sure who won. Nobody cared.

Kids give my life perspective. When you spend your work week dealing with mostly overpaid pro athletes who bitch about their working conditions and whine if someone else has one more zero at the end of his paycheque, there's nothing like going out in the rain and wind and mud on a Saturday morning and having some little kid say: "Whadya mean, we can't play? Gimme the ball."

Real animals — dogs, cats, ducks, elephants, horses, hoofed, clawed, wild, tame, beaked or toothy — flat scare the hell out of me. If they're on my side of the fence, I'm gone. Imaginary animals are much better. You can make up stories about them and they won't bite or call their agent. Kids, now, kids are sneaky. Without half trying they can tie knots around your heart.

Sometimes I think the best thing I ever did was bring the oranges to my son's soccer games when he was six, because once you bring the oranges they've got you. You get to watch them play and learn and grow, and before you know it you're league chairman and screaming at parents who think their kid is the new Pele and should turn pro at nine.

To shut them up I invented a new position: Right By Me. When a parent complained that his boy was playing the wrong position I'd bring him off the field, stand him next to me, look at his father and say, "This is his new position: Right By Me. Now go away, or he'll play it all game. And if we go indoors, he'll play Left Outside."

They are, thank God, exceptions. But that doesn't make them any less dangerous. Someday I may write a piece in which they're pecked to death by imaginary ducks ...

KID STUFF

December 23, 1988

In the business of organized play, only the sport and the faces change. The story remains the same. Mostly, it's a good story, but a lot of times it goes bad. When it does, this is how it happens: Adults organize kids' league. Kids play. League expands. More adults and organization needed. Dissension breaks out at adult level. Kids get caught in wringer. Adults fight some more. Board meetings grow endless. Eventually, most kids play — but some kids quit.

When it happens that way it's usually because the two adult sides of the triangle, the Big People and the Coaches, have forgotten about the third side, the only side that matters. If I was a kid, I might write it like this:

Dear Mom and Dad and Coach and all the other people involved in juvenile (insert sport):

THANK YOU for fixing it so I can play. Now, please let me.

DAD, you tell me stories about how you had to play on vacant lots and choose up sides and nobody had uniforms. Gosh, that sounds like fun.

Did your folks get into fights with other parents over who was how old or who should play on what team? Did they have to go to meetings that went on for hours and come home so angry that it made you feel bad that you were causing all that trouble? Maybe what we need, Dad, are more vacant lots.

MOM, I really appreciate the way you keep my uniform neat and drive me to practices and games and hardly ever forget when it's your turn to bring the oranges. But could you do me one more favour? Could you maybe get Dad to stop running up and down the sidelines yelling at me about how I should play? It's embarrassing, Mom, and it gets me all confused because the coach says to do one thing and Dad yells to do something else and either way I'm wrong.

COACH, can I play as much as the other kids, please? I know I'm not as good, but I try hard. And I'm never going to get any better on the sidelines. Winning is neat, but to be honest, I'd rather play and lose than sit and win.

MOM, DAD, I hope I'm not a big disappointment. Some of my friends are good athletes and maybe they're going to be pro someday and make their parents proud. But I'm not. I know that. But gosh, it's sure fun to play.

So thanks for reading this. I'm not complaining or anything. I know how hard everybody works getting the equipment ready and making sure us kids have a good place to play. It's just that sometimes you get so upset on the sidelines or after the meetings we wonder if the game is for us, or for you.

Remember when we went to registration and Joey said he didn't want to play and his dad told him he had to and it would make a man out of him? Joey and me, we're 11 years old. We don't want to be men right now. For a while, we just want to be kids.

I love you.

Your son.

TWO BRUNOS FOR A FANG

April 5, 1991

The problem with all-engulfing stories like the NHL player strike is that other stories of even greater significance get lost in the backwash. Case-in-point: Doggie trading cards.

One lousy sentence it got in this paper, which is one more than it got in the other one. I myself almost missed it, buried down at the very bottom of the Collectors' Corner column: "*But there is a 100-card set for the Iditarod dogsled race ...*"

My heart skipped a beat. Doggie trading cards. Heaven without the dying part!

A thousand questions sprang to mind. Questions like: "Are there really people out there dumb enough to collect picture cards of assorted dogs and goggled people buried so deeply in frost-covered parkas you couldn't tell the winner from a mogul?"

Or: "How do they possibly get 100 different shots out of a dog race?"

"Look, Mom, I got the whole Iditarod set! See? Here's Fang ... and King ... and Lassie ... and Bruno. Here's Bruno's driver ... and Bruno eating his driver's arm ... and ... Gosh, Mom, what's King trying to do to Lassie? And look! On the next card the driver's pouring water on them ... Boy, when they said action cards, they weren't kidding!"

Don't get me wrong. I like dogs. We had a collie for 14 years. When we were kids in Saskatchewan we used to play with the neighbour's huskies. One of them almost ripped my brother's face off. I didn't care. He was a nice husky, and I had another brother.

Now we have a Dalmatian puppy that so far has only eaten two sports jackets and the frame of my glasses. We're into puppy training, and after only two lessons she's taught me how to fetch her stick. And her leash, and her meals.

But dog trading cards?

I yield to no one in my admiration for the brave menpersons and womenpersons who make that trek across the frozen north, placing their lives in the paws of four-footed creatures fully capable of tearing their throats out if they don't like the *Alpo de jour*. But will collectors really get turned on to picture cards in which almost all of the subjects have doggie breath?

Assuming the card people can get the dogs to sit still for signing sessions without jumping off the podium every five minutes and heading for the nearest tree, tire or chesterfield leg, how many kids will line up for pawtographs?

Frankly, I think the card people are pushing it on this one. Sets of Striking Baseball Millionaires is one thing. Sports Cars of NHL Picketers, maybe. Jocks for Jail is an obvious bull market.

But dogs? Who'd be dumb enough to deal in doggie futures?

Wait a minute.

Why is the trading-card business booming? Because the people who collect them and dream of making a killing down the road haven't figured out that the more cards are issued, the quicker the bubble will burst.

Yeah. For these people, dogs might work.

DON'T FORGET THE STAIN REMOVER

February 26, 1995

The first name on the list of athletes nominated for the Canadian Sports Hall of Fame fairly leaps off the form. Runner, jumper, Olympian, World Cup champion — the list of his accomplishments covers three full pages.

As a selection-committee member, my hand is already itching to put that X beside his name, to watch him march proudly to the podium at the annual dinner to accept his nation's highest sporting honour.

There is just one problem. What if he poops on the carpet?

Could we ever live it down? Would the Hall be held to ridicule if Big Ben — arguably one of the finest athletes this country has ever produced — were to lean forward as the ribbon is placed around his manly neck, stare out over the black-tie audience, and release a calling card?

Five weeks from voting day, and the committee is in a social and moral quandary. The athlete's qualifications are beyond question. He has served his country long and well. There's no saying for certain that he'll make it, because the competition is tough — but what if he does?

How can we be sure he won't get, uh, nervous? You know how horses are when they get nervous. And once they start, they tend to be big on quantity.

We could check with Ian Millar on his regularity (Ben's, not Ian's). But is that discriminatory? Would we have to ask the other nominees? If Ben gets the nod, should we have a guy walking behind him to the podium with a shovel and a bucket? If we do, should he be black tie?

These problems come to us through the courtesy of Barbara M. Ring, a Toronto housewife who has submitted an Honoured Member Nomination Form for Big Ben.

She has listed his name, address and telephone number. (I phoned, and got voice mail. Presumably he'll call back.) She has given his place of birth in Belgium, his birthday (April 20, 1976), and the year he arrived in Canada (November, 1983). She has stipulated that she wants him considered as an athlete, not a builder, and enclosed a superbly detailed list of his accomplishments as this country's greatest show jumper.

The horse qualifies. An argument could be made that we should put him in the Hall now rather than later because he's 19 human years old, which is Lord knows how many in horse, and he should be honoured while he's around to enjoy it and has better control of his bodily functions.

There is, of course, the matter of Canadian citizenship. Did Ben ever get a green card? Is he a citizen or landed immigrant? No matter. He's ours. The CBC has done a special on him, and you can't get more Canadian than that.

Not to let out any secrets, but Ben's got my vote.

How can you not love an athlete who has beaten the world over and over again, never once gone on strike, held out for more grain or demanded a trainer be fired; an athlete who has done a lot of snorting in his day, but never anything illegal; an athlete who hits the bottle only during the mandatory urine tests; an athlete who has resisted all blandishments to write a book or do a mini-series or squeal on the gay stallions, and has no interest whatever in appearing on Barbara Walters?

In 1991, when this country was debating whether that other Ben named Johnson should be allowed to run again after being nailed as an Olympian cheat, Big Ben underwent abdominal surgery for the second time and came back to have one of his finest years. The other Ben got bigger headlines for finishing up the track. With neither a whine nor a whinny, Big Ben just kept on winning.

We thank Ms. Ring for her nomination, and for the generous post-script: "Assuming the obvious, that Big Ben will be elected to the Sports Hall of Fame this year, I would hope you would also include Ian Millar, as they are truly an outstanding team and athletes."

True. And with Millar, we wouldn't have to worry about the carpet.

"IT WAS THIS LONG! I SWEAR!"

August 12, 1992

Well, it's about time.

I've been suspicious of fishing derbies since the time in the '70s when the winner of the first-prize boat in the *Vancouver Sun* Free

Salmon Derby was discovered to have bought the fish elsewhere and brought it to Deep Cove to smuggle onto his boat early on Derby Day.

But for one tiny mistake, he might have gotten away with it. He brought the fish to the marina by taxi. Strangely enough, he was the only person all day to climb into the back of a cab toting a huge dead fish and ask to be taken to the ocean. As I recall, the home address on his entry form turned out to be a vacant lot. Fishermen are not here on scholarship.

Pause here to admit to a certain bias.

My first job in newspapers was typing out the individual entries for the King Fisherman derby run by the *Daily Colonist* in Victoria. Catch a fish, you got your name in the paper along with your address, type of lure, weight of fish and place it was caught. If you caught 10 fish, you were in there 10 times.

For two summers that was almost all I did, all shift: type fishing entries by the thousands. They finally let me off when I crossed my eyes and explained to the managing editor that I was getting an irresistible urge to go upriver and spawn.

As a result, I do not like fishing derbies. Once, when the late Stu Keate ordered a column on the *Sun* derby, I wrote a piece about aliens fishing the planet Earth for young fish (called Kids) by dangling lures shaped like hot dogs in places called Schools. "Haul 'em in, stick a knife there in the belly button, and you gut 'em with one up-and-down stroke," the alien explained. "Fillet and pan-fry 'em and they taste great. And don't worry about the hook. Kids don't feel pain. It's a scientific fact."

They never asked me again.

Anyway, about the Kenora derby and the lie-detector test. Organizers say that with $85,000 in prizes there's always the temptation to break the rules, so they made the winners take a polygraph test, run by a Winnipeg private investigator. Mike Hammerhead, maybe, or Oarlock Holmes.

Good on them, as far as it goes, which personally I don't consider far enough.

Fishermen are always talking about what great sportsmen they are. Anyone who's listened to all those stories about the big one that got away has to know these people are on some kind of hallucinogenic drug. Let 'em pee in a bottle like all the other big-time athletes.

Tinkle, tinkle, little angler,
Take a sample from your dangler.

Not that all fishermen are liars. For instance, I never questioned the veracity of Denny Veitch, the former general manager of the B.C. Lions, when he illustrated the length of the one that got away. But then, Denny has only one arm.

DONALD, WHERE'S YOUR TROUSERS?

December 17, 1992

Personally, I'm *glad* that the NHL has gone Mickey Mouse and let in The Mighty Ducks of Anaheim. Maybe now we'll get some answers to the questions that really matter, like how come Donald Duck doesn't wear pants?

Everybody from the late Walt Disney himself to current Disney boss Michael Eisner has dodged that one.

Here's this duck with no visible means of support, living with and apparently raising three little boy ducks named Hughie, Louie and Dewey who are supposed to be his nephews (although we've never been offered one shred of proof) *and all four of them are wandering around without pants.*

In fact, if memory serves, when Donald's girlfriend, Daisy, drops in she doesn't wear pants, either. And in the last few years there's been a little girl duck named Webbigail wearing nothing below her waist but shoes.

So where are the social workers when you really need them? Why hasn't someone noticed that the kids are hardly ever in school? Where does Donald get the money to feed them? Aside from a Navy hitch and some factory work during the war, what's he ever done? Is he exploiting the kids? Is it blackmail? Has he got pictures of Uncle Scrooge McDuck (the world's richest duck) getting it on with a teenage mallard?

Are the NHL governors really sure they want to climb into bed with people who condone behaviour like that? Or are they tolerating Donald in the hope of getting next to Scrooge and his money bin in much the same manner they have tapped into Bruce McNall?

There's something else the governors should be asking, a question that has plagued mankind almost from the day Mickey first appeared in *Mickey Mouse Magazine* in 1935: If Mickey is a mouse and Donald is a duck and Pluto is a dog — what is a Goofy?

Pluto barks and chases cars. Goofy talks and drives cars. He looks like a dog — beagle-ish kind of face, big black nose, long floppy ears — but he walks upright. (Okay, he wears pants. A good thing, too, because he spends all his time on his hind legs. It's either pants or a trenchcoat.) He has a home. He goes skiing and sky-diving. What kind of an animal is he?

You know what we're talking here, don't you?

Steroids.

If this is a dog, he's on something. The folks at Disney have built themselves a better dog. Not a smarter dog, but bigger and a shade more dexterous with his front paws. And you know what that could mean.

Think about it. Here we have a big, ungainly, tangle-footed creature who falls down a lot but keeps getting up and in his very ineptitude comes off both lovable and marketable. Is that or is that not the perfect player for a team destined to lose game after game?

Maybe, all these years, the Disney people haven't been building a movie and entertainment empire after all. Maybe it's been a cover-up. Maybe what they've really been building toward all along is an all-Goofy NHL franchise.

Is it coincidence that in several Disney cartoons Goofy has been seen ice-skating? Not very well, but on an expansion franchise who'd notice?

Lovable dogs, half-naked ducks and Mickey Mouse at the ticket window. Look around the NHL and tell me it wouldn't work.

TIME OF THE TIGER

April 15, 1997

At a banquet where his son would be named *Sports Illustrated*'s sportsman of the year for 1996, Earl Woods laid out his expectations — no, his certainties — for the young Tiger.

"Tiger will do more than any man in history to change the course of humanity," he said.

Not the course of sport, or the course of golf, or even the course of the Red Sea. The course of humanity. When someone asked if that included Nelson Mandela, Gandhi and Buddha, he said yes, it did, "because he has a larger forum than any of them." When he called his son the Chosen One, the capital letters were a given.

SI must have bought it. The cover photo of Tiger Woods was made to look like stained glass. Saint Tiger, Lord of the greens, the tee box and all that lies between. Saint Tiger, for whom all but perfection is deemed failure.

He is 21 years old, and already he has been spared the measure held to mere mortals, greatness maintained over time. Nicklaus, Palmer, Trevino, Player — some of the greatest ever to swing a club are calling him the best ever.

Not potentially the best. Just the best, period. Careers are measured over time, not over a few tournaments — but in Tiger's case, time seems the only part of the game he cannot mould to his personal specifications.

And you found yourself wondering, as he pulled on the green jacket at the Augusta National course where, not that many years ago, the competitive colours were green, magnolia and Caucasian, if it is humanly possible that he can keep it up.

Not the golf. With that honeyed swing, the unbelievable distance, the iron-willed composure and the well-disguised cockiness of youth, the golf will be the easy part. Carrying the world like a cosmic golf bag might be something else.

Arnold Palmer came out of Pennsylvania with that chopping drive likened to a dockworker dropping a crate. His assignment was to beat a course to death, and he did. He was of the world. No one ever told him he had to change it.

Lee Trevino graduated from dirt greens and putt-with-a-pop-bottle side bets he didn't dare lose because his pockets were empty. He had no Nike ads suggesting there were courses he couldn't play. No one found his minority status marketable. He laughed at it. ("I used to be Mexican, but now that I've got money, I'm Spanish.") His burdens were his own, and he carried them with a bubbling joy that made him, in his own way, as popular as Arnie.

Nicklaus was Fat Jack, jeered at first for his girth, despised because he dared to challenge and beat the beloved Arnie. He pared his body, styled his hair and destroyed the record book. But no one said he had to be Gandhi.

Tiger Woods turned pro and with one stroke of a pen made more money than Arnold Palmer earned on the course in all his years as a pro — some $43,000,000 to embrace the Nike swoosh, other deals boosting the total to $60,000,000 before he ever swung a club as a pro.

He's 21 and a multimillionaire, and his time is not his own. Everyone wants a piece of it: an hour here, a banquet there. "It's scary," says Johnny Miller. "Any tournament he's not in becomes second-rate." And Earl Woods expects him to change the world.

It is not the golf that could get him. It's that he is allowed no margin for error. He tells a slightly racy joke in a cab, and it's in the tabloids. He skips a banquet and he is arrogant. He admits that sometimes the crowds get to him, and he is going high-hat. And when he goes to bed at night, he knows that it's only going to get worse.

He is the Chosen One. It's been planned since he was five. "I don't know exactly what form this will take," admits Earl Woods. "But he'll have the power to impact nations. Not people. Nations! The world is just getting a taste of his power."

And for the Chosen One, there can be no days off.

GROOMING THE TIGER

May 20, 1997

The weekend-shift hair-suit-and-teeth guy doing sports on *Newsworld* has just announced that Tiger Woods has signed another $30,000,000 endorsement deal, this time with American Express.

To earn the money, plus an additional $1,000,000 that goes to his charitable foundation, he basically has to smile for the next five years and tell the world that he never leaves home without his AMEX card.

You can see where that would be important.

He's just a kid, and kids are always running short of cash. What if it's Friday night and he wants to take Betty-Lou to the movies, or maybe buy Augusta National? He checks his wallet and — omigosh, he left his $120,000,000 in endorsement money and his PGA earnings in the vault. Don't you just hate it when that happens?

"Don't worry, Betty-Lou," he cries, whipping out his personalized platinum AMEX card with his picture in the middle riding the Nike swoosh. "This card is accepted almost anywhere in the world! And it has no credit limit, so even with extra butter on the popcorn we'll still be able to buy a mountain with a really neat view so we can park and make out in private! Not only that, but Dad says I can stay out 'til 11 as long as I promise to win the Grand Slam and become more famous than Gandhi."

"Oooh, Tiger," coos Betty-Lou. "Won't that be hard?"

"Naah! The Slam part's easy, and I'll have my marketing people get on the Gandhi thing first thing in the morning. Couple of photo ops of me hitting a driver across the Ganges — no, the LENGTH of it, driver and wedge. Maybe a Tiger Woods line of Gandhi caps — I mean, the dude was cool, all right, but what did HE ever shoot at Augusta ...?"

Call me cynical, but I am growing just a tad weary of Tiger Woods. Not the kid who can hit a ball over the curvature of the earth. What's not to like?

It's the Corporate Tiger, the Image Tiger, the father who writes a book in which he says his first marriage and children were God's way of giving him the training he would need to raise Tiger; the IMG people who are smart enough to turn him into an instant icon, and stupid enough to let him come off back-to-back 64s at the Byron Nelson and say, "I don't have my A game yet."

The commentators fawning on him. The networks running an hour-long tribute to Tiger before the Masters, pretending it's journalism when it's actually a pre-packaged IMG production sugared and honeyed and loaded with his sponsors' logos and narrated by an announcer who also happens to be an IMG client. We'll be right back with more hard-hitting, in-depth journalism, but first — another shot of his Titleist ball!

The fried-chicken-and-collard-greens controversy. Fuzzy Zoeller made a thoughtless remark and the America-wide knee-jerks are loud enough to crack windows. K-Mart ends a 21-year relationship because Tiger is perceived in America to be black. But his own reported penchant for off-colour and gay jokes, though published in *GQ* magazine, is virtually ignored or written off as one of the foibles of youth.

Tiger Woods may become the greatest golfer who ever swung a club. Certainly he will be the richest — and may be already. Given the pressures already placed on him, he may also crack like a walnut. If he does, he'll need more than an AMEX card to make it back.

BUM STEER IN MISSISSIPPI

September 16, 1992

Fool that I am, I thought the high-school football coach who bit the head off a toad had achieved the ultimate in inspirational speeches.

It happened in Texas a few years ago. Come to think of it, maybe it was a newt. Whatever it was, it wandered across the practice field while he was whipping his boys into a frenzy over what they were gonna do to those pissants in the Big Game come Friday night, and he just flat grabbed that sucker and chomped.

There was considerable fuss.

They might still be talking about it down there if it wasn't for another high-school coach whose team was about to play a team called the Eagles. He painted a chicken in the school colours, threw it out onto the field and screamed at his players to "Stomp that eagle!"

A surprising number of people took offence, which makes me wonder how Jackie Sherrill is going to fare at Mississippi State now that he's castrated the bull.

Well, what else was he supposed to do? The damned thing was too big to bite its head off. It might not have liked being painted Texas burnt orange and white, and probably wouldn't have stood for a stomping.

Besides, those are high-school stunts. This is university. You got to think grown up and big. So, when Jackie Sherrill was psyching up his Bulldogs in the days before the big game against Texas Longhorns and they admitted they didn't even know what a steer *was* — well, hell, he had to do *something*. So, he had a calf castrated by its owner on the practice field. Presto: instant steer.

Now that a complaint has been filed with the state Animal Rescue League and the associate dean of MSU's school of veterinary medicine has deemed the event "out of place" on the practice field, Sherrill has felt moved to justify his actions.

"One, it's educational," he said. "That's probably the biggest reason. And motivation."

Asked how he thought viewing a castration would motivate his players to go out and beat Texas, he replied: "That's everybody's different perception."

Yes, indeed.

"Uh, coach? I been studyin' the Texas game films and I notice the QB tends to stand a little bit spready-legged. If we were to get in there quick-like and combine this castration thing with the chomp that high-school coach put on the toad, we could maybe get him out of his offence real fast."

"Hot damn, Billy-Bob, you're right. Hit 'em low, hit 'em fast, and chomp, that's the stuff! It's like that Churchill guy said: 'Give us the tools, and we'll finish the job.' "

Sherrill stands by his motivational techniques. "They were going to perform the castration anyway," he says. "We didn't do anything inhumane to an animal ... I don't think the calf was embarrassed by anyone watching him."

Besides, didn't his Bulldogs beat those Longhorns 28-10? Just goes to show you: there ain't nuthin' beats a college education.

BIG WORLD, SMALL SHOULDERS

July 26, 1996

You want to know what's wrong with the Olympic Games? Look at the pictures of American gymnast Kerri Strug plastered across sports pages all over the world.

Look at the soft cast already on her right leg. Look at the wan, half-hearted smile on her face as she waves to the crowd. Compare it to the happy grin of coach Bela Karolyi as he carries her from the podium. Read his answer when she said, before the final vault that gave the U.S. its first-ever team-gymnastics title, "I can't feel my leg."

"Shake it out," he said. "We need one more good vault."

So Kerri Strug, who didn't know what was wrong with her leg or what would happen to it when she landed, went out and made a final vault, essentially landing one-legged. Karolyi hugged her and told the world, "She showed everything that a great athlete can show."

Then, and only then, they took her to hospital to find out what was wrong.

It was a lateral strain on her left ankle, suffered when she missed her previous vault. Nothing serious. But it could have been. It could have been a muscle tear or a pinched or torn nerve or a stress fracture or any one of a number of things. The point is that Karolyi didn't know — couldn't know — before he sent her out for that final vault.

But he sent her. "I knew she will not say no," he said later. "There was no hesitation. This is a once-in-a-lifetime experience."

Not for Karolyi, it isn't. He's been there before. He was there at the Montreal Olympics in 1976 with a shy, waif-like little girl named Nadia Comaneci, who reeled off perfect 10s with seamless precision and ended each with a brief, mechanical little smile — not because she was happy, as it turned out, but because she'd been taught that a smile like that at the end could mean an extra fraction of a point from the judges.

She was a little girl with gold dangling around her neck. But she had to be taught how to smile. We are doing something wrong. We are looking too much to the result and not enough to the effort.

How else can you explain the words of then-American women's swim-team coach Flip Darr at the 1975 World Aquatic Games in Cali, Colombia? Victory, he told reporters at a media conference, would go to the swimmers who could push themselves furthest past the wall of pain.

"What would be the maximum?" someone asked.

"Well," he said, "I guess the maximum would be death."

It doesn't have to be that way.

At those same Games I had a brief conversation with a 13-year-old, 113-pound bubble of a girl from Halifax named Nancy Garapick, who'd come out of nowhere in the past months and was now being hailed as Canada's best hope to win gold.

"I feel like I've got a whole country on my shoulders," she said. "Gee, I wish I could just swim."

That night she stood on the blocks in the 100-metre backstroke between East Germany's Birgit Treiber and Ulrike Richter, a dinghy between twin destroyers. She held on for a bronze. Two nights later she broke the world record in the 200-metre, but settled for silver behind Treiber.

When she came out of the water there was a suspicion of tears in her eyes. "I tried," she said. "I really tried."

Her coach, Nigel Kemp, scooped her into his arms. "Sunshine," he said, "you did just fine."

Bela Karolyi would never have understood.

MACHO JIM (CON'T.)

October 23, 1992

The Even Further Adventures of Macho Jim: Sportsman, Animal Lover and Outdoorsy-Type Guy ...

As I've often said, even city-type guys can have outdoorsy-type adventures in which ferocious (well, barking and mewing and whinnying) animals play a vital role. You don't even have to leave home.

Remember Y'Arba Samantha, the horse I bought my daughter? Teresa gathered and packaged Sam's manure and sold it for 50¢ a bag to help pay the expenses. Then I noticed that it was costing me more to fill the front end than she was making unloading the back. I swear the damned horse smiled.

Remember the two ducks, Poopsie and Poopsie, who landed in my swimming pool and wouldn't go away because they fell in love with the decorative decoy?

Remember when we woke up to the smell of burning insulation or wiring, called the fire department, and the firemen rushed in with their axes, sniffed the air and said, "Skunk! Your dog's run into a skunk!"? And we didn't have any tomato juice to wash the smell away so we used V-8 and the dog looked like something in the Emergency Ward after a knife fight?

Those were the easy ones.

The time in Thailand when I climbed on the elephant ready to pound my chest, holler, "Ungowa, Tantor!" and give the cry of the great bull ape, and the guide made me fasten my seat belt, that was humiliating. Especially when he told me that all elephants in Thailand were called Chang and I said in North America all elephants were called Gerald in honour of the great jazz singer, Elephants Gerald. "Get off elephant," he said.

But now things are getting serious.

We have a new dog, a year-old Dalmatian named Risky for reasons soon to become obvious. She got out of the yard only once, just often enough to come back with her left hind leg raised and obviously hurting.

"No break," said the vet as I paid the bill. "It will clear up."

It did, but Risky was now so used to running on three legs she wasn't using the other one. Back to the vet.

"Give her physiotherapy," he said as I paid the bill. "Move the leg up and down 10 minutes twice a day."

We gave the dog physiotherapy, moving the leg up and down and telling her to put pressure on it. She paid no attention. Maybe it's true: Maybe Dalmatians *are* hard of hearing. She was just getting back to using it a little when she started limping on the other back leg.

"She has a tear in her paw," said the vet.

Hey, how tough could that be?

"And an intra-digital cyst," he said. "It's infected. It'll have to come out. Surgery. No food after 10 p.m. tonight, bring her in tomorrow. We'll put her under and remove it."

She's coming home today. I can hardly wait. She won't walk on her left hind leg and now she won't be able to walk on her right hind leg. Leg-wise, she's hitting two-for-four. What's she supposed to do for the next week, handstands?

"Never mind," my wife said sweetly. "It could be worse."

"How?" I demanded.

"You could have bought an octopus."

BACKLASH

February 23, 1997

We were talking soccer a couple of years ago, a bunch of coaches, managers, line-runners and orange-bringers looking ahead to another season of the chaotic wonderment that is working in minor sport, when somebody said, "Remember: no hugging the kids."

Excuse me?

"Don't hug the kids," he repeated. "These days, you hug a kid, you pat him on the ass as he goes on the field, somebody might get the wrong idea, and you could be in serious trouble ..."

And that is the backlash of the evil that has seeped through the lives of people like Sheldon Kennedy and places like Maple Leaf Gardens as pedophiles fish the streams of childhood.

In a latchkey society loaded with single-parent families and kids in need of hugs, the people who can give them — the teachers, the coaches, the team managers, the volunteers, the people who are there when parents can't or don't choose to be — have to pause and consider the possible consequences.

Even writing this brings a stomach lurch. What if people read it wrong? What if they somehow think you're *defending* these animals? You work with kids, or used to, and will again. How will this look? What if ...?

But the parents of the thousands upon thousands of kids they send into minor sport need to face up to two chilling certainties:

*Pedophiles will always stalk the rinks and playing fields as surely as hunters stalk waterholes, because that's where their prey congregates.

*Most of you aren't doing a good enough job watching your kids.

You're good parents. You work at it. When your child enrolls in school you meet the teachers, talk to the principal, maybe join the PTA, because these are the people who'll be influencing and guiding your child in the coming year.

Then you enroll that child in soccer or hockey or baseball or lacrosse and turn him over to someone like me, to practise twice a week after school in a local park and play games on a weekend that most of you never see. I probably have as much or more influence on that child as his teachers, because I decide whether he makes the team. I decide whether he *plays.* And most of you don't know who the hell I am.

This is not a call for a witch hunt. It's a call to get involved. Talk to the people who coach your kids. Get to know them. Watch the way they interact. Meet the other parents. Watch the system at work, because it's a great one and does an enormous amount of good. Be happy that your kids can be part of it, and that there are people who will take the time to make it happen. But watch.

As for the hugging, which I will never stop doing as long as there are kids who look to need it — two small stories of two small boys.

Dustin was on one of the teams my son, Chris, and I coached from age 11 to 17. He's on his own now. One day Chris visited his apartment and found a blown-up snapshot of the two of us on the wall.

Dustin was embarrassed. "Oh, I guess I never mentioned it," he said. "But sometimes you two were about all I had."

And then there was Jonathan, age 11, whose earnest ineptness often drew the ire of his teammates. One day he left the practice crying. I asked him what was wrong.

"Nobody likes me," he sobbed.

I put my arm across his shoulders and hugged. "I like you," I said. "Chris likes you."

He looked up and gave a little smile. "I know," he said.

Chapter Ten

PSST! WANNA BE A PUBLISHER?

In September of 1995 a man waved a bunch of money in my face and convinced me that giving up a daily sports column I'd written for 25 years to write for a new sports weekly was a hell of an idea.

They would also give me a title: Associate Publisher, which I later found out was taken from the Latin and meant "Responsibility Without Power." Who could resist?

Sports Only lasted exactly one year: an exasperating, frustrating, maddening, exhilarating, mind-bending, ulcer-twinging 12 months I wouldn't trade for a clean shot at a Pulitzer. We were under-staffed, under-financed and under the guns of Vancouver's two-pronged Daily Monopoly — Southam's one-building, two-paper *Sun* and *Province* — which reacted by throwing about a million extra bucks into services they didn't have to provide when they were the only game in town.

But, Lord, it was fun.

We were a tabloid that didn't outlaw three-syllable words, never believed that there was no tomorrow or that when the going got tough, the tough got going or that athletes were anything more or less than people with muscles who sweat a lot and could probably win any spitting contest this side Spittoons 'R' Us.

And we were a tabloid with broadsheet space, unfettered by the to-hell-with-the-story, tell-it-in-this-much-space-or-we'll-cut-it-to-fit mentality of the daily tabs, where the Second Coming would have to be done in 15 inches under a head that said, "HE'S BACK!"

Along the way, we got to sit down with tryers and hopers, winners and losers, dreamers and schemers and a horse named Ruth who was actually a stallion, had his own fan club, and would nip whatever protruding part you were foolish enough to put within range.

They told us their stories and we got to write them. It's what the business used to be about ...

GARRY SAWATZKY: UNCAGED LION

B.C. Lions' training camp, June 1995. The kids from the detention home approach Garry Sawatzky with a curious hesitancy, some smirking, others trying desperately to be cool. "They can't fool me," he says. "I've been there. I cut through to their souls."

He was 27 years old and doing life for murder when he decided to play pro football. Life 10, they call it: Life behind bars and maybe full parole after 10, the maybe hung out there like a candy you can't quite reach.

There was no logic to the decision. He hadn't played since high school. He had no way of knowing when he'd get out or how he could go about it when he did. He was just another big, tough kid who'd found the weight room in Manitoba's Stony Mountain Penitentiary. For three years, he'd trained like an animal, twice a day, six days a week. "In prison, lifting defines who you are," admits Garry Sawatzky. "But it doesn't matter a damn if you can't fight."

Along the way, he developed an interest in philosophy (he's currently five credits short of his BA) and, although he is not of Native blood, in the teachings of the tribal elders who visited the prison's Native population. He was sitting in a sweat lodge, weak from the heat and the fasting, almost hallucinogenic, when it came to him out of nowhere: He would play pro football. That was where he made his deal.

"I made a promise to myself, and maybe to my Creator," he says. " 'If you give me football, I'll spend the rest of my life working with kids — young offenders, kids headed the wrong way.' I have done some bad things, but I keep my promises."

He joined a group of lifers speaking to kids visiting from drop-in centres, making friends and laying out the truth as he'd lived it. He ran a Children's Wish Foundation in the prison, staging boxing matches to raise the money. And a strange thing happened: The more he did, the more he got little breaks that inched him closer to football.

"They ask me what happened, and I tell them, 'If you're going to carry a knife, you're going to use it, or somebody's going to take it away and use it on you ...' "

— Garry Sawatzky

"I'm not a victim," Sawatzky insists. "That's crap. I was a kid who grew up angry, with a lot of negative energy. My dad was a hard person, more into work than family. He had a farm around Stonewall, Manitoba. The family came second, but the barn had better be clean. My parents split when I was 16, and it got rough. We had it out physically. I was 17 and I finally won one. That was when I left home."

He worked two jobs, on the docks and unloading trucks for a courier company, saving for a Harley. He got it, met Colleen, and joined a motorcycle club called Los Brovos. "I hated it," Colleen Sawatzky says. "Not the bikers, the life. I could see it going nowhere and taking Garry with it."

It took him to an 18-month sentence for robbery. Then on the long weekend in May of 1985, it took him on a club run for a barbecue at the park.

"The police knew we were coming. The weapons the club carried — legal, registered firearms — were all in the trunk of one car. Every motorcycle club on a run has them, just in case a rival gang should come along and decide to put us away. But this was a barbecue, nothing more, and we were well away from the main campground."

Sawatzky, on day parole after the robbery, wasn't surprised to be there. But he walked into the main campground, just talking to people he knew.

"A truckload of guys, blind drunk, showed up from town. They were doing just what we used to do — go to a party and beat up the guys from Winnipeg. And I was wearing motorcycle-club colours. "

Someone shoved him. Sawatzky responded with "a light slap on the face. I could have let it go, but they were playing tough-ass. The fight was on. Pretty soon they were all over me, pulling chunks out of my hair."

As he was falling, he pulled out his knife and started stabbing into the pile. "I honestly thought I was stabbing arms," he says softly, "making them let go. When they got off me, I walked away, but I'd stabbed him through the heart and his lung." Wayne Paul Doyle was dead. He was 19 years old.

"We were married in prison, wedding dress and silk flowers that had to be there three days early so they could be checked. There was a chaplain, and bridesmaids and guests, and someone inside had baked a cake. When it was over, as we crossed the yard to the conjugal-visit trailer, the warden wanted me strip-searched. They settled for patting me down."

— Colleen Sawatzky

The 10 months awaiting trial were spent in solitary confinement in a provincial institution in Headingley, Manitoba, the result of an argument with a guard at the remand centre in Winnipeg.

Colleen, 19-month-old Clinton in her lap, was sitting across a table from Sawatzky in the visiting area. They could lean across the table to kiss. Otherwise, they couldn't touch. The guard accused Sawatzky of caressing Colleen's breast. Sawatzky threatened to get him. "The guard got so mad, they strip-searched the baby," Colleen says. "Even lifted his bum and looked into the diaper."

Colleen Sawatzky looking through the bars in the solitary cell at Headingley — the bunk, the open toilet, the rats, the ice on the walls, her husband in shackles, leg irons and dirty overalls. "He looked like an animal. There was just the toilet and the cot. The smell of urine was everywhere. Criminology students on tour could look right at him. For exercise, they took him into a yard in chains like a dog, and led him around in a circle."

While Colleen protested and demanded that, at the very least, the handcuffs be removed when she visited with the baby, Garry Sawatzky plucked threads from his overalls and fashioned a noose. "I wanted to catch a rat," he says. "I wanted to see what they'd do if I proved that they were there."

The trial lasted a week. Sentence was passed on Valentine's Day, 1986. Second-degree murder. Life. They stared at each other through the glass. "Get on with your life," Garry told her.

Instead, her family and friends behind her, she went to work, raised their son, took criminology courses because they might help her understand what he was going through, and built her family around four trailer visits per year, 72 hours apiece, for nine years.

Two days before Colleen Sawatzky's first visit, the biggest snowstorm of the year hit Winnipeg. The city was virtually shut down. She pulled on snowsuit and mukluks, and headed their beater into the snow. "I made it," she says. "Fifteen miles. I'm still not sure how."

"I'd visit him two to three times a week, 15 miles to Stony Mountain. And every four months, he could hold me and his son. People used to kid about what a wreck I'd be from having sex 45 times in three days, and razz me for taking Clinton. It's not like that. Of course I took him. There was a TV and a living room and two bedrooms. Every four months, we could be a family."

— Colleen Sawatzky

The relationship, rocky before the killing, strengthened under stress. On October 26, 1987, they were married in prison. When their daughter, Cheyenne, was born, Garry got a pass to be at the hospital. And they waited for the parole that might not come.

"I'd try to talk about the future and he'd get upset," Colleen says. "He didn't let me dream. Dreaming was a luxury we couldn't afford."

"He's the most incredible physical specimen I've ever seen. He's changed. Why can't we?"

— Blue Bombers' coach Urban Bowman, 1992

The road to pro football began by chance with a visit to the prison by former Winnipeg Blue Bombers' running back Tim Jessie. He passed the word to Urban Bowman, Bombers' interim head coach as Cal Murphy recovered from his heart transplant.

Bowman gave Sawatzky an evaluation on a day-pass trip. He was grass green, but 312 pounds and quick. Newspapers and TV stations became interested. He might have won a training-camp shot. But the manslaughter case was too close to home. As the interest and the controversy grew, the prison responded by transferring him out west.

"Basically, they wanted me out of their hair, and it cost me another year in jail, because if the Bombers had taken me, there would have been a parole. But it was the best thing, because I got out here [to B.C.] and met [line coach] Gary Hoffman."

At his parole hearing in B.C., he said nothing about football. He went out and got jobs to rebuild his family. But football was still his plan A. He just didn't know how he'd work it.

He was still working with kids, and doing his gym time. Again, fate stepped in. During one workout in 1994, he met George Chayka, the Lions' director of marketing. Chayka mentioned him to coach Dave Ritchie, and he had his second shot.

The Lions let him attend a tryout camp, then he got a spot on the practice roster, working during the day, seeing the family afterward, and checking back into a halfway house at night.

"Coach Ritchie told me everything was against me — my age [32], my inexperience, everything. But he said he wouldn't stand in my way. He and [GM] Eric Tillman gave me the chance. Michael Gray, the DL coach, actually put the pads on and went at me during the tryout. And coach Hoffman just worked and worked with me. He's like a teacher. He gave me assignments, notebooks with this new language I had to learn. I was terrible. I was learning."

This year, he has made it to the roster as the backup offensive lineman. He does not play often, but he can feel the progress, feel himself getting comfortable, feel the instincts taking over.

"I can feel myself accelerating, getting better at a faster rate. I know now that I can play this game for four or five more years."

Meanwhile, the work with the kids goes on — singly, in groups, for organizations or on his own, kids alone or kids in gangs. There is no preaching. He hangs out with them, even goes into prison and walks the yard with them.

"I'm not trying to change the world," he says. "I know you can't reach them all. But when I talk to some of these kids, I see them listening. They say 'Everything you said, that's me.' I tell them I know they cry into their pillows at night because I did. They know I'm not lying."

"I was void of any social conscience. I left home in a hostile mood, I was in the gym to let off all that hostility. Looking back, it's like seeing another person."

— Garry Sawatzky

Sawatzky steps into the Vancouver apartment, filling the tiny hallway. He weighs 290 now, 20-some pounds lighter than he reached in prison. He's picked up Cheyenne, three, from day care.

Clinton, 11, is at the Nintendo. There is a normalcy to it that still catches him by surprise.

He has lived with his family only since his full parole came through. The halfway-house days are over. It's taken some getting used to. "We have a normal life and everything," he says, "but I still can't get used to sleeping in the same bed with someone. I use a cot in my son's room."

The planning is not over. The spirituality he learned in prison has grown. He has his own medicine bag, and sometimes burns sweetgrass during meditation. And the promise is still there for the keeping. Down the road, he sees a farm — Dream Farm, he calls it — where troubled kids with dreams can come and learn a trade. He doesn't know how he's going to do it, only that some day he will.

Colleen Sawatzky sits in her living room, reliving the memories and smiling at her kids. Clinton is proud of his father, who plays for the B.C. Lions. She has her work as a dental assistant and apartment-block residential manager, she has her family, and on Saturdays she can indulge her passion for garage sales. Finally, she can afford to dream.

PAVEL BURE:
ROCKET LAUNCH

He thought for a while about going to Siberia, where the money was good because conditions were so bad — 14-hour days, no toilets, no showers, nothing but work and cold. If he could stand it for a couple of years, he could bring some money home for his family. And maybe, just maybe, he could buy himself a car ...

Pavel Bure comes to the interview in sweats, hair still damp from the shower after another of the workouts that inch him closer to the day he can play hockey again. He does not look like a hockey player or a millionaire at 24. He looks like Ron Howard playing Opie, Tom Sawyer after Aunt Polly made him take a bath. Okay, he drives a Mercedes — but he will never forget the Lada.

"In Russia, is big difference," he says. "You can't just go out and buy a car. You had to line up, to get on a list, some people for years. But if you do something special, something big like win a world championship, then you get a favour: You still have to buy the car, but you go to the top of the list.

"I remember, we go to Bern and win the world championship and I go to the coach [Victor Tikhonov] and say, 'Can I get a car now?' He says, 'No.' I have to do something else. So we go to the Goodwill Games, which is very big, almost like the Olympics for us. We win that, too, and I say, 'Now can I get it?' He says, 'Yes you can.' Even then, I waited six or seven months, so it was a big deal, getting that Lada."

Even then, by Moscow standards, he had it all: The car, the apartment, the great clothes, the money — "not like here, but not many people at 19 have these things there, so I was a pretty big level. At 19, if you have a car, it is a huge deal. Here, at 19 you've got a car, so what?

"The police used to stop me all the time because they could see me driving this car. In Russia, you're not allowed to drive your father's car without special permission. They would stop me and ask for driver's licence, then ask whose car it is. I say, 'Mine' and they say, 'How come?' Then: 'Oh you must be hockey player. Is okay, then.' "

"I never thought of NHL, but I remember I say to my folks and to my friends, 'Listen, I don't know how, but someday I'm going to have a lot of money. Maybe it will be something else. But I'm going to have money.' "

By the time he was 16, Pavel had tried rich and he'd tried poor. It was no stretch to figure that rich was better.

"We had money," he says. "We weren't rich like here, but my father [Vladimir] was a great athlete, a champion swimmer who swam in the Olympics, so we got money — not money like hockey players got, because hockey and soccer are the two main sports, but we could afford an apartment, car, good clothes. We could go for vacation. So we had some money. But when he retired in 1979, after a couple or three years, it was gone. Because he couldn't swim anymore, he couldn't make good money. He was professional coach, but coaches in Russia don't make much.

"So basically from 11 to 16 it was a really hard time. We weren't starving, but it was hard. My mom, she never worked before. She had to go to work as manager in supermarket and it was hard for her because she had lived well, and now she had to do this."

He knew that somehow he had to change all that, and thought of the logging camps of Siberia. But just about then, things started to get good. Suddenly, he was playing hockey for money.

"My first hockey salary, I was 14, and it was 40 rubles [five rubles per U.S. dollar at that time] every month for playing junior hockey with the Red Army team. My mom was making 180 rubles for managing a supermarket, and I was making 40. The next year, they start to pay me 70, and when I got to the main professional team at 16, the salary was 120 rubles. But I would get only 10, because the rest of the money I would give to my mom."

He discusses money only because the subject was raised, and to correct a common misconception of a poor kid from a foreign country suddenly faced with the twin pitfalls of North America and sudden wealth.

"There was no big-headed, no jump," he says. "My father, when he was swimming, made 300 rubles a month. Normal people were making 150 and at 16 I was making 120. It was quite a bit, you know? At 18, I make the national team and they start to pay me in dollars if you win something big. The first time we win the Worlds, they gave us $1,200 and it was, like, huge. When I was a kid, we would come to Canada for 15 days and they would give us 100 bucks, and this time they gave us $1,200 and it was really big money. A year later, I went with the national team and won the world championship and they gave us $10,000.

"So, it is not like suddenly I had everything. It came slowly: A little more money every year, then the car, then the apartment. So when I came here, I thought, 'Okay, maybe I get a better car'. And I got a Toyota Camry."

He had taken the next step. He was in the National Hockey League. Now all he had to do was prove he belonged. But he was used to that.

"Yes, my dad pushed. I think you have to push. If he had come up to me 15 years ago and said, 'You are the best, you're great, you don't have to work anymore,' I would have said, 'Hey, I'm great, I'm the best. Why should I work?' But he would say, 'Yes, you're good, but do you know how many players on the Red Army team and the national team are better than you? You have to work harder.' "

You listen to Pavel Bure, and time and countries melt into one. In Moscow, the young Pavel dreams of owning a car, as a young Wayne Gretzky did in Brantford, Ontario, a decade earlier. In Moscow, Bure knew that someday he would have a lot of money. In Brantford, Gretzky's grandma Mary reached back to her European roots and said he would, too. "Hairy arms," she explained. "You have hairy arms. It means you will be rich."

In Brantford, the pre-teen Gretzky wants to sleep rather than attend an early practice. "Okay," says Walter Gretzky. "But when you're an adult taking a lunch kit to work, you remember what you had a chance to be, and gave it up." Gretzky gets up, and goes to practice, the work ethic given stronger root. In Moscow, the pre-teen Bure gets another best-forward trophy and Vlad is there beside him. "Congratulations," he says. "But it's no big deal. You may be the best player here, but there are lots better than you. You have to get better."

Vladimir Bure began working with his two sons (Valeri, three years younger, is in the Montreal Canadiens' chain) when Pavel was six. He was a swimmer who knew nothing about hockey. "He would go watch the Red Army or the national team," Pavel says, "and when he sees someone doing something he would bring it back to me and say, 'Do this. Learn this move.' "

His conditioning methods were based on what he taught as a professional swimming coach. "Usually, kids could do nothing in the summer," Pavel recalls. "He would give me 20, maybe 25 days off, then send me to train with the swimmers."

He thinks sometimes about those lost summers, but never for very long. More often his thoughts go back to the endless hours spent after his own practice, sitting in the stands with his dad, watching the Red Army or national team work out, dreaming of the day when he would be like Valeri Kharlamov or Boris Mikhailov or Vladislav Tretiak as Gretzky had dreamed of being Gordie Howe. And Vladimir would look at him and say, "If you want to get there, you've got to work hard. You're not supposed to drink, you're not supposed to smoke, you're just supposed to concentrate on the hockey."

"The first time my dad was really happy," Pavel says, "was when I got the best forward on the world junior team in Anchorage. 'You're almost there,' he told me, 'but it's another step to be on the national team.' And the next year, I made it."

The first year in Vancouver, he admits, was very bad.

"I would go home to watch TV, just the pictures because I couldn't understand the words. I could not understand the news, the movies, the game shows. It was like when I was 16 and the coach took me, just me, to Japan to show the drills where he was doing clinics. Just me and my coach. 'Here's the hotel. Here's the rink.' Nothing else. No one to talk to. It was lonely."

Here, the loneliness was short-term. Igor and Lena Larionov took him in. He lived with them for the first two weeks, played with their kids, spoke Russian. "They help me in everything," he says. "I couldn't even call a cab myself because I didn't know the words. Then my mother arrived with my girlfriend, and my dad a few weeks later, and I had a family. So I was never by myself.

"English? When I got here, none. If I don't know the word, I would ask. Like 'What is that? Fork? What is fork?' And they show me and I say, 'Fine, that is fork.' Sometimes I would write them down to remember. I learn sometimes three words a day, sometimes five."

His parents are divorced, Vladimir remarried, Pavel's girlfriend history. ("Don't ask me questions like that," he grins when asked about his current social status. Then: "You can say I don't have my old girlfriend.") More comfortable with the language and the media ("They asked me questions I didn't have the words to answer"), he concentrates now on rehabilitating the injured knee that will keep him out of the game for the season, and on keeping the injury in perspective.

"When it happened, it goes through my mind: 'Well, it could be worse.' A real tragedy is something like Grinkov [30-year-old Russian Olympic figure-skating star Sergei Grinkov, who collapsed and died of a heart attack while he and wife and skating partner Ekaterina Gordeeva were practising for an ice show]. A knee is just something you have to work through."

The game is still the game of his childhood, only better, because here the ice is smaller and it takes less time to score. "In Europe," he grins, "you enter the zone and there is still a long way to go. Here, as soon as you get into the zone you can shoot. And every shot could go in.

"Much better," he grins. "Much better."

He leans back, scoffing a sandwich, staring out over the floor of GM Place where, in a matter of hours, a superstar named Michael Jordan will put on a show of his own in the building that was supposed to be his showcase. He is 24, and the games lie ahead beyond number. "Maybe," he says dreamily, "I will play 'til I'm 40."

Siberia is a universe away.

ERNIE "PUNCH" MCLEAN: JUST A TAD STUBBORN

The two best times, he says, are early mornings when he listens to the silence, and early evenings when he looks for the gold.

Between the two there are 14 hours of shovelling gravel into a sluice box. Because that's what gold mining is — shovelling gravel into a box with water powering through it, turning off the water, and looking in to see what's sunk to the bottom.

"And the next day," says Punch McLean, his one good eye a-twinkle, "you get to do it all over again ..."

Punch McLean isn't exactly certain just when he decided to get out of the construction business.

It could have been the time the bulldozer fell on his face. Or the day he put his light plane into the trees in northern Saskatchewan, when he broke his jaw in four places, permanently lost the sight in one eye, and the bloody haze covering the other almost spoiled the view of the rescue planes that flew overhead eight times without noticing him.

Or maybe it was later, when he grew weary of waiting to be rescued and decided to walk out on his own. There was plenty of time to think: It took him 23 hours to crawl the four km to a farmhouse and help. Or it might have been the day the chain snapped on a load and shattered his left elbow. Or the time he fell 40 feet off one side of a narrow bridge while peering over the other. Any time in there, a man could rightly contemplate the benefits of a career change.

There was the hockey, of course. He could have stayed in that, because no one ever matched the run he'd had as coach of the New Westminster Bruins from 1975 through 1978: Four straight trips to the Memorial Cup final and victory in the last two. Teams that produced the likes of Barry Beck, Brad Maxwell, Miles Zaharko and Paul Shmyr — and later, when he came back to New Westminster for a 19-month stint in 1987, players like Bill Ranford and Mark Recchi. Maybe the NHL would have continued to ignore him, but there'd always have been a place in hockey for Punch McLean.

So how did he wind up panning gravel so high in the wilds of B.C. that the birds flew north for the winter because it was a shortcut? Why Atlin? Why mining?

Maybe it's because miners, like hockey coaches, have to be optimists, each beginning with crude ore and dreaming of nuggets.

Nobody did optimism like Punch. When the bulldozer fell on him as he was working under it, he took solace from the fact that the blocks were higher than the blade and thus his face was squeezed rather than pulped. Fourteen days after the plane crash — in 1971, when he was flying survey — and three days after he left hospital peering through his remaining eye, he was in New Westminster, negotiating to transfer his Estevan Bruins to Queens Park Arena.

For a guy who thinks like that, why not gold mining?

When he got the bug, he flew to Atlin to negotiate a contract. The deal fell through, but he loved the country. He came home, and in two weeks he raised $200,000. Just like that, Punch McLean was a miner. Hey, how tough could it be? He knew about moving dirt. He'd run the family construction business. Wasn't that what miners did — moved the dirt until the gold showed up?

"Four years later, my partners and I were about $500,000 in," he says. "It was what you might call a rude awakening."

They started on Boulder Creek and stayed four years. On a lot of days, the gold on the bottom of the box wouldn't cover wages. Then one evening in 1987 like any other evening, one of the cleanup crew reached in and pulled out a 27-ounce nugget. Gold was running around $700 and more per ounce. "You get one that big — and I think there's been only two up there in 15 years — you don't take it to the mint," he says. Instead, they sold it to the Golden Nugget in Las Vegas for display in the casino. The take: $65,000.

After Boulder Creek, it was Smith Creek for five years. Then, in 1990, they moved to the current site of Davenport Creek. All they had to do to get there was build 45 km of road. "It's 2 1/2 hours to the highway, another two to Whitehorse," McLean says happily. "No drop-ins. Once in a while, in hunting season, you might see one vehicle. And it's at the point where it could be lucrative for the next 10 years."

Seven people work the claim, April through October. McLean's wife, Frances, doubles as cook. The hours are long, but they are good hours, quiet hours. Coming back to the city is like leaving home, not returning. "People down here are always pushing and shoving to get to some place," McLean says. "At camp, we're already there."

They have fallen in love with the life, the country, and the history.

"The camp at Atlin started in 1898," McLean begins, trying to share his sense of wonder at what it must have been back then. "The people who found the original Discovery claim came from Russia. It took them a year to get there from Juneau, but they had a map, so someone had been there before.

"The next year the railway was being built from Skagway to Whitehorse. When word got out that gold had been discovered nearby, 1,500 men left the railroad in one day. There was one area about three blocks long being worked by thousands of men, each with his 50-foot claim, marked with a tag on the post. They changed hands so often there were posts covered in so many tags it was hard to tell who owned it."

You can almost hear the itch in his voice, the yearning of a man perhaps born a century too late.

Punch McLean is 63, and hockey has been much of that life. He can look back to the day he climbed aboard the train in Estevan for the trip to Winnipeg and a look-see from the New York Rangers. He sat in the dressing room next to Andy Bathgate, played centre in the intra-squad game. When he decked a young phenom and the coaches fretted, Harry Howell tapped him on the butt and said, "Way to go, kid." Memories ...

Two years of junior for Humboldt, and the decision not to take a chance away to go to Hershey. He knew there were players better than he was. There was the family construction business. He thought he was through with hockey, until Scotty Munro moved the Bruins from Humboldt to Estevan and asked Ernie to help out. Scotty moved to Florida in '62 and suddenly he was coach. Then the Bruins, and the tempestuous years building tough, winning teams led by a coach who routinely threw garbage cans and sticks to motivate his team, and once reached out to pluck a toupée from a passing linesman. "It's a question," he says, "of generating enthusiasm."

If there is a regret, it is that he never got to coach the Vancouver Canucks. He thought he had a chance in '84. So did a lot of other people. Instead, they hired Bill Laforge, who lasted a matter of weeks.

"I think I might have done pretty well," says Punch McLean.

He sounds a little bit wistful. But it's November, it's hockey season, and he is a long way from home. Come April, when the road is open and the river is running and the air is so clear that the clouds are like neighbours, he'll be fine. At home the gold in the sluice box is extra.

CHARMAINE CROOKS: WOMAN ON THE RUN

They met at Whistler, and she was drop-dead gorgeous, so naturally he had to make a move.

"What do you do?" he asked.

"I run," she replied.

"Uh, you any good?"

"I'm ranked fifth."

"Really!" he said. "Well, where do the top four Canadians come from?"

"I meant fifth in the world," she said.

"Oh," he said. Somewhere Cary Grant moaned softly.

Charmaine Crooks has been running so long she almost can't remember when she wasn't. "Even when I was little, I had these long, long legs," she says. "It was like I was up on stilts. But I could run. And now here I am at 33 years old, and I'm still running. What does that tell you?"

She laughs when she says it. She laughs a lot, does Charmaine Crooks — laughs and giggles and rolls her eyes when she talks, which she concedes is usually. Because she knows what it tells you, and what it's going to tell the world a few months down the road in Atlanta: That the little Jamaican-born stilt girl is competing on her fifth Canadian Olympic Games team.

Not in her fifth Olympics. The politicians put the asterisk to that one with the boycott in 1980. But she made the team. She would have run in Moscow, 18 years old, up against the world, flying down the track to — what?

Whatever. It's irrelevant. Moscow was then, Atlanta is now, and "Yesterday" is a pretty good song by the Beatles. Treasure the 16 years of world-class competition. But focus on Atlanta and the 800 metres. Get ready for then, and get ready for after. Push ...

She wanted to be a ballerina and was forever phoning ballet schools, but ballet is expensive and running is cheap, and when you're one of nine kids in a family newly emigrated from Jamaica, that counts. Besides, there was this park, Earls Court, across the street from the house in the Italian district of Toronto, with a track and a pool for swimming in summer and skating in winter. When her dad came home from his job as a welder and went jogging, the six-year-old with skinny legs would go with him. By 17, she was national champion over 400 metres and off to the University of Texas-El Paso to use one of the many scholarship offers.

Along the way, she'd learned the lesson that comes with being part of a family mob scene: You don't wait, you do. The work is there to be done, and when someone else needs help, you pitch in. At 12 she was a candy-striper in a hospital cancer ward. She joined Army cadets. The vitality that kept her going also kept her healthy.

"I was never sick," she says. "That made me the nurse whenever the other kids were."

In later life, those roots of commitment would lead her into work with drug-abuse programs, breast-cancer clinics, youth organizations and a fund-raiser called "No Laughing Matter," a comedians' revue that has sold out in each of its first two years. Back then she was just a kid with a million involvements, trying to fit them all in.

No matter what, though, there was always time to run. She could be good. She knew that. Push ...

"You're pushy," suggests a visitor to the North Van apartment where Charmaine Crooks and her husband of three years, timber broker, Internet surfer and hockey nut Anders Thorsen — yes, the Whistler guy; eat dirt, Cary — work on the post-Atlanta plans and the marketing campaign that can help make it all happen.

And she is. The pushing — the degree in psychology, the sales jobs ("Listen, if you can cold-sell photocopiers, you can sell anything!"), the public-speaking course, the voice lessons, the charity work, the acting, even the stint singing with the band (World Class and the Olympians) has opened doors, created opportunities that would never have been there had she been content to sit back and let herself be defined only by her sport.

Without the push and the preparation, there could have been nothing like *Cycle*, the CBC national television show she co-hosts, which has been renewed for its fourth year, colour commenting at the world track-and-field championships, the song-writing (in 1992 she wrote, co-produced and recorded "Circles of Love"), the motivational-lecture circuit. Talent and work will keep the doors open, but it was the push that broke the locks.

"Well, okay, maybe pushy that way," she concedes with a trace of exasperation. "But, you can't just sit around and wait."

So, they have put together the full marketing package: produced the seven-minute promo tape, made their own shoe deal with Reebok, worked to get the endorsements and support of companies like Nature

Made Vitamins, KINeSYS sports-care products and Maple Leaf Springs, talked to some of the big American sports agencies — and hit the wall.

For Thorsen, who is also into marketing, it is less a matter of concern than of amusement.

"In marketing, she has three problems," he says. "She's not in the biggest sport on earth — well, maybe she is, but not here. She's a woman, and she's a black woman. In Europe — in Brazil, for Pete's sake — they hold out pictures for her to sign. But recognition in Canada — there's some, sure, but a lot of it is 'Hey, she's the woman on that TV cycling show.' "

It's not easy, marketing an athletic career when you're not into the North American establishment sports: baseball, basketball, football, hockey, tennis or golf. "I called one of the big American agencies and laid it out for them," he recalls. "Five Olympics, has her own TV show, personable, well-spoken, attractive, the whole package. The guy told me they get 20 calls a day like mine, maybe two of them are worth looking at, and maybe only one of them will even get called back."

He is not speaking only of Charmaine Crooks. "In Canada there's some kind of barrier with the companies," he contends, "and to be honest it probably has a lot to do with Ben Johnson. The fallout from that is never going to go away. We've got Bruny Surin and Donovan Bailey out there, and they're never going to get the recognition they deserve.

"Do I get frustrated? I'm looking beyond that. But you can't help but be aware of differences. There were 192 countries represented at the world track-and-field championships, where figure skating might draw 30. And Donovan goes out and wins the world title. If he was a European, he couldn't walk the street without getting mobbed. Here ...?"

The laugh is genuine, if a tad rueful. A shrug puts it all to one side. All that is for later, and there is a sense of confidence that down the road it will all get done.

For now the plate is full of Atlanta, an experience to be savoured all the more because it is the last of the five and the finale of a career. Leaving demands your best. Push ...

The medals, the trophies, the mementos of a life on the tracks of the world, sit on shelves in a corner of her apartment. Lying flat most of them, not on display so much as there to be picked up and examined at the rush of a particular memory: The silver medal for the

4 by 400 from the '94 Commonwealth Games in Victoria after a year out of track with a leg injury; some of the nine Canadian championship golds collected by the only Canadian woman to break two minutes in the 800 at 1:58:52. The dreams of Atlanta are cut from more modest cloth.

"I want to make the finals," she says. "That's the only way I'll truly measure my success, to make the darn finals. You go there, and you never know what kind of a draw you'll have in the heats, so you've got to prepare yourself for the toughest heat possible. I'm trying to do some different things to get ready this time — more cross country, more lifting. This is my last shot and I want to give myself every opportunity to make those finals.

"Because if you get there, anything can happen. You never, ever count yourself out. We've gotten so much inspiration from Donovan, and we've got a team atmosphere that is conducive to doing very well. But on the track I'm all by myself, focusing on making it through the rounds, because that's what you've got to do."

And if you don't?

"Life goes on," she laughs. Then: "You know, at the Barcelona Olympics, my time was ninth and I didn't make the finals. Three of the women who did make them have since been busted for 'roids. So I could have been there. But you can't dwell on things like that. You've got to keep looking at the big picture: Where am I going to be in 10 years? Where are they going to be?

"Things happen. The injury in '93 turned my life around because it gave me the time and the opportunity to do the *Cycle* show and the colour commentary. If I hadn't been hurt, I might have missed it all. So who knows what's next? All you can do is work to be ready for it. That's what I'm trying to do.

"Not just in Atlanta," she adds. "In everything."

Push ...

GORD RACETTE: "THIS WASN'T WHAT I HAD IN MIND ..."

"Hey, I was there! I had my shot, and I went as far as I could. When you can say that, what's to regret?"

— Gord Racette

He was going to be Rocky IV — or V, or VI or whatever. Sylvester Stallone said so. Would Sly lie?

So he'd started too late — later, even, than the 26 he called himself when he came out of the So You Think You're Tough? rumbles and the kick-boxing circuit and announced that, without an amateur bout to his name, he was going to become a heavyweight pro. Wasn't that what Rocky was all about — the pursuit of the impossible dream and the gloves waved triumphantly aloft at the fadeout?

He had a manager, a guy named Tony Dowling who'd scuffed around the edges of the game for a long time (and, in a rare moment of candour, admitted that in his own hungry days he'd once thrown a fight). He had the commodity that the fight mob is always seeking and never admits: In a sport dominated by Afro-American fighters, he was pleasingly Caucasian. And now here was Sly Stallone, old Rocky himself, taking him to Los Angeles, making him a part of his Tiger Eye stable, the one that was going to produce an assembly line of champions. What could possibly go wrong?

As it turned out, a lot of things.

Gord Racette comes into the office swinging a cane from which he draws occasional support. Nothing serious, he insists, the knee just goes sometimes.

He is surprised to be there. He's a referee now, a family man with two small kids, working on a degree in rehab medicine and a pilot's licence, teaching martial arts, collecting black belts (he has three), building a home, working with young offenders through the Department of Corrections, getting on with the rest of his life. "I'm old news," he says. "Been there, done that, so what?"

But he is more than that. As a Canadian who rushed headlong into the fight game at an age (he still won't specify what) when a lot of guys are giving it up, he is a living textbook, a case study for aspiring local fighters like Troy Roberts, who steps up a notch to meet the aging but dangerous Bonecrusher Smith in the feature of an upcoming card at the UBC gym, where Racette will referee.

He fought Trevor Berbick and Jim Young and Tony Tubbs. He played with the big boys, saw how the game can engulf you and how quickly it can spit you out. The lessons are there for the learning in the limp, the neck surgery, the battered nose, the old bone breaks. "I've given my body to sports," he shrugs. "No regrets, but no retirement plan, either. Hey, it happens."

Yes, it does. But not often like this ...

He grew up in Port Alberni knowing there had to be something better than getting a job in the mill. If there was a game, he could play it. That was it, then: he would become a professional athlete. But fate kept strewing banana peels.

Three months before a scheduled tryout with the B.C. Lions — an ex-player friend who'd seen him destroying people at floor hockey said he should try football — he was hit by a car and had his heel torn off. They sewed it back on. "My doctor said it was okay," Racette says, "but one day he was sick and another doctor said it was gangrene and they cut it off again. So on Saturday I'm planning to sue my doctor and on Sunday he dies of a heart attack."

He'd never played rugby, but he'd never played a sport with his brother, either, and his brother played for the James Bay Athletic Association in Victoria, so he wandered down and made the team. But there was no pro rugby.

He saw a game of Senior A lacrosse, another sport he'd never tried. But there was a pro league now. He spent the winter in the wind and rain at the lacrosse box, learning to handle the stick. That summer he made the senior C team in Nanaimo, then senior A. That was the year the pro league folded.

About then, the So You Think You're Tough? phenomenon was at its peak: bikers, bar-room brawlers and assorted thugs and wannabes stepping into a ring to do for money what they'd been doing on weekends for free. Racette was into martial arts (as a kick-boxer he was 42-6). It was worth a shot.

He entered one in Delta. ("Out of town, so my friends wouldn't see me if I got licked.") No danger. He won that one and the next five. He ran out of opponents. "You wanna keep fighting, kid," the promoters told him, "you gotta turn pro."

Dowling was cornerman for one of his victims.

"The guy asks Tony, 'How do I beat this guy?' " Racette says. "Tony says, 'Head-butt him.' So he did, for six stitches." Racette hung in and won anyway. "If you ever wanna turn pro," Dowling said, "call me."

In June of 1979, 26 going on whatever, Racette started down the pro trail, Dowling his manager and trainer. "If you look at my first fight picture, I didn't even know how to pose as a fighter," he says. "And because of the neck injury [from the martial-arts days], sometimes when I got hit my whole left arm would go limp as a noodle. But there I was, a pro."

People said he fought too often and wasn't careful enough about picking opponents at his own level. He doesn't disagree.

"I wanted to find out fast if I had what it took to get into the ring, because if I didn't I wanted to get out. Actually, having no boxing background was a benefit because I didn't have all those years of head-pounding that comes with that. I had a clear head. What kind of clouded it was guys like Berbick and Tubbs."

Three years later, nowhere near ready, he met Berbick in Nanaimo and basically got his butt kicked. Standing in the dressing room, he looked in the mirror at the welts on his face and the blood in his eyes. "To tell the truth," he said, "this wasn't what I had in mind."

But by that time Stallone had heard of him during the Vancouver filming of *First Blood*, the movie that spawned the Rambo series. Richie Giachetti, who'd later gain fame as a Mike Tyson trainer, fronted the operation.

"They took me and my wife and Tony to Los Angeles," Racette says, "and what basically happened was nothing. Tony cashed in his chips and left. I wanted him to stay, but Stallone had Giachetti, and there was Sly saying I'd make $25,000,000, so what was I supposed to do?"

He and Giachetti never hit it off. "The guy takes me to a basic all-Black gym to train, and here I am, Sly's boy, sure to make money, and most of these guys aren't making any. He kind of threw me into the ring and said, 'Defend yourself.' That was a long, hard time."

His career with Tiger Eye lasted four fights. Along the way he became part of the party group, which offered everything but training.

"There was no training. Richie kept telling me to go outside and run. There was smog and I was allergic to it. My nose kept bleeding. The guy I replaced as Stallone's heavyweight was a gym fighter — you know: looks great in the gym, but in the ring his heart shrinks? He'd find an excuse and pull out. That's why they loved me, because I'd show up any time and fight anybody."

Two weeks after he returned to Canada for major surgery on his nose, under strict orders not to fight for six weeks, he got the call from Tiger Eye and fought Tony Tubbs. He spent the two nights prior to the Jimmy Young fight under a blanket trying to sweat out the flu. "When he floored me in the eighth, I wasn't hurt. I just had no strength to get up."

It couldn't last, and it didn't. Tiger Eye dropped him. Racette sued — he met his lawyer wife, Nives, when she worked on his case —

and won a settlement he's legally bound not to discuss. Just like that, the fight career was over, promises and dreams unfulfilled.

"I guess there might be one regret," concedes Gord Racette, biting into a hamburger. "I never worry about what might have been, but I wonder what I might have been if I'd started younger. But when I was a kid I said I'd be a pro athlete, travel the world, meet interesting people, and I've done that."

When he talks to the kids in the correctional institutions, his message is as quick and sharp as the Ali jab he never quite learned to throw, the never-give-up, be-all-you-can-be work ethic distilled by his time in the seediest game on earth. "If you're willing to suck shit through a straw long enough, you can achieve anything."

So, no regrets. Why should there be, for a busy ex-athlete, ex-barroom bouncer and ex-professional boxer with an old *Ring Magazine* rating him 19th in world heavyweight rankings in the closet next to a world super-heavyweight kick-boxing championship belt, a wife and kids, a home a-building and a future full of dreams that work can turn to reality?

"I never got the brass ring," he says, giving the cane a half-twirl, "but I got close enough to reach for it, and I tried my damnedest."

No regrets, and over time, even the bad memories can be viewed with a certain affection. He was there. He had his shot. A man can't ask for much more.

SILKEN LAUMANN: "MY LIFE IS ON HOLD ..."

One month after the accident that all but tore her right leg to pieces, Silken Laumann crawled back into her racing shell and resumed training. She had to crawl, because she still couldn't walk. "I can be a stubborn person," she says.

She was 15 years old, staring out over the water at a women's rowing crew in training, knowing that it wasn't for her. "It looked so brutal," she says. "The women were really big and they all dressed in black and had grease marks and blood all over their hands. I said 'Where's the fun in that?' "

Besides, she was a runner, not a rower — 800 metres and pretty good, really. Provincial level, at least. Weighed 110 pounds and stood 5' 9", the perfect runner's build. She was an athlete. In Germany, her father had been a soccer player, her mother a long jumper. Rowing meant canoes and backpacks and those old movies where some guy in a coonskin coat is strumming a mandolin and rhyming moon with lagoon. Forget it.

It took a stress fracture to get her into a shell. Her sister Daniele, 19 (with whom she would win a doubles bronze in the 1984 Olympics), kept telling her how much fun it was. So okay, she'd row to stay in shape while she recovered. But she wasn't a rower. The club was close to her home in Mississauga, her sister was there, it was a way of conditioning without pounding down on the legs. But once she got better, she was gone. She was a runner, not a rower. Everybody clear on that? Okay.

Two things happened: Like Topsy, she jes' growed. Not big as in chubby — big as in stronger and longer, a body capable of pushing itself to heaven-knew-what heights. And suddenly she burned with the need to discover where that limit lay. The timing was perfect: She had fallen hopelessly in love with a sport that could challenge her to find the answer.

Consider the ducks floating along over the waters of the Elk Lake training centre. Above the water, nothing moves. Beneath the surface, they are paddling like hell. Rowing is like that, she says.

"On a nice day when the sun is shining and the water is flat and your boat is gliding along, it feels effortless — beautiful, you know? It's relaxing, and yet you're still working hard. Your heart rate is up, you're muscling it, you're using your whole body. So there's always that contradiction between being powerful and strong and explosive and really raw, and the other side where it's esthetic and beautiful and pretty. Those things are always being thrown together, and it's an odd mixture."

It frustrates her, sometimes, that so many of the people who cover this sport she has helped to bring to the forefront of Canada's athletic nationalism have fallen into the trap of accepting the beauty and the competition without truly understanding what goes into making it seem so simple. "They write about us, they say things about us, and they just don't know because they've never taken the time to learn," she says. "If they could spend six hours in a coach boat in the rain and the cold watching us work, they'd have a better understanding of what's really happening.

"Most of the time when we're training, we're working at a high level, a heart rate of 175 and over, several hours at a time. You have to be focused: Is the boat running out, the way the blades are entering the water, the way you're moving your trunk forward, the level of your hands at the catch, the movement of your head."

The very repetitive nature can be a trap. An undetected error in technique can become ingrained through hundreds of repetitions. Making the change slows you down, makes it easy to slip back into the old habit. It has to be fought until the better way is itself ingrained. The battle towards perfection is never-ending. But that's all right. Without the battle, there couldn't be The Rush.

The irony of the Great Drug Fiasco of 1995 has not escaped Silken Laumann. There she was, stripped of a gold medal along with her teammates in the quadruple sculls event of the Pan-American Games because she took the wrong type of Benadryl for her asthma — not just unknowingly, but on the advice of the team doctors — and all along she has been hooked on something far more powerful, a drug she may have trouble shaking when she finally puts away the oars: The pure, unadulterated adrenaline.

"When you're out rowing, your world becomes very narrow, very small with the focus on excelling, the focus on the immediate, the here, the now. It's like life outside your boat disappears. And we do that several hours per day."

"I'm addicted to the adrenaline, the physical and mental high of performing. I love the pressure — I hate the pressure, but I love the pressure. I love challenging myself to get better and better, of never being totally satisfied, of always looking for what else I can do. People ask what I get out of it now. I get all the things I used to but more, because I'm more focused, more in control than when I was 17 or 18. I'm 30 years old and in the driver's seat. I have to seek the help, to find the tools that will make me better. It's exciting, it's wonderful to have the passion, to have something you feel so strongly about."

The scars of the Pan-Am drug mess are healed. The loss of the medals didn't bother the others in the boat with her ("We won the race by 13 seconds. It was a fun race, and in rowing, the Pan-Ams are a B regatta"), and the uproar was a wake-up call.

"We'd never talked about drugs or doping or what we should or shouldn't take. It wasn't important to us. Rowing hadn't had a positive result for a couple of years, world-wide, in any meet during random testing, so it was never addressed. What this did was set off alarm bells. Everybody was cleaning out the medicine cabinet and wondering if there was anything there that shouldn't be. Because everyone realized, 'Wait a minute, this could have happened to me.' "

As to suggestions in the ensuing cover-your-butt competition, that she had been pretty dumb not to know what she was taking when the book of prohibited drugs is right there for the reading: "When you look back you can say, 'Why didn't I look at the book?' I'm sure the doctors feel the same way: 'Why didn't I ask to see the drug, why did I assume that Benadryl was Benadryl was Benadryl?' It's always easy in retrospect. Maybe we'll all be better for it."

The other scars, the ones on the right leg, are there forever. Ten weeks before the 1992 Olympic Games, during warm-up at a meet in Essen, she was crashed into by a German men's pair. Her right ankle was broken, all the muscles on one side of the leg severed. The surgery to re-attach them, the incredible comeback, the bronze medal in Barcelona, the stuff of which the completed-but-as-yet-unreleased movie is made, cannot disguise the fact that this is not the same rower who dominated the world before the accident. As good, possibly better, but not the same.

"It affects everything," she says. "The way I walk, the way I move. Muscles that aren't supposed to be stretched that much are being asked to do something at an incredibly high level, so I have problems with my back and my hips and my knees.

"I apply pressure with my legs differently and I don't have that much feeling on the outside of my foot, so even though I'm pushing with both legs I don't have the perception of pushing on the right side, so everything's different. It's not bad that it's different. It's just different, so it makes your body move differently."

And, inevitably, out of it comes a positive, an account to be drawn upon when things get tough: "Mentally, it's made me stronger. It showed me what's possible, that no matter what the challenge, I can get through it. That's nice to know."

Silken Laumann and husband John Wallace (a rowing gold medallist in 1992) live in a rambling old house near the Elk Lake training site. In the first 18 months, she was in the house exactly 21 days.

"In university," she recalls, "I did my degree in four years and there were two Olympics in there. I got up at 4:30 and rowed, went to school, rowed again, studied all night. Rowing was early mornings and late nights." Now, because of her profile, her medals, her four sponsors (IGA, Nike, McDonald's and Subaru) and as much public speaking as she wants to do, she has reached the point where rowing pays the bills. "I don't have to work AND train," she says. "And that, in our sport, is a luxury."

"Most people in our sport don't have a home. They're renting something for $300 per month or less, and they live with a whole bunch of people. They get by on one carded athlete cheque per month plus whatever mom and dad and their friends and their one sponsor can provide. That's the reality of being a rower and that was my life for 10 years."

It is also a huge advantage, allowing her to train in San Diego for the next seven months, to get an apartment there, to focus fully on the dream that is Atlanta '96. It doesn't ease the training, it just provides the best environment for it to happen.

Until then, the house is on hold, a refuge to be enjoyed in the scattered private moments along with the luxury of just sitting back and reading a book, or maybe listening to music, or sharing the day with John, who makes so many things possible just by being there.

"He has put his life on hold for me," she says. "He's my right-hand man. He helps with everything — the training, the business side. That's hard on a relationship, but ours is incredibly strong. I have so much respect for him. To give up so much, and so willingly, to be really happy doing it, that's pretty special."

And so it goes on, the dream and the never-ending toil to make it a reality — 12 hours at the boathouse or on the lake, every day but Saturday. Come January, she will slam the door on the appearances and interviews, narrowing even further the focus on Atlanta and the Games and the podium with the three steps to the top that, but for the injury, she might have climbed four years ago. "It might seem arrogant," she says, "but it's something I have to do. I'm looking forward to the rest of my life, but this is my last chance to do what I'm doing *now*."

Pressed to put the drive into words, she pauses for a moment as though to sort it out.

"Rowing is an avenue for excellence," she says. "It's not what I do to relax, it's something I do well. I'm always moving forward, always to the next step. It's my chosen field. It's not writing, it's not music, it's rowing."

She shakes hands goodbye — carefully, babying the wrist a little in deference to a touch of tendonitis. "It's the way I train," she says ruefully. "I train hard. I push myself 'til I get sick. It means I get injured, more than most, but it's the way I am, and I'm stuck with it."

At least, until Atlanta. After that, there will be time to write, to read the books and listen to the music, on the wonderful post-podium day when she can finally push the button that takes the rest of her life off hold.

MANNY SOBRAL:
JUST LIKE IN THE MOVIES

When you're 14 and fat, your choices are limited. You can resign yourself to going through school as "Chubby," and try to be the life of the party to overcome it. You can answer one of those ads on the back of comic books promising to mould you into a mound of muscle who punches out bullies and walks off with the dream girl. You can say, "Hey, this who I am," and get on with your life.

Manny Sobral went looking for a gym.

"I was in Grade Eight, 20 or 30 pounds overweight," he says in that low-pitched, whispery voice that belies the tiger inside. "My grandma just over-fed me, and I ate it all. My idea was to start jogging, turn the page and start losing some weight. So I looked in the Yellow Pages under 'Gyms' and found this place, the Inner City Gym, on Main and Hastings. Not the best neighbourhood, but it said they had weights. I figured it was worth a look ..."

There is a back-lot, B-movie quality to the Manny Sobral story, a tale told in infinite variation in Saturday matinées and nostalgia channels. There is even a Canadian precedent: Ottawa, 1955. Fat kid decides he wants to be in showbiz. Joins a gym, pares off the weight, gets his nose fixed, writes "Diana," becomes teenage singing idol and winds up writing "My Way" for Sinatra and the *Tonight Show* theme for Johnny Carson. Paul Anka, tubby Canadian teenager with a dream and a plan to make it work. So why not Manny Sobral?

He went to a gym. He had his nose fixed — the hard way, in 126 amateur bouts that included 40 KOs and only nine losses. He has the dream, to box for the world welterweight title, and he has The Plan. Why not Manny Sobral?

Fade to flashback. Chubby kid enters seedy-looking gym in rundown neighbourhood. An old man, most of his teeth missing, face showing the marks of too many punches, wanders over and asks him what he wants.

"His name was Steve, an older gentleman who said he sparred with Rocky Marciano," Sobral recalls. "My parents didn't like me going to the gym because of the neighbourhood, and when school started in September, I had to stop. But for two months in the summer, Steve would open the gym at 11 a.m. He held the pads for me, taught me how to box, work the speed bag, skip a little bit. He took me under his wing. Old Steve, he was the one who got me hooked."

Through the school year, Sobral shifted his training to the Hastings Community Centre, but it was only three nights a week, not enough for a kid who had a taste of it and wanted more. Summer came and he was back at Inner City, run now by an American named Bob Decker who'd coached a lot of good amateurs and liked the quiet kid with the big punch. Suddenly, there were lots of fights — 40 in one year, as Decker took fighters to the U.S. Sobral did well, then had to find a new coach as Decker left the country.

The early pattern of his career — meet the right person at just the right time — held true. At the Astoria Gym, he met George Angelomatis, who managed him through his amateur career, and in 1987, a construction foreman and boxing trainer named Nelson Kitchen. "Nelson was helping with the coaching at the club, and right away I liked the way he taught," Sobral says. "He was really technical, and I like that aspect of the sport. So George would get me in really good shape and work on motivation, and Nelson would teach me technique. It was a good balance."

The team lifted Sobral to the Canadian welterweight title in 1987 and 1988, and to the Canadian squad for the 1988 Olympic Games, where he won two and then lost to eventual bronze medallist Yoni Nyeman of Finland. He was 20 years old and hit like a jackhammer. He could turn pro, meet some contenders, and then ...

"Cut! What is this, Disney Goes to Madison Square? We need a problem here! You can't have a happy ending without a crisis! Somebody give me a crisis!"

Manny Sobral came home from the Olympics, and quit.

Not cold. He'd still go to the gym, work out, stay in shape. He was just tired of it, tired of balancing boxing and school and construction work to stay alive. He'd quit college after a year to concentrate on the Olympics. It was time to look after the future. He went back to college, working on his phys. ed. degree. Boxing was done. He would be a teacher.

The resolve lasted three years. Then he saw an ad for a Tough Man competition, entered it in the hope of picking up some cash, and won $10,000. And all the things he loved about the game came flooding back. But there was a price: The win took him out of the amateur picture, and killed any thought of the 1992 Olympics. If he fought again, it would have to be as a pro.

"Cut! You call that a crisis? Gimme crisis! Gimme a happy ending!"

He had his first pro fight on April 22, 1992, and five or six in the next 10 months. They were hairy days, because that was also his collegiate grad year. Something had to give, and something did: Both shoulders. The cartilage in the joint between the shoulder blade and collarbone had demineralized, literally worn away through the years of pounding.

"We went to a lot of doctors who said cortisone or an operation. But Nelson had been a ski racer and still had trouble with his knees. He just looked at me and said, 'Manny, do you want my knee problems in your shoulders for the rest of your life?' That was it. I just retired."

"Cut! This is a happy ending? Happy! I want happy!"

Sobral went back to coaching boxing, just to help out. He was teaching now. That was his life. Boxing was a memory. Then a friend told him about a dentist and homeopathic doctor who'd cured some ankle problems with a combination of acupuncture and injections of what Sobral calls "some sort of plant extract."

"I went for treatments for four or five months. The shoulders were feeling better all the time. I started hitting the bag again, sparring with some of the kids at the club. One day I called Nelson and said, 'I'm ready to go.' "

At first, Kitchen was having none of it. "You're kidding yourself," he told his friend. Eventually he relented. Team Manny was reunited, the storybook re-opened.

In 1996, Manny Sobral is 17-0 as a pro, the latest a first-round KO of someone called Sean Crowdus in Edmonton, where he was also named Canada's pro boxer of the year. He is Canada's super-welterweight champion, a title taken in November with a third-round KO of Del Ritchie. He has become a crowd favourite in shows at the Lucky Eagle Casino on the Chehalish Indian reservation in Washington, where he is known as "The Teacher." He is beginning to attract the attention of people who offer to sponsor him if he'll take a year off teaching, and promoters aching for a piece of the white kid who can hit.

All the signs point up. But as decision day draws near, Manny Sobral stops to give himself frequent reality checks.

He knows the stories of other Canadians who were told how good they could be, people like Olympian Shawn O'Sullivan and kickboxer-turned-heavyweight Gord Racette. He knows about the sharks that circle the game, ready to feast on a fighter's blood. He can relate to the tales of bright young fighters who now hear phones that no longer ring.

"I know the pitfalls," he says. "But even the smart ones get caught up in it. Why is Evander Holyfield fighting again? He has the money, the fame, everything. I think I've put in safety nets, people I've known for a long time who will tell me when it's time to stop. There comes a time when your skills have eroded. I trust these people. They will tell me when it's time to quit, and I believe I will accept their opinions."

Meanwhile, he and Kitchen share his management contract and control his career. ESPN and *Showtime* have been sniffing around, talking about putting him on a big fight undercard.

"I'm pretty much breaking even now," says Manny Sobral. "It's tough with the teaching [Burnaby North Secondary] and being sponsor for the school wrestling team and training and boxing. I don't have a girlfriend. Where's the time? The money is still four-digit 'tip-money,' the promoter at the Eagle calls it, and it's a fact that a few fighters get all the money and the rest of us scramble.

"But I want to do this thing, to try it. If I take a year off and box every two months, I can make it. If it doesn't work I can go back to teaching, which I love and find fulfilling.

"There'll come a point where I have to decide how far to take it," concludes The Teacher. "If my mind says no, then I go back to my career."

He is in the gym now, removing the glasses, winding the tape around his hands, doing the stretching, sprawling on the floor to take the medicine ball dropped again and again onto his stomach — enjoying the ritual of his game. Note the eagerness as he climbs into the ring to spar. The mind will find it hard to say no.

DEBBIE BRILL: LEAP OF FAITH

The former Haney Hick is gigglingly aghast. "Migawd, look at me," she says. "Forty-two-year-old mother of three, house in the suburbs, married to a doctor, two dogs and a hot tub. What happened?"

Debbie Brill looks, well, contented — as though, after all those turbulent years when the spotlight and the uncertainty and the searching for Lord-knew-what kept getting in the way of the happiness, she has faced up to the questions and found most of the answers. And she is high-jumping again. Eight years away from it and she's back for the best of all possible reasons: the sheer, unadulterated joy ...

"There's a second, at the top of the jump, when it's like everything goes motionless and you're hanging over the world. But then you come down. You always come down."

— Debbie Brill, 1972

She was 18, sitting moist-eyed in a residence hall at UBC, trying to explain to a stranger why she had quit high-jumping at the top of her game when the country was saying she shouldn't, that she somehow owed it something, that there was an obligation to bring it gold or silver or bronze.

After winning Pan-Am gold, touring Europe and twice tying her record, she'd been beaten at a paltry 5' 6" in South Africa, Saskatoon and Winnipeg — and told a reporter she didn't care. It was as though she'd spat upon the flag.

"It wasn't that I didn't want to win," she said back then. "It's that it wasn't terrible any more when I lost. When you're really young and you start, it's like a game. You go out and jump and don't feel any pressure at all. When you're older, you've made the adjustments to pressure. But there's a time in between when you fail the whole country every time you miss. That's where I've been, and that's why I quit. There's a whole bunch of worlds. I can't stay trapped in just one."

She didn't. After a virtual last-minute decision to compete in the Munich Olympic Games (finishing eighth at 5' 11½") she left the sport — for good, she thought — and dove into other universes with reckless abandon, going her own way, letting others think what they might. She travelled, lived on a subsistence farm near Vanderhoof, washed dishes in a Boston Bar hotel, worked on the conveyor belt in a Maple Ridge cannery. She went back to university in Victoria and lived in a tent, doing math by flashlight.

"I don't think celebrity is a particularly healthy state," she says now, looking back at the troubled times. "It was what drove me out. There was this developing persona of Debbie Brill. People were looking at me differently. I was the kid who was the first ever to jump backwards. I was winning. Nothing had changed inside me, but the two Debbie Brills were getting further and further apart. To me, nothing was making sense. The world was going a little bit crazy. Part of me always wanted to live up to it, and the other part was saying 'Wait a minute, this is nuts.' "

So she walked away.

And in September of '74, she came back to the track, this time on her terms, and stayed at it through 1987, when Achilles tendon surgery finally put an apparent end to a career that then spanned 18 years. The only break came in 1980, when she called a press conference to announce her pregnancy — and got Adidas to sponsor it.

"I didn't want it to sound like some kind of accident," she said. "I'd been living with Greg [Ray] for a long time. We wanted a child, and I was not going to have Neil born under some cloud. Besides, I was number one in the world, and I wanted them to know I had no intention of quitting."

When she resumed competition, the baby went with her. She'd cuddle him, pass him to one of the other competitors, jump, and come back to take him again. He was in the infield at the Sunkist meet in Los Angeles, six months old, being spoiled by the women she was beating, when Mom (eligible because her own mother was American-born) set the U.S. indoor record at 6' 5".

"I've never said that the government should pay my way if I want to jump. But if the government wants me to jump, then the support should be there. If it isn't, how do our kids get better?"

Motherhood didn't change everything. A rebel she was, a rebel she remained.

When Canada joined the Moscow Olympics boycott and Sport Canada huffed that it just might send a team anyway, she was asked to comment. "I don't compete with countries who put tanks in other people's streets," she said.

When Sport Canada sent out the applications and conditions for grant support, she routinely crossed out all the clauses that bothered her before she signed it. The money came anyway.

"This funding cutback for athletics," she says now. "I wonder if they know what they're doing. There's no grassroots support. Neil [now 14] came home from school the other day and said none of the kids are really interested in getting involved in amateur sport. When I asked him why, he said, 'Because they know that you can't be good if you come from Canada.' I was shocked, but then I remembered that I used to think that way myself. It's not impossible; it's just a lot harder."

When she finally quit for good, Debbie Brill made one mistake. She slammed the door. It took eight years to discover that she could leave it open and walk freely between the two worlds she loves best.

"I'm jumping again," she chortles. "Isn't that a hoot? Eight years out and here I am, jumping in Masters competitions and loving it. I did my first meet in February, the U.S. Masters, and it was a BLAST! I was really nervous because I hadn't competed for so long, but it was so much fun. There were 65-year-olds high-jumping and enjoying it and talking about their training. Some are competitive, some not at all, some were good athletes, some never were and only started competing when they were older.

"But, you see, it's not the centre of their lives, just like it's not the centre of mine. They've got other lives, and it felt very much like it did when I first started in sports, just out there to enjoy something physical. No sponsorship, and not looking for any. Just something I do on my own money, for myself, because I want to.

"At the start, for years, I didn't train. I just jumped. I was extremely gifted, so lucky. But I never considered myself an athlete. I used to think, 'This is silly. I can just go out there and do this all the time, forever, and everybody thinks it's great, and I'm doing nothing.' "

In the basement of the new home shared by Debbie, Neil, husband Doug Coleman and their two children, Katie, five, and Jake, three, there is the weight room. It is here that Debbie Brill trains the three girls she's coaching and works on the business of getting fit ("My whole life is different when I'm fit. I have more energy, approach everything with a more positive attitude") and the challenge of a new goal: To become the first woman over 40 to clear 6' 3½", higher than in Reno, where she set "a pathetic" world age-class Masters record.

One of her pupils, 25-year-old Michele Laviolette, arrives to work the weights. When Debbie Brill leaped backwards out of Haney, Michele wasn't born. Soon, Debbie says, the teacher will jump with the pupils as the new push begins.

"Those people back then were right," she admits. "When I lost, I wasn't taking it as hard as they were. Because, what the heck, I'd jump again.

"One of the silliest sayings in sport is that there's no tomorrow. Of course there is. What an awful way to go through life. I want the girls I coach to recognize that everything is a process, and the mark of a great athlete is not only to compete well, but to do well consistently, over time. That means you have big ups and big downs, little ups and little downs. And you work through them, and go on."

Jake bounds into the room to show off a loop he's made of plastic toys. "That's wonderful, Jake," enthuses Mrs. Mom. But it's the Haney Hick who looks up and grins at the picture she knows it makes. The process is working just fine.

A BOY NAMED RUTH: HORSE MEETS MEDIA

It was hatched in a bar, as so many good ideas are.

The *Sports Only* management committee was dreaming up ways to let the public know there was a new game in town, a weekly newspaper devoted — as the name cleverly implied — only to sports.

"How about we buy a horse?" a guy said.

"Better yet," I sneered, "why don't we just take a bunch of hundred-dollar bills into the bathroom and flush them down the john while one of you bites me on the butt?

"Horses hate me. Every time I come near the stable they play odd-and-even — which isn't easy when you've got hooves — to see which one gets to bite me this time. I owned a horse once. It cost more than my wife, and it didn't even have a charge card."

"That's what we need — experience!" they enthused. "You can be chairman."

"Chairman of what?"

"The fan club. See, what we do is, we buy a horse, form a fan club, and put all the membership money into a fund to be donated to the B.C. chapter of the Canadian Breast Cancer Foundation. Everybody has fun, the dough goes to a great cause ..."

"Fine. We can probably pick up a decent horse for 25 grand, maybe 30 — hey! Where'd everybody go?"

Fortunately, we didn't have to buy the horse. Jim Harrigan "sold" us a pretend share in a horse named P.E.I. Ruth, who turned out to be a guy whose name was supposed to be Big Mikey — which went to a filly because Harrigan got the registration papers mixed. "Perfect," we said at the next meeting. "If ever a horse needed a fan club ..."

There were initial problems, caused in part by the fact that none of us knew anything about horses. In one of our pub pop quizzes, four out of five thought palomino meant "friendly Italian".

Next, we had to deal with the unfounded rumour that Ruth was a gelding. At first we thought it meant he was in a union like our beloved American Newspaper Geld. When the term was explained we lost three full glasses of beer from guys crossing their legs. And in the end, Ruth proved to be guy clear through.

The P.E.I. Ruth Fan Club was an instant success. Ruth had his own Talking Yellow Pages hot line. Fans loved the idea of coming to the track to watch their very own horse — sort of — in action. Free admission on the days Ruth raced, cool *Sports Only* hat, a launch party in the barbecue tent, no feed bills, no vet bills — "Ownership without the manure," we called it. And all for a $20 donation to the breast-cancer fund.

Came Ruth's first race. Seventh pole position in the seventh race for a seven-year-old horse with seven previous wins and ridden by a jockey named Winnett. What could go wrong?

Ruth lost by a nose.

Hey, no problem. Fan-club members went to the winner's circle anyway and had their picture taken with Ruth just as though he'd won. Winnett looked ready to bolt. What were these people doing here? You're supposed to come here if you win. Otherwise they'd have called it the loser's circle.

The management committee held another meeting.

"Nostril uplift," we said. "We lift the nose an inch, maybe puff the nostrils out with that stuff Julia Roberts uses on her lips."

Ruth ran again, and finished further back.

"A handicap," we said. "We stick him in a handicap race. Give him his own wheelchair. Get Rick Hansen to coach him. Better yet, get the Canucks and Grizzlies to coach the other horses."

But then it occurred to us: It didn't matter whether Ruth won or lost.

We wanted him to win. His fan club was growing. Many members had never visited a track pre-Ruth. They were getting to know one another. They were learning to speak Horse. They were learning Exciting Horse Secrets, like how to split an apple in half by sticking your thumb into one end, and how if you feed it to the horse in one piece it hits his stomach like a bowling ball hooking into the 1-3 pocket.

The provincial chapter of the Breast Cancer Foundation got every cent of the membership fee, allowing fan-club members who got caught sneaking off to the track to explain to their spouses that they were out checking their charitable donation.

Plus, it gave me the chance to make up horse jokes ...

RUTH II: FOLLOW THE BOUNCING DUDE

The most-asked question about P.E.I. Ruth, *Sports Only*'s adopted wonder horse is: "If I join the P.E.I. Ruth Fan Club, can I ride him?"

No, you cannot.

You can cheer him. You can commiserate with him — and a male horse saddled with a name like Ruth deserves all the commiseration he can get.

You and your family can get into Hastings Park Racecourse free any day Ruth runs by flashing your official P.E.I. Ruth membership card — looking cool all the while in your coveted free *Sports Only* hat.

You can scan your free program and sneer at the other horses doomed to eat the dust of our celebrated non-gelding.

You can sit in the barbecue area of the infield at a fan-club party, watching the race and pretending you're an owner with big bucks involved instead of a fan who's donated $20 to the Breast Cancer Foundation (B.C. chapter) and gets all the club privileges for free.

You can have a rip-snorting, throat-rasping, manure-free good time. You can even bet a bob or two on Ruth.

But you cannot ride him. Trust me, this is not necessarily a bad thing.

Horses are meant to be ridden by jockeys or apprentices or other people who speak Horse. They know what they're doing. More importantly, the horse knows that they know what they're doing. Therefore, it does not do to them what it is programmed to do to ordinary, unsuspecting people coerced into climbing aboard by other family members who know how to ride and live to see daddy fall off.

To illustrate:

Buffeted on all sides by pleas, promises and teeth-on-edge whining, I once took my family to a dude ranch. The first night, as I sat in the outdoor biffy contemplating the insanity of man, I was bitten on the buttock by a large and obviously fanged horsefly.

The next morning we went riding — or, in my case, bouncing. Each landing brought the bitten buttock into harsh contact with the saddle. Naturally, the bite festered. It was like hitting a boil with a hammer.

It got worse. The horse selected for me by the kindly cowboys was ancient enough to have a bony spine and a gastro-intestinal disorder that made him, uh, break wind, at every step. Thirty feet from the corral it was determined that I ride at the end of the line.

So there we were, all in a row: My happy wife, son and daughter riding happily along in front of me while I ate dust and bounced my boilish buttock on the saddle to the accompaniment of a farting horse.

God intervened.

It was 10 a.m. The other horses proceed merrily down the trail. Not my horse. My horse decides it's time for lunch. It wheels, breaks into a gallop that bounces me back and forth from ears to tail, and heads for the barn.

"Tell him 'whoa'," my wife suggests.

I make a counter-suggestion.

The horse dashes back to the ranch, through the corral, into the barn — and stops dead. I do not. I go over his head into a pile of manure.

I curse out the horse, who stands there, munching lunch. I curse him again.

He looks at me. He has one fart left.

TERESA FANTILLO:
THE REAL NUMBERS GAME

She stood at the podium, slender and big-eyed under one of those chic slashes of colour that are the badge of the breast-cancer fighters — the hats and scarves and caps and tams that cover the shorn heads and bravely try to cover the fear.

Teresa Fantillo, age 32. Wife of Dino, mother of Gillian, seven, and Sophie, four. Teresa Fantillo, breast-cancer victim, trying to get across a message no one wanted to hear.

She knew she was in tough. This was a Vancouver Grizzlies luncheon, and while the Canadian Breast Cancer Foundation (B.C. chapter) was to benefit from the team's charitable enterprises, she was there only as a representative, given two minutes at the end, after the Grizzlies shoe raffle, to catch a restless, mostly male audience peering at wrist watches and anxious to be gone.

"GM Place," she said, "has a seating capacity of over 17,000. Imagine, if you will, 17,000 female fans at tomorrow's game against Sacramento. That is the number of women diagnosed with breast cancer last year, and the number that will be diagnosed again this year. That is 17,000 mothers and daughters, grandmothers, sisters, wives and friends.

"I hazard a guess that there are approximately 5,400 professional athletes in North America — hockey players, skaters, golfers, tennis players, race-car drivers, soccer players, basketball players. Now, imagine if this entire membership of professional athletes was wiped out *every year*.

"This represents the number of women who died of breast cancer in Canada last year. That number has not changed in years."

No one was looking at a wrist watch now, or inching toward an exit. The Grizzlies, the dignitaries, the crowd, the media — every eye was pinned on the young woman in the bold, brave hat, putting a face on the unspeakable.

"As ugly as the disease is," she said, "the treatment is even uglier. Losing a breast is usually followed by highly toxic chemotherapy that leaves even the strongest of us feeling like we would rather die than have another treatment. Living without hair has been a big challenge for me. I look forward to burning all my caps when my hair grows back. All but my Grizzlies one, of course ..."

Teresa Fantillo sits in her Burnaby living room, serving tea and cookies. The hair has grown back into an attractive, close-cropped look, showcasing eyes that sparkle and roll with the joy of laughter as she hears the stereo shift into the Eagles doing "Get Over It".

"Don't I wish," she says.

Her chemo and radiation treatments are over, but the battle is not and never will be. For breast-cancer survivors there is no magical test, no finish line. Every three months, or six, or whatever, she'll live with the knot in her stomach waiting for the test results that will stretch the happiness until the next one, or tell her that the enemy is back and the fight begins anew.

That speech to the Grizzlies' luncheon has left her much in demand as a face, speaker and message-carrier in the other fight, the one to raise public awareness and with it the funds for the research that might someday slay the loathsome dragon. She does them all and looks for more, and only she knows at what cost.

"You know what cancer is?" she asks. "It's something someone else gets. Not someone I know, or someone in my family, not me. Maybe, because I'm 32, I can help get the message across that the threat is there for everybody and it's got to be fought."

"Do you ever get tired of being brave?" she's asked.

"Not yet," she says. "Not yet."